W9-BNN-133

After School and More

After School, Weekend and Holiday Programs for Children and Youth with Disabilities and Special Needs in the Metro New York Area

Resources for Children with Special Needs, Inc.
116 East 16th Street, 5th Floor
New York, NY 10003
(212) 677-4650 Phone ▪ (212) 254-4070 FAX
info@resourcesnyc.org ▪ www.resourcesnyc.org

Resources for Children with Special Needs'
Publication Program has been made possible
through the generous support of

The Achelis and Bodman Foundations

The Altman Foundation

The Arkin Foundation

The Citigroup Foundation

The Independence Community Foundation

The JM Foundation

The Joseph LeRoy and Ann C. Warner Fund

The Metropolitan Life Foundation

The Milbank Foundation for Rehabilitation

The New York Community Trust

The New York Times Company Foundation

Pfizer Inc

The Pinkerton Foundation

The Stella and Charles Guttman Foundation

The United Hospital Fund

Published in the United States of America by
Resources for Children with Special Needs, Inc.
116 East 16th Street, 5th Floor, New York, NY 10003
Copyright © 2002 by Resources for Children with Special Needs, Inc.

ISBN: 0-9678365-5-7

1234567890

Who We Are

The Staff

Karen Thoreson Schlesinger, Executive Director

Helene F. Craner, CSW, Associate Director

Judith H. Sussman, APR, MA, Director of Development

Linda Lew, MLS, Director of Information Services

Dianne Littwin, Director of Publications

Nina E. Lublin, MEd, Program Director

Roberto Romero, Program Director

Miguel Salazar, MA, Program Director

Gary Shulman, MS Ed, Program Director

Carol Khoury, CPA, Financial Manager

Maxine Silent, MPA, Database Administrator

Jean Mizutani, Program Associate

Veronica Feliciano, Information Assistant

Keachi Coleman, Advocate

Martina Moran, Data Entry Associate

Iliana Velez-Howard, Administrative Assistant

Yvette Cruz, Administrative Aide

Board of Directors

Laura Shapiro Kramer, Chair

Nina M. Hill, Ph.D, Vice Chair

Patrick Owen Burns, President

Ellen Miller-Wachtel, Secretary

Leigh J. Abramson, Treasurer

Helene F. Craner, CSW

Matilda Raffa Coumo

Katharine P. Darrow

Evan A. Davis

Robert E. Dineen, Jr.

Michael B. Exstein

Virginia M. Giddens

Judy Lee Greenhill

Diana E. Herzog (Honorary Member)

Richard Hofstetter

Owen P.J. King

Jamie H. Klein

Marcus N. Lamb

Tondra Lynford, CSW

John J. McGuire

Joseph T. McLaughlin (Honorary Member)

Marko C. Remec

Karen Thoreson Schlesinger

Dania M. Seiglie

Renee A. Simon, CSW

Geraldine Telchin

Board of Advisors

Alan Wachtel, MD, Chair

Elizabeth Sharpless, PhD, Co-Chair

Dena Birnback, PhD

Judith R. Birsh, EdD

Judith Ginsberg, PhD

Fatima Goldman

Jay Kramer

Jeffrey Lyons

Dr. Ann Marcus

Karen Redlener

Blanche Saia, MA

Sandy Rochelle Schachter

Penny Schneier

Elaine Yudkovitz, PhD

Table of Contents

Publisher's Note

After School and More is the fourth directory published by Resources for Children with Special Needs. It provides critically needed, up-to-date information on "what's out there and how to get it" to parents and caregivers of children with special needs and the people who work with them.

This directory follows publication of *Camps 2002*, the English/Spanish annual publication highlighting camps and summer programs; *Schools for Children with Autism Spectrum Disorders*; and *The Comprehensive Directory*—1,000+ pages featuring more than 2,600 agencies and the broadest range of services and programs together in one publication.

Like Resources' other three directories, this publication would not have been possible without the strong support of our funders and our Board of Directors, and the hard work of every member of our staff.

I continue to be convinced that the success of this program, the dissemination of information to the audience that needs it most, will depend on you. I urge you to fill out the form at the back of the book and send your suggestions for new publications to us. We will, in turn, give you the directories and guides you need most. And please, don't hesitate to contact us with any updated information you have about the agencies in this directory, or about programs and services we have missed.

Visit our Web site (www.resourcesnyc.org) often for information about forthcoming books, including our forthcoming titles, *Camps 2003* and a new guide on the process and programs of transition from school to adult life services, plus announcements about our training workshops, and Camp Fair, and other information about Resources' services to children, parents, caregivers and professionals.

Dianne Littwin
Director of Publications

Introduction

Resources for Children with Special Needs, Inc. (Resources) is an independent, not-for-profit organization founded in 1983 to insure that New York City children and youth with disabilities and special needs and their families obtain the programs and services they need and to which they are entitled. Resources provides information, referral, parent support, advocacy services, training, publications, and special events for New York City and metropolitan area parents and professionals. Resources is designated as a Parent Training and Information Center by the U.S. Department of Education and as a New York Parent Center by the New York State Education Department.

From the beginning, our services have been built on accurate, comprehensive information.

The technology that makes it possible to organize and retrieve information is a tool that expands possibilities for children and youth with disabilities. Technology helps to connect a child, parent, professional, student, advocate or policymaker to school, daycare, respite, housing, summer camp, independent living, health care, therapies, legal assistance, and more—in short, to the universe of available resources. *After School and More* and the directories before it—*The Comprehensive Directory, Camps 2002* (published annually), and *Schools for Children with Autism Spectrum Disorders*—are products of our continually developing resource database.

Resources' publications are a natural extension of our belief that information is power, and that parents of children with special needs, and the professionals who work with them, must have access to accurate information in order to make informed, effective and appropriate choices for children. We thank the foundations that have provided support for the establishment of the publications program. Their belief in the importance of information has moved us from a vision to reality.

A great many people have worked tirelessly to produce *After School and More*. Our heartfelt thanks go to Dianne Littwin, director of publications; Maxine Silent, MPA, database administrator; Martina Moran, data entry associate, Linda Lew, MLS, director of information services and Veronica Feliciano, information assistant. We also wish to thank a volunteer, Gabrielle McDonough, who helped us gather data, the Resources staff, who checked and rechecked the directory content; and Gary Shulman, after-school expert extraordinaire.

Resources for Children with Special Needs, Inc.
New York City, September 2002

A*fter School and More* provides information about programs serving children and youth, and their families, who live in New York City and the metropolitan New York area and who have any kind of disability or special need.

Obtaining Information

Information about the programs has been obtained from questionnaires, from brochures and material sent to us by the organizations, and from information gathered by phone up to the point of publication. Programs and services, as well as personnel and contact information, change often. We urge you to contact each program in which you are interested to confirm information. We apologize for errors or omissions and invite all readers to notify us of out-of-date information or of new programs that should be added to the next edition. Updates will be posted regularly on our Web site and we plan new and updated editions of the Directory every two years.

Resources for Children with Special Needs, Inc. is not an accrediting or certifying agency. Information in *After School and More* comes from the programs themselves, and we do not assume responsibility for any of the individual resources listed.

Using the Directory

The listings in this directory make it a valuable tool for many users. Parents and caregivers can find immediately needed services, and can identify programs that might be appropriate in the future. Professionals can use the directory as a portable, one-stop guide to all types of after-school programs that will help their consumers, and as an overview of available programs for New York City's children with special needs and their families.

Program Information

We have included all available relevant information for each agency. The descriptive labels include:

- **Contact Information:** Name, address, phone and fax numbers, e-mail addresses and Web sites. Note that the number in brackets [222] in the phone listing is the extension number.
- **Contact Person:** The director or most appropriate contact person in the organization.
- **Affiliation:** The program's parent organization, if there is one.
- **Area Served:** The specific geographic region the agency or program serves. This can be a city, borough, ZIP code, neighborhood, county or country.
- **Languages Spoken:** Languages other than English that program staff speak.
- **Sites:** Contact information for each site run by an agency is listed with an assigned number.
- **Services:** The specific services of an agency or program. Similar services are grouped together. Specific program names appear in capital letters above the services provided by the program. The identifying number of the site(s) at which each service is provided is shown under each group of services.

- **Service Description:** A short overview description of the after-school, weekend or holiday services provided by the agency.
- **Population Served:** The disabilities or special needs served. If a program serves "all disabilities," it serves a wide range of physical, developmental, learning and emotional disabilities.
- **Ages:** Ages served.
- **Wheelchair Accessible:** Shows whether or not there is wheelchair accessibility.
- **Program Capacity:** How many children each program serves.
- **Staff/Child Ratio:** Number of children per staff.
- **Program Hours:** Days and hours of programs.
- **Fees**
- **Method of payment:** What type of payment is accepted.
- **Medication Administered**
- **Transportation**

See the diagram below for a sample of an agency listing, and all the features we have included.

Key to Information on Agency Pages

- Contact Information
  - Languages

ALIANZA DOMINICANA, INC.
2410 Amsterdam Ave.
New York, NY 10033

(212) 740-1960 Administrative
(212) 740-1967 FAX

www.alianzadominicana.org
info@alianzadominicana.org

Moisés Perez, Executive Director
Languages Spoken: Spanish

Sites

1. ALIANZA DOMINICANA, INC.
   2410 Amsterdam Ave.
   New York, NY 10033

   (212) 740-1960 Administrative
   (212) 740-1967 FAX

   www.alianzadominicana.org

   Moises Perez, Executive Director

2. ALIANZA DOMINICANA, INC. - LA PLAZA
   COMMUNITY CENTER
   515 W. 182nd St.
   New York, NY 10033

   (212) 928-4992 Administrative
   (212) 927-8095 FAX

   José Duran, Supervisor

3. ALIANZA DOMINICA, INC.
   2346 Amsterdam Ave.
   New York, NY 10036

   (212) 795-5872 Administrative
   (212) 795-9645 FAX

   www.alianzadom.org

   Felix Arias, Administrative Director

- Site Listing

Services

Athletics Programs
Camps/Day
English as a Second Language
Homework Help Programs
Recreational Activities
Service Description: A comprehensive community facility offering recreation and sports activities, after school programs, summer day camp, counseling, tutoring, community organizing activities, cable access program production, GED classes for youth and ESL classes for adults, peer mediation training and drug prevention.
Sites: 2

Services

- Descriptive Information
- Number Indicates Site where Services are Offered

Child Care Centers
Sites: 1

Computer Classes
Homework Help Programs
Recreational Activities
Sports Instruction
Tutoring
Ages: 6 to 12
Population Served: Learning Disability, Speech/Language Disability
Area Served: All Boroughs
Program Capacity: 20
Program Hours: School year: 3-6 p.m., Summer and School Holidays: 8 a.m-5:30 p.m.
Fees: Sliding scale, determined by ACD
Medication Administered: No
Transportation Provided: No
Wheelchair Accessible: Yes
Service Description: A city-funded agency providing pre-school and after school programs. Sports are included only in summer and during school holidays.
Sites: 3

Services Continued

- Descriptive Information
- Number Indicates Site where Services are Offered

Additional Services, Contacts, Location Information

Many organizations serve people with special needs from birth through their adult lives and may offer many more services and programs than we include in this directory. Consult our other directories for more information on these services, call Resources at 212 677-4650, or email us at info@resourcesnyc.org for additional information on any agency.

The Appendix, Legal Services, (page 151) includes many local and some national legal services specializing in disability rights.

Since location is a very important part of the selection process for an after-school program, in addition to a service index and a disability index we provide a City/Town index, with listings by borouogh, as well as a zip code index at the back of the book. Every organization in the Borough of Queens is listed under its postal address. In the City/Town index, the following postal addresses are all located in Queens: Arverne, Astoria, Bayside, Bellerose, Cambria Heights, College Point, Corona, Douglaston, East Elmhurst, Elmhurst, Far Rockaway, Floral Park, Flushing, Flushing Meadows, Forest Hills, Fresh Meadows, Hollis, Jackson Heights, Jamaica, Laurelton, Little Neck, Long Island City, Ozone Park, Queens Village, Rego Park, Ridgewood, Springfield Gardens, St. Albans, Whitestone, Woodside.

After-School Programs

After School and More includes programs that are available to children with disabilities and special needs outside of normal school hours. Although we use the term "after school," the programs may be before-school programs (especially valuable for working parents), Saturday and weekend programs, holiday programs, and programs that are run in the weeks between camp and school.

Why Might I Need an After-School Program?

There are many reasons for seeking an after-school program and there are various options available for children with special needs. What would you like your child to be doing? Do you want a continuation of schoolwork? Does your child need to learn appropriate social skills? Does your child need the opportunity to make new friends? All children need to have fun and all children need to feel important. They need to grow and develop and to maximize their skills and talents. An after-school program can provide a stimulating environment in which children can spend some of their free time.

Types of Programs

There are a wide variety of programs available throughout the city. We divide these into three basic types:

- <u>special programs</u> that work only with children with disabilities.
- <u>inclusion programs</u> that include children with and without disabilities and have staff experienced in working with children with special needs.
- <u>mainstream programs</u> that accept children with special needs. Under the Americans with Disabilities Act of 1990 (ADA) all non-sectarian mainstream programs are required to make reasonable accommodations for children with special needs. They are not required, however, to provide extensive training for staff about including and working with children who have disabilities.

All three types of programs are included in *After School and More.*

Selecting the Right Program

Consider your child first. Does your child need a <u>special program</u> that works solely with children with disabilities? This type of program provides a specially trained staff and, often, a high staff-to-child ratio, allowing for more individualized attention. Or could your child benefit from an <u>inclusion program</u> that offers the opportunity to play with, socialize with, and make friends with children with and without disabilities? Or could he/she participate in a <u>mainstream program</u>, with less attention from staff? It is up to you to clarify what accommodations your child needs to succeed in any program.

Program Locations

After-school programs take place in public and private schools, community centers, neighborhood houses, Y's, Boys and Girls Clubs, churches, offices, parks, organization headquarters, museums, and elsewhere, depending on the activity and the purpose. When you select a program, consider the program environment. You may also want to consider the location relative to your child's school and home, and the transportation options available for the program.

Activities, Activities, Activities

- "My child needs more tutoring and help with his homework. His after-school activities should be a learning experience."
- "My child loves to sing. Music is her passion."
- "My child has a real talent for drawing."
- "My child needs to see more of the world."
- "My teenage son wants to socialize on the weekends."
- "My child and I need respite."

There are programs for tutoring and instruction, music, art, cultural enrichment, sports, swimming, arts and crafts, equestrian therapy, writing, dance, drama, computer instruction, and just making friends. When making a choice, involve your child as much as possible. The more a program focuses on your child's interests, the greater the chance of success. If your child loves art, an after-school museum program might be appropriate. If your child is really good with his/her hands, or needs more help in developing fine motor skills, an arts-and-crafts program might be just right.

We have included many museums and parks in the directory. Wherever possible, special programs, including school-hour programs given at the museum, or in some cases, in the classroom, are identified. In the descriptive information, the fees indicated usually relate to the special program, not the general admission. Most museums and parks are wheelchair accessible, and open during after-school hours, on weekends, and many holidays. They provide a stimulating and enjoyable experience for families.

Important Considerations

There are as many issues for a parent or caregiver to consider in selecting a program as there are unique personalities and needs in children. They include:

- **Staff**: What are the qualifications of the staff, teachers, or caregivers? Who does the tutoring, or conducts sports activities or music or art? Who supervises the travel program? What training have they had; how much experience? This is important for all activities.
- **Accessibility**: If your child uses a wheelchair, you will need to focus on those programs that are wheelchair accessible.
- **Medication**: If your child needs to take medication during program hours, make sure the staff will arrange for medication administration or supervision. Programs licensed by the New York City Department of Health should have a health coordinator on staff who can administer or monitor medication. The Americans with Disabilities Act (ADA) would

consider medication administration a reasonable accommodation to enable a child with a disability to participate in a program. Even if such a feature is not noted, you should inquire about whether that accommodation can be made if everything else in the program is right for your child.

- **Transportation**: If your child needs transportation to and/or from a program, is it available or can you arrange it? Children who receive transportation to special education programs in New York City may be eligible for transportation to after-school programs. Parents should inquire about a PM Drop-Off form at their local school district.
- **Personal Needs**: If your child needs help with toileting, can the staff be counted on?
- **Behavior**: If your child has behavior problems, does the program know about behavior management?
- **Communication**: Is the program willing to talk with you about techniques that seem to work well for your child?
- **Parental Needs**: Does the program meet your needs as well as your child's?
- **Philosophy and Attitude**: What is the philosophy of the program supervisor and the staff who will be working with your child? Is there a feeling of acceptance of differences? Does the language used by the staff reflect this? Visit the program and observe the interactions of staff and children. Is there consistency and consideration for all?

A Note About Respite and Child Care

After School and More includes programs that provide respite and child care. Respite means temporary relief, a break! Usually, these are programs specifically for children with developmental disabilities or mental illness, or who are in foster care. Respite programs might be after school, on weekends, or even overnight. It is important to visit programs before you enroll your child to learn whether or not the program will meet your child's needs. If a program does not want to arrange a site visit, consider another program. Speak with other parents if possible to get feedback about programs.

Child care programs are designed to provide a safe, structured environment for children while parents are at work or away from home. More and more child care programs are also offering an educational component, or they may combine recreation and education.

Your Right to Accommodations

The Americans with Disabilities Act (ADA) mandates that all programs, except those run by religious institutions, must offer reasonable accommodation. As noted above, medication administration is considered a reasonable accommodation. For more information regarding the ADA you can contact the ADA Hotline at the U.S. Department of Justice: 800 514-0301 or 800 514-0383 (TDD). If you believe that your child is the victim of discrimination under the ADA, call Resources for Children with Special Needs, Inc. or any of the organizations listed in the Appendix to learn more about what you can do if a program discriminates.

After School and More includes hundreds of options for after-school care for your child, and holiday and weekend programs. Happy hunting.

Agency Name Index

Agency Name Index

Agency Name Index

Agency Name Index

Agency Name Index

Agency Listings

81ST PRECINCT COMMUNITY AFFAIRS

30 Ralph Ave.
Brooklyn, NY 11221

(718) 574-0411 [433] Administrative
(718) 574-8722 FAX

Cynthia Herrera, Contact

Services

Field Trips/Excursions
Homework Help Programs
Mentoring Programs
Sports, Individual
Sports, Team/Leagues

Ages: 7 to 21
Program Hours: Monday - Friday: 3:30-9 p.m.
Program Capacity: 150
Staff/Child Ratio: 1:10
Fees: None
Medication Administered: No
Transportation Provided: No
Wheelchair Accessible: No
Service Description: Provides a variety of after school programs and activities for all children. Children with special needs are considered on a case-by-case basis.

92ND STREET YM-YWHA

1395 Lexington Ave.
New York, NY 10128

(212) 415-5600 Administrative
(212) 415-5626 Special Needs
(212) 415-5637 FAX

www.92ndsty.org

Melanie Mandel, Director, Children with Special Needs

Services

CONNECT JEWISH AFTER SCHOOL
Acting Instruction
Arts and Crafts Instruction
Music Instruction
Storytelling
Tutoring

Ages: 5 to 10
Area Served: All Boroughs
Program Hours: September - May, Mondays: 3:30-5:30 p.m.
Fees: $850 for one child ($750 each additional child)
Method of Payment: Check, Money Order
Medication Administered: No
Transportation Provided: No
Wheelchair Accessible: Yes
Service Description: Children spend one afternoon each week exploring the beauty and excitement of Judaism. This unique program connects children with their religion, customs and heritage in an atmosphere that is both secure and engaging.
Contact: Deborah Mittman, Connect Principal

NESHER PROGRAM FOR CHILDREN WITH DEVELOPMENTAL DISABILITIES
Acting Instruction
Arts and Crafts Instruction
Exercise Classes/Groups
Homework Help Programs
Sports, Individual
Sports, Team/Leagues
Swimming

Ages: 4 to 20
Population Served: Autism, Developmental Disability, Mental Retardation (mild-moderate), Speech/Language Disability
Area Served: All Boroughs
Program Hours: Monday - Friday: 3:30-5:30 p.m.; Sunday
Program Capacity: Monday - Friday: 80, Sunday: 125
Staff/Child Ratio: 3:1, 1:1 is also available
Fees: $1,150 per year
Method of Payment: Cash, Check, Credit Card, Money Order (scholarships available)
Service Description: An after school program where children can engage in a variety of activities and programs.

NOAR AFTER SCHOOL CENTER
Arts and Crafts Instruction
Dancing Instruction
Exercise Classes/Groups
Homework Help Programs
Music Instruction
Sports, Individual
Sports, Team/Leagues
Swimming

Ages: 5 to 11
Area Served: All Boroughs
Program Hours: Monday - Friday: 3-6 p.m.
Fees: Call for information
Medication Administered: No
Transportation Provided: No
Wheelchair Accessible: Yes
Service Description: Offers a variety of educational and recreational programs for all children.
Contact: Rick Vargas

A - 1 UNIVERSAL CARE, INC.

352 Fulton Ave., Suite 7
Hempstead, NY 11550

(516) 485-2646 Administrative
(516) 485-8797 FAX

Linda Woods, Executive Director
Languages Spoken: Spanish

< continued...>

Services

AFTER SCHOOL/WEEKEND RESPITE
Arts and Crafts Instruction
Child Care Centers
Dancing Instruction
Exercise Classes/Groups
Homework Help Programs
Music Instruction
Respite, Children's Out-of-Home
Sports, Individual
Sports, Team/Leagues

Ages: 6 to 22
Population Served: Attention Deficit Disorder (ADD/ADHD), Autism, Cerebral Palsy, Developmental Disability, Mental Retardation (mild-moderate), Mental Retardation (severe-profound), Pervasive Developmental Disorder (PDD/NOS)
Area Served: Nassau County
Program Hours: Weekend Respite: 10 a.m.-2 p.m., Afterschool: Tuesday, Wednesday, Friday: 2:30-6 p.m.
Program Capacity: 25
Staff/Child Ratio: 2:10
Fees: None
Medication Administered: No
Transportation Provided: School district provides transportation for after school program only. No transportation provided for weekend respite.
Wheelchair Accessible: Yes
Service Description: Both programs offered off-site; call for details.
Contact: Claire Elcock, Program Coordinator

A PLUS CENTER FOR LEARNING

254 Smith St.
Brooklyn, NY 11231

(718) 596-1986 Administrative
(718) 596-1681 FAX

www.aboutaplus.com
apluscenter@yahoo.com

Richard Bourbeau, Executive Director
Languages Spoken: Chinese, French, German, Italian, Japanese, Russian

Services

English as a Second Language
Homework Help Programs
Music Instruction
Tutoring

Ages: All Ages
Population Served: Attention Deficit Disorder (ADD/ADHD), Autism, Developmental Disability, Learning Disability, Mental Retardation (mild-severe), Neurological Disability, Underachiever
Area Served: All Boroughs, Nassau
Program Hours: Summer: 8 a.m.-7 p.m., School year, Weekdays: 3:30-7:30 p.m., Saturday: 11 a.m.-7 p.m.,

Sunday: 12-5 p.m.
Staff/Child Ratio: 1:1; groups 1:3
Fees: Hourly, call for information
Method of Payment: Credit Card, Check: Payment Plan available
Medication Administered: No
Transportation Provided: No
Wheelchair Accessible: Yes
Service Description: Provides tutoring for a wide range of children, both mainstream and special needs. In-home tutoring is available, hours are flexible by appointment. ESL is offered in home or office. Music instruction is provided in home or in schools and community organizations. A learning disability specialist is available, as are speech improvement teachers.

A.D.D. RESOURCE CENTER, INC. (THE)

215 W. 75th St.
New York, NY 10023-1799

(212) 721-0049 Administrative
(914) 763-5648 Administrative
(212) 724-4519 FAX
(914) 763-5581 FAX

addrc@mail.com

Hal Meyer, Executive Director

Services

Recreational Activities
Social Skills Training
Study Skills Assistance

Ages: 7 to 12; 18 and up
Population Served: Asperger Syndrome, Attention Deficit Disorder (ADD/ADHD), Learning Disability, Pervasive Developmental Disorder (PDD/NOS)
Area Served: NYC Metro, Westchester
Program Hours: Call for information
Fees: Call for information.
Transportation Provided: No
Wheelchair Accessible: Yes
Service Description: Offers socialization skills training for children; parenting skills training, and coaching for time management, organizational, job and study skills.

ACCESSIBLE JOURNEYS

35 W. Sellers Ave.
Ridley Park, PA 19078

(610) 521-0339 Administrative
(800) 846-4537 Toll Free
(610) 521-6959 FAX

www.disabilitytravel.com
sales@disabilitytravel.com

< continued... >

Howard McCoy, Executive Director

Services

Travel

Ages: 8 and up
Population Served: Physical/Orthopedic Disability
Wheelchair Accessible: Yes
Service Description: Domestic and international travel for slow walkers or persons using a wheelchair or moterized chair. Travelers must provide their own companion if assistance with activities of daily living is required. No medical professionals on trips. Trips are year round, but are not arranged in summer, and on school holidays and weekends.

ACHILLES TRACK CLUB, INC.

42 W. 38th St., 4th Fl.
New York, NY 10018

(212) 354-0300 Administrative
(212) 354-3978 FAX

www.achillestrackclub.org
achillesclub@aol.com

Karen Lewis, Director, Achilles Kids
Languages Spoken: Spanish

Services

Sports, Individual
Sports, Team/Leagues

Ages: 4 to 21
Population Served: Deaf/Hard of Hearing, Developmental Disability, Neurological Disability, Physical/Orthopedic Disability, Visual Disability/Blind
Area Served: All Boroughs
Program Hours: Call for information
Fees: Call for information
Medication Administered: No
Wheelchair Accessible: Yes
Service Description: A long distance running/walking/"rolling" program in a mainstream environment available on weekend mornings for children and adults with physical disabilities, developmental disabilities, neurological and sensory impairments. The program is designed to encourage all children and youth with disabilities to participate in running. No previous athletic experience is necessary. Siblings are welcome to participate. Parent or guardian must accompany their child.

ACTORS THEATRE WORKSHOP, INC. (THE)

145 W. 28th St., 3rd Fl.
New York, NY 10001

(212) 947-1386 Administrative
(212) 947-0642 FAX

www.actorstheatreworkshop.com

Thurman E. Scott, Executive Director

Services

BUILDERS OF THE NEW WORLD
Acting Instruction
Arts and Crafts Instruction
Mentoring Programs
Theater Performances

Ages: 8 to 12
Population Served: At-Risk
Program Hours: One weeknight (Tuesdays in 2002).
Fees: None
Medication Administered: No
Transportation Provided: No
Service Description: The program is held at the Harriet Tubman Housing Project. It is a creative arts program designed especially for homeless children. Summer program is two full days a week. Can accommodate children with special needs.
Contact: Matt Meis

ADD JOY TO LEARNING

240 Second Ave.
New York, NY 10009

(212) 995-1137 Administrative

ajlmusic@consentric.net

Audrey J. Levine, Executive Director

Services

MUSIC INDUSTRY SEMINAR
Music Instruction

Ages: 16 and up
Area Served: All Boroughs
Program Hours: Friday: 3-4:30/5 p.m.
Fees: None
Medication Administered: No
Transportation Provided: No
Wheelchair Accessible: Yes (limited access)
Service Description: Every week a music industry person is invited to the seminar to explain to adolescents and young adults interested in pursuing a career in the music industry what their particular job consists of and how they obtained it. Adolescents and young

<continued...>

adults with special needs can be accommodated.

AFRICAN AMERICAN PARENT COUNCIL

180 Parkhill Ave.
Staten Island, NY 10304

(718) 876-9195 Administrative
(718) 876-0514 FAX

aaparentcouncil@aol.com

Minnie Graham, Executive Director

Services

Arts and Crafts Instruction
Homework Help Programs

Ages: All Ages
Population Served: Developmental Disabilities
Program Hours: Monday - Friday: 3-6 p.m.
Fees: Mainstream: $55, Disabilities: Free
Method of Payment: Cash, Checks, Money Orders
Wheelchair Accessible: Yes
Service Description: After school services provided for both mainstream and special needs population.
Contact: Minnie Graham, Executive Director

AFTER SCHOOL WORKSHOP, INC.

530 E. 76th St.
New York, NY 10028

(212) 734-7620 Administrative

Services

Homework Help Programs
Recreational Activities
Tutoring

Ages: 5 to 13
Population Served: Attention Deficit Disorder (ADD/ADHD), Developmental Disability, Learning Disability, Mental Retardation (mild-moderate), Neurological Disability, Physical/Orthopedic Disability, Speech/Language Disability, Underachiever
Program Hours: Call for information
Fees: Call for information.
Transportation Provided: No
Service Description: Offers individual and group tutoring, as well as homework help programs for all children.

AFTER-SCHOOL CORPORATION, THE (TASC)

925 Ninth Ave.
New York, NY 10019

(212) 547-6950 Administrative
(212) 547-6983 FAX

www.tascorp.org

Charissa L. Fernandez, Deputy Dir./Operations, Special Projects

Services

Arts and Crafts Instruction
Computer Classes
Homework Help Programs
Mentoring Programs
Music Instruction
Sports, Individual
Sports, Team/Leagues

Ages: 5 to 18
Area Served: All Boroughs
Program Hours: Monday - Friday: 3-6 p.m.
Staff/Child Ratio: 1:10
Fees: None
Wheelchair Accessible: Yes (at some sites)
Service Description: TASC provides funding, training and other resources to community-based organizations to operate after-school programs in public schools. Program capacity ranges from approximately 150 to 400, depending on the site. The programming at all sites includes a balance of academics, homework help, performing arts, and recreation, but the specific activities vary from site to site. For more information about specific activities, contact the program directly. Also, the sites sometimes change from school year to school year. Call TASC for detailed information. Programs are open only to students currently attending the school where the program is located. Children with disabilities and special needs are considered on a case-by-case basis, depending upon the availability of appropriate facilities, transportation and staff.

BRONX

American Museum of Natural History
CES 42
1537 Washington Avenue
Bronx, NY 10457
Wendy Edge
718-583-7366

Children's Aid Society
CS 146
968 Cauldwell Avenue
Bronx, NY 10456
Tisha M. Jermin

< continued... >

718-861-5935

Children's Aid Society
IS 123
1025 Morrison Avenue
Bronx, NY 10472
Patrice Shand
718-860-3490

Citizens Advice Bureau
CES 90
1116 Sheridan Avenue
Bronx, NY 10456
Claudia Bostick-Bailey
718-293-0727 x251

Citizens Advice Bureau, Inc.
PS 130
750 Prospect Avenue
Bronx, NY 10455
Kenneth Greene
718-292-3452

Committee for Hispanic Children and Families
PS 59
2185 Bathgate Avenue
Bronx, NY 10457
Hugo Fernandez
718-584-4598

Committee for Hispanic Children and Families, Inc.
PS/MS 279
2100 Walton Avenue
Bronx, NY 10453
Helena Yordan
718-584-4186

East Side House Settlement
PS 43
165 Brown Place
Bronx, NY 10454
Maria Delgado
718-292-4502 x136

East Side House Settlement
PS 220
468 E. 140th Street
Bronx, NY 10454
James L. Blakeney
718-292-7394

Episcopal Social Services
MS 52
681 Kelly Street
Bronx, NY 10455
Gracie Johnson
718-993-7358

GDOC
General Development and Orientation Council
PS 157
757 Cauldwell Avenue

Bronx, NY 10456
Gladys Lopez
718-292-5255

Gloria Wise Boys and Girls Club
PS 111
3740 Baychester Avenue
Bronx, NY 10466
Maria Lopez
718-379-2830 x285

Inwood House
PS 198
1180 Tinton Avenue
Bronx, NY 10456
Kenyatta Funderburk
718-617-6571

Kingsbridge Heights Community Center
MS 143X
120 West 231th Street
Bronx, NY 10463
Yvonne McNair
718-796-8170 x203

Kips Bay Boys & Girls Club
IS 158
800 Home Street
Bronx, NY 10456
Andrew McFall
718-893-8600 x308

Mosholu Montefiore Community Center
PS/MS 95
3961 Hillman Avenue
Bronx, NY 10463
Michael Gray
914-416-6495

Mosholu Montefiore Community Center, Inc.
PS 8
3010 Briggs Avenue
Bronx, NY 10458
Charmaine Swearing
646-529-4662

New Settlement Apartments/ The Crenulated
Co. LDT
CES 64
1425 Walton Avenue
Bronx, NY 10452
Theresa Winokur
718-410-7743

New York City Mission Society
CES 28
1861 Anthony Avenue
Bronx, NY 10457
Aida Maldonado / Adriana Madera
718-583-5400

NYU Metro Center for Urban Education

< continued... >

PS 197/ PS 196/ PS 195
1250 Ward Avenue
Bronx, NY 10472
Catherine Barufaldi
718-542-9356

Pathways for Youth Boys and Girls Club
PS 60
888 Rev. James A. Polite Avenue
Bronx, NY 10459
Wanda Morales
718-860-0602

Phipps Community Development Center
CS 6
1000 E. Tremont Avenue
Bronx, NY 10453
LaShana Williams
718-542-8333x38

Pius XII Youth & Family Services
PS 79
125 East 181st Street
Bronx, NY 10453
Tori Ann Prevost / Dely Ramos
718-584-5158

Pius XII Youth and Family Services
Adlai Stevenson High School
1980 Lafayette Avenue
Bronx, NY 10473
Katherine Brauer
718-518-0565

Pius XII Youth and Family Services
PS 3
2100 Lafontaine Avenue
Bronx, NY 10457
Ingris Coronado
718-584-3658

SCAN
Supportive Children's Advocacy Network
CES 53
360 East 168th Street
Bronx, NY 10456
Ken Thompson
718-681-7955

SCAN
Supportive Children's Advocacy Network
CES 55
450 St. Paul's Place
Bronx, NY 10456
Rebecca Rajswasser
718-699-1899

Sports & Arts in Schools Foundation
MS 127
1560 Purdy Street
Bronx, NY 10462
Edwin DeLeon

718-824-4831

Supportive Children's Advocacy Network
PS 212
800 Home Street
Bronx, NY 10456
Ms. So-Yun Lee
718-617-0662

Supportive Children's Advocacy Network
CS 66
1001 Jennings Avenue
Bronx, NY 10460
Nancy Kowalski
718-584-5860

WHEDCO
CES 218
1220 Gerard Avenue
Bronx, NY 10452
Davon Russell
718-839-1118

BROOKLYN

Antioch Development Corporation, The
PS/IS 25 - Eubie Blake
787 Lafayette Avenue
Brooklyn, NY 11221
Charmaine Noel
718-443-9100

Brooklyn Bureau of Community Service
PS 306
970 Vermont Street
Brooklyn, NY 11207
Larry Yancy
718-649-4119

Brooklyn Bureau of Community Service
PS 91
532 Albany Avenue
Brooklyn, NY 11203
Vashia C. Rhone
718-756-0243 x216

Brooklyn Bureau of Community Service
MS 246
72 Veronica Place
Brooklyn, NY 11226
Nina Johnson
917-378-0806

Brooklyn Chinese-American Association
PS 160 - Willian T. Sampson School
5105 Fort Hamilton Parkway
Brooklyn, NY 11219
Sydney Li Fang Huang
718-438-8711

Builders for Family and Youth
PS 106

< continued... >

1314 Putnam Avenue
Brooklyn, NY 11221
Jaime Zelaya
718-574-0261

Carter G. Woodson Cultural Literacy Project
PS 150
364 Sackman Street
Brooklyn, NY 11212
718-346-2619

Chinese American Planning Council, Inc.
PS 153
1970 Homecrest Avenue
Brooklyn, NY 11229
Eduardo Alexander Rabel
718-627-6373

Church Avenue Merchants Block
PS 109
15 Snyder Avenue
Brooklyn, NY 11212
Rohan Jeremiah
718-469-8064

Church Avenue Merchants Block
IS 62
Ditmas 62
700 Cortelyou Road
Brooklyn, NY 11218
Daniel Kreiss
718-856-2341

Church Avenue Merchants Block Association
MS 391
790 East New York Avenue
Brooklyn, NY 11233
Nadia Bryan
718-493-8920 x229

Clearpool
PS 26
1014 Lafayette Avenue
Brooklyn, NY 11221
Sherry Ormond
718-453-7004

Community Counseling and Mediation Services
PS 138
760 Prospect Place
Brooklyn, NY 11216
Shalawn Langhorne
718-735-9112 x22

Community Counseling And Mediation Services
MS 320
46 McKeever Place
Brooklyn, NY 11225
Nicole Alyssa Creary
718-282-8721

Cypress Hills Local Development Corp.

PS 7
858 Jamaica Avenue
Brooklyn, NY 11208
Michelle Hammett
888-500-1669

Educators for Social Responsibility Metropolitan
Area, Inc.
PS 24
427 38th Street
Brooklyn, NY 11232
Marisol Ramos
718-832-9366 x201

El Puente de Williamsburg
El Puente Academy
211 South 4th Street
Brooklyn, NY 11211
Edwin Diaz
718-387-0404 x23

Federation of Italian American Organizations of
Brooklyn (F.I.A.O.B.)
PS 48K
6015 18th Avenue
Brooklyn, NY 11204
Maria Cosentino
718-236-3187

Good Shepherd Services
PS 27
27 Huntington Street
Brooklyn, NY 11231
Stacey Billups
718-222-9561

Good Shepherd Services
PS 32
317 Hoyt Street
Brooklyn, NY 11231
Steve Kennedy
718-330-6394

HeartShare Human Services of New York
PS 102 Bayview School
211 72nd Street
Brooklyn, NY 11209
Patricia Di Dino
718-567-2365

New York Urban League
PS 92
601 Parkside Avenue
Brooklyn, NY 11226
Autumn King
718-756-3031 x21

Project Reach Youth, Inc.
PS 124
515 4th Avenue
Brooklyn, NY 11215
Peter Berkowitz

< continued... >

7

718-499-9699

Project Reach Youth, Inc.
PS 230
1 Albermarle Road
Brooklyn, NY 11218
Carol Prud'homme-Ross
718-436-7196

Ralph - Lincoln Service Center
PS/MS 12
430 Howard Avenue, Rm. 130
Brooklyn, NY 11212
718-773-3165

Research Foundation of CUNY-Brooklyn College
Community Partnership for Research and Learning
New Utrecht High School
1601 80th Street
Brooklyn, NY 11214
Karen Baker
718-232-2500 x281

Research Foundation of CUNY Brooklyn College
Community Partnership for Research and Learning
Bushwick High School
400 Irving Avenue
Brooklyn, NY 11237
Moe Mpela
718-381-7100 x249

Research Foundation of CUNY/Medgar Evers College
ACE
PS 181
1023 New York Avenue
Brooklyn, NY 11203
Andre Lake
718-703-3633

Ridgewood Bushwick Senior Citizens Council
PS 86
220 Irving Avenue
Brooklyn, NY 11207
Tyese Brown
718-574-4736

Safe Horizon (formerly Victim Services)
IS 292
300 Wyona Street
Brooklyn, NY 11207
Tracey Haqq
718-498-6560 x1148

Shorefront YM-YWHA
PS 253 - Ezra Keats International Elementary School
601 Oceanview Ave
Brooklyn, NY 11235
Shirley Pineiro
718-332-3331

Sports & Arts in Schools Foundation
PS 40

265 Ralph Avenue
Brooklyn, NY 11233
Philippe Cadet
718-455-9445

Sports & Arts in Schools Foundation
MS 143/MS 267
800 Gates Avenue
Brooklyn, NY 11221
Michael O'Keefe
718-443-0268

Sports & Arts in Schools Foundation
IS 211
1001 East 100th Street
Brooklyn, NY 11236
Shauna Murphy
718-251-4411

Spring Creek Community Corp.
PS 346
1400 Pennsylvania Avenue
Brooklyn, NY 11239
Lousie Rojas
718-942-1789

St. Christopher Ottilie/Center for Family Life in
Sunset Park
PS 1
309 47th Street
Brooklyn, NY 11220
Sharoya Lopiz / Helene Onserud
718-788-3500

St. Nicholas Neighborhood Preservation Corp.
PS 250
108 Montrose Avenue
Brooklyn, NY 11206
Noelia Rodriguez
718-599-8610

St. Rosalia-Regina Pacis Neighborhood
Improvement Assoc.
Edward B. Shallow IS 227
6500 16th Avenue
Brooklyn, NY 11204
Jenya Iuzzini
718-621-3483

St. Rosalia-Regina Pacis Neighborhood
Improvement Assoc.
The Irving Gladstone Elementary School
PS 186
7601 19th Avenue
Brooklyn, NY 11214
Kim Nielsen
718-621-3088

YMCA of Greater New York
PS 205
6701 20th Avenue
Brooklyn, NY 11204

< continued... >

Fran D'Apolito
718-234-2655

YMCA of Greater New York
PS 243
1580 Dean Street
Brooklyn, NY 11213
Denise Robinson
718574-2404 x19

YMCA of Greater New York/Brooklyn Central YMCA
PS 8
37 Hicks Street
Brooklyn, NY 11201
Mike Dogan
718-834-6722

YMCA of Greater New York/ Brooklyn Central YMCA
PS 20
225 Adelphi Street
Brooklyn, NY 11205
Marlon Williams
718-237-8774

YMCA of Greater New York/Flatbush YMCA
PS 208
4801 Avenue D
Brooklyn, NY 11203
Donna Ottey
917-748-6855

MANHATTAN

Alianza Dominicana, Inc.
IS 143
515 West 182nd Street
New York, NY 10033
Jose Duran
212-928-4992

Children's Aid Society- Manhattan Ctr.
280 Pleasant Avenue
(East 116th St. & FDR Dr.)
New York, NY 10029
Karen Kramer-Ruben
212-423-9630

Children's Aid Society
PS 152
93 Nagle Avenue
New York, NY 10040
Aledia Suarez
212-544-0221

Children's Aid Society
PS 8
465 West 167th Street
New York, NY 10032
Anu Doddapaneni
212-740-8655

Children's Aid Society

The Vito Marcantonio School - PS 50
433 East 100th Street
New York, NY 10029
Alejandro Carrion/ Delia Salas
Community School Directors
212-860-0299

Children's Aid Society
The Mirabel Sisters School - IS 90
Janet Heller
21 Jumel Place @168th Street
New York, NY 10032
Danny Pena
212-923-1563

Dance Theatre of Harlem
PS 153M
1750 Amsterdam Avenue
New York, NY 10031
Debra Clarke
Assistant Coordinator
212-927-8644

Educational Alliance
PS 64
600 East 6th Street
New York, NY 10009
Juliana Cope
646-879-4841

Educational Alliance, Inc.
School of the Future
27 East 22nd Street
New York, NY 10010
Mitzi Sinnott
212-475-8086 x200

14th Street Union Square Local Development
Corporation (The)
Washington Irving High School, #460
40 Irving Place
New York, NY 10003
Jenny Bailey
212-358-0165

Friends of the Family Academy
PS 241
240 West 113th Street
New York, NY 10026
Mina Fasolo
212-749-2830 x285

Harlem Children's Zone, Inc. (Previously
Rheedlen)
PS 194
244 West 144th Street
New York, NY 10030
Rita Knight
212-234-4500

Harlem Dowling West Side Center for Children
and Family Services

< continued... >

PS 129
425 West 130th Street
New York, NY 10027
Beverly Brumell / Sheryl Anderson
212-926-3040

Harlem Dowling West Side Center for Children and
Family Services
PS 125
425 West 123rd Street
New York, NY 10027
Griselda Hernandez
917-312-6431

Harlem Dowling West Side Center for Children and
Family Services
PS 161
499 W. 133rd Street
New York, NY 10027
Jenny Fernandez
917-806-8192

Henry Street Settlement
PS 110
285 Delancey Street
New York, NY 10002
Erika Fulton
212-254-3100 x260

Henry Street Settlement
PS 134 - Henrietta Szold School
293 East Broadway
New York, NY 10038
Rebeeca Beers
212-254-3100 x228

Interfaith Neighbors, Inc.
PS 38
232 East 103rd Street
New York, NY 10029
Victoria Mancilla/ Michelle Simon
212-410-7310

Learning Through an Expanded Arts Program, Inc.
PS 191
210 West 61th Street
New York , NY 10023
Taishya Adams
212-678-2947

Lincoln Square Business Improvement District
MLK, Jr. HS
122 Amsterdam Avenue
New York, NY 10023
Rebecca Fabiano
212-501-1200

Loisaida, Inc.
PS 188
442 East Houston Street
New York, NY 10002
Rachel Breitman

646-602-0465

Louise Wise Services
PS 30
144-176 East 128th Street
New York, NY 10035
Nathallie Kiser Negron
212-427-1781

New York City Mission Society
PS 154
250 West 127th Street
New York, NY 10027
Carl Harris
212-690-5820

NYU School of Education, Metro Center
PS 84
32 West 92nd Street
New York, NY 10025
Helen Barahal
212-222-7540

NYU School of Education, Metro Center
PS 171
19 East 103rd Street, Rm. 201
New York, NY 10029
Jan Greyson/ Bruce Martin
212-992-9434

Sheltering Arms Children's Services
PS 96
216 East 120th Street
New York, NY 10035
Thomas Peyton
212-679-4242

Stanley M. Isaacs Neighborhood Center
PS 198/ PS 77-Lower Lab School
1700 Third Avenue
New York, NY 10128
Shana Khun-Siegel
212-828-6342

Teachers College, Columbia University
Heritage School # 71
1680 Lexington Avenue
New York, NY 10029
Andrew Lappin
212-828-2857 x309

University Settlement
PS 63
121 East 3rd Street
New York, NY 10009
Tameeka Ford
917-418-6743

Manhattan Youth Recreation and Resources
IS 89
201 Warren Street
New York, NY 10282

< continued... >

Mr. Theseus Roche
212-571-2392

NYU School of Education
Seward Park High School
350 Grand Street
New York, NY 10002
Rachel Swaner
212-674-7000 x315

University Settlement
PS 137 - The John L. Bernstein School
327 Cherry Street
New York, NY 10002
Elizabeth Speck
212-602-9800

Vision Urbana
JHS 56 - Magnet School for Technology and Education
for the 21st Century
220 Henry Street
New York, NY 10002
Debra Chinnery Smith
212-577-9160

YMCA of Greater New York/ Chinatown YMCA
PS/IS 126
80 Catherine Street
New York, NY 10038
Josette Bailey
212-240-9443

YWCA of the City of New York
Murry Bergtraum High School for Business Careers
411 Pearl Street
New York, NY 11038
Sarah J. Goldoff
212-964-9610 x249

QUEENS

F.E.G.S.
PS 105
420 Beach 51 Street
Far Rockaway, NY 11691
Chris Felton
718-474-0828

F.E.G.S.
JHS 8
108-35 167th Street
Jamaica, NY 11433
David Anderson
718.206.1360
718-739-6883 x504

Forest Hills Community Houses
JHS 217
85-05 144th Street
Jamaica, NY 11435
Ron Velez
718- 262-9234

Goodwill Industries of Greater New York &
Northern New Jersey, Inc.
PS 40
109-20 Union Hall Street
Jamaica, NY 11433
Gilda Bain-Pew
718-526-1904

Goodwill Industries of Greater New York &
Northern New Jersey, Inc.
PS 111
37-15 13th Street
Long Island City, NY 11101
Tyrone Green
718-349-3429

Greater Ridgewood Youth Council
IS 93
66-56 Forest Avenue
Ridgewood, NY 11385
Giselle Ayala
718-456-5437 x229

Greater Ridgewood Youth Council, Inc.
PS 71
62-85 Forest Avenue
Ridgewood, NY 11385
Walter Welsh
718-456-5437 x228

Jacob A. Riis Neighborhood Settlement House,
Inc.
IS 126
31-51 21st Street
Long Island City, NY 11106
Albert Pollard
718-784-7447 x128

Maspeth Town Hall, Inc.
PS 229 - Emanuel Kaplan
67-25 51st Road
Woodside, NY 11377
Stephen Powers
718-289-5229

Mount Sinai School of Medicine
Queens Gateway to the Health Sciences
150-91 87th Road
Jamaica, NY 11432
John Madera
718-739-8080 x2241

Police Athletic League, Inc.
PS 140
116th Ave. & 166th Street
Jamaica, NY 11434
James Wright
718-298-5002

Police Athletic League, Inc.
PS 118

< continued... >

190-02 109th Road
Hollis, NY 11412
Valerie Littleton-Cohen
718.264-1402

Queens Child Guidance Center
PS 89
85-28 Britton Avenue
Elmhurst, NY 11373
Francis Wood
718-565-5702

Queens Child Guidance Center
PS 24 Q
141-11 Holly Avenue
Flushing, NY 11355
Doreen The
718-445-8176

Queens Child Guidance Center
PS 22
153-31 Sanford Avenue
Flushing, NY 11355
Frances Lee
718-762-2636

Samuel Field Bay Terrace YM&YWHA
PS 115Q
80-15 261st Street
Floral Park, NY 11004
Iris Shaw
718-225-6750 x333

Samuel Field YM & Ywha, Inc.
MS 158Q
46-35 Oceania Street
Bayside, NY 11361
Roxanne J. Stark
718-423-8100 x150

Sports & Arts in Schools Foundation
IS 125 Q
46-02 47th Avenue
Woodside, NY 11377
Rebecca Kind Slater
718-752-9210

Sports & Arts in Schools Foundation
PS 122
21-21 Ditmars Blvd.
Astoria, NY 11105
Janis K. Vazquez
718-728-6210

Sunnyside Community Services
PS 199
39-20 48th Avenue
Sunnyside, NY 11104
Madeline Delgado
718-786-6958

Sunnyside Community Services

PS 150
40-01 43rd Avenue
Sunnyside, NY 11104
Erik Osugi
718-392-3635

YMCA of Greater New York
PS 197
825 Hicksville Road
Far Rockaway, NY 11691
Tara Bowser
718-479-0505 x171

YMCA of Greater New York
PS 139
93-06 63rd Drive
Rego Park, NY 11374
Kristy Lebron
718-459-4404

YMCA of Greater New York
PS 95
179-01 90th Avenue
Jamaica, NY 11432
Rosemay Francois
718-558-0709

YMCA of Greater New York/ Flushing Branch
PS 120
30-48 Linden Place
Flushing, NY 11354
John Cavalcante
718-353-7810

STATEN ISLAND

Police Athletic League, Inc.
PS 14
100 Tompkins Avenue
Staten Island, NY 10304
Catherine Mudd
718-981-3976

Police Athletic League, Inc.
The Michael J. Petrides School
715 Ocean Terrace
Staten Island, NY 10301
Michelle Schluter
718-815-7556

YMCA of Greater New York/ Staten Island
PS 44 - The Thomas Brown School
80 Maple Parkway
Staten Island, NY 10303
Voula Lagoudis
718-420-1832

YMCA of Greater New York
PS 22
1860 Forest Avenue
Staten Island, NY 10303
Deanne DeNyse

< continued... >

718-556-0521

AGUADILLA DAY CARE CENTER

656 Willoughby Ave.
Brooklyn, NY 11206

(718) 443-2900 Administrative
(718) 443-2905 FAX

Ms. E. Martin, Executive Director
Languages Spoken: Spanish

Services

Arts and Crafts Instruction
Child Care Centers
Recreational Activities

Ages: 6 to 8
Population Served: Emotional Disability,
Speech/Language Disability
Program Hours: School year, Monday - Friday: 3-6
p.m.; Summer: 7:30 a.m.-6 p.m.
Fees: ACD determines fees.
Medication Administered: No
Transportation Provided: Yes (only from PS 304, PS
59 and PS 23)
Wheelchair Accessible: No
Service Description: The after school program at this
city-funded day care center provides transportation from
local schools. Others must be taken to the center.

AGUDATH ISRAEL OF AMERICA

42 Broadway
New York, NY 10004

(212) 797-9000 [284] Administrative
(646) 254-1600 FAX

Mashi Kaufman, Executive Director

Services

Respite, Children's Out-of-Home

BNOS CHAVIVOS INTEGRATION PROGRAM
Recreational Activities

Ages: 6 to 30 (males); 14 to 30 (females)
Population Served: Developmental Disability
Area Served: Brooklyn, Manhattan
Program Hours: Males - Saturday afternoon; Females -
Saturday evening
Transportation Provided: Yes
Wheelchair Accessible: No

ALIANZA DOMINICANA, INC.

2410 Amsterdam Ave.
New York, NY 10033

(212) 740-1960 Administrative
(212) 740-1967 FAX

www.alianzadominicana.org
info@alianzadominicana.org

Moisés Perez, Executive Director
Languages Spoken: Spanish

Sites

1. ALIANZA DOMINICANA, INC.
2410 Amsterdam Ave.
New York, NY 10033

(212) 740-1960 Administrative
(212) 740-1967 FAX

www.alianzadominicana.org

Moises Perez, Executive Director

**2. ALIANZA DOMINICANA, INC. - LA PLAZA
COMMUNITY CENTER**
515 W. 182nd St.
New York, NY 10033

(212) 928-4992 Administrative
(212) 927-8095 FAX

José Duran, Supervisor

3. ALIANZA DOMINICA, INC.
2346 Amsterdam Ave.
New York, NY 10036

(212) 795-5872 Administrative
(212) 795-9645 FAX

www.alianzadom.org

Felix Arias, Administrative Director

Services

LA FAMILIA UNIDA DAY CARE CENTER
Child Care Centers

Sites: 1

Computer Classes
Homework Help Programs
Recreational Activities
Tutoring

Ages: 6 to 12
Population Served: Learning Disability,
Speech/Language Disability
Area Served: All Boroughs
Program Hours: School year: 3-6 p.m.,
Summer and School Holidays: 8 a.m-5:30 p.m.
Program Capacity: 20
Fees: Sliding scale, determined by ACD
Medication Administered: No
Transportation Provided: No

<continued...>

Wheelchair Accessible: Yes
Service Description: A city-funded agency providing pre-school and after school programs. Sports are included only in summer and during school holidays.
Sites: 2 3

English as a Second Language
Homework Help Programs
Recreational Activities

Service Description: A comprehensive community facility offering recreation and sports activities, after school programs, summer day camp, counseling, tutoring, community organizing activities, cable access program production, GED classes for youth and ESL classes for adults, peer mediation training and drug prevention.
Sites: 2

ALL CHILDREN'S HOUSE FAMILY CENTER

171 E. 121 St.
New York, NY 10035

(212) 996-2263 Administrative
(212) 996-3268 FAX

Elizabeth Mendez, Director
Languages Spoken: Spanish

Services

Arts and Crafts Instruction
Field Trips/Excursions
Mentoring Programs
Tutoring

Ages: 6 to 10
Population Served: Developmental Disability, Emotional Disability
Program Hours: Monday - Friday: 3:30-6 p.m.
Medication Administered: No
Transportation Provided: No
Service Description: Provides a variety of after school activities for children with special needs. Also offers counseling for individuals and families, primarily supporting children with emotional difficulties, placing emphasis on preventive services.
Contact: Chris Velatoro

ALLEY POND ENVIRONMENTAL CENTER

228-06 Northern Blvd.
Douglaston, NY 11363

(718) 229-4000 Administrative
(718) 229-0376 FAX

www.alleypond.com

Jill Weiss, Assistant Educational Director

Services

Arts and Crafts Instruction
Nature Centers/Walks
Parks/Recreation Areas
Zoos/Wildlife Parks

Ages: 5 to 7
Area Served: Bronx, Brooklyn, Manhattan, Nassau County, Queens
Program Hours: Twice per week. Call for days.
Fees: Call for details
Transportation Provided: No
Wheelchair Accessible: Yes
Service Description: Provides after school recreational activities for mainstream and special needs population.

AMERICAN CRAFT MUSEUM

40 W. 53rd St.
New York, NY 10019

(212) 956-3535 Administrative
(212) 459-0026 FAX

www.americancraftmuseum.org
amy.kuzniar@amerciancraftmuseum.org

Amy Kuzniar, Coordinator, School and Children's Prog.
Languages Spoken: French, German, Italian

Services

CRAFT DISCOVERY PROGRAM
Arts and Crafts Instruction
Museums

Ages: 6 and up
Area Served: All Boroughs
Program Hours: Tuesday - Friday: Sessions are 90 minutes long. Call museum for exact times.
Fees: $75, call for reservations
Medication Administered: No
Transportation Provided: No
Wheelchair Accessible: Yes

AMERICAN MUSEUM OF NATURAL HISTORY

Central Park West at 79th St.
New York, NY 10024-5192

(212) 769-5200 Reservations
(212) 769-5100 Administrative
(212) 769-5304 Education Department

www.amnh.org

Languages Spoken: Spanish

<continued...>

Services

Museums

Wheelchair Accessible: Yes
Service Description: The museum runs a variety of programs for children and families.

The Science and Nature Program for Young Children offers weekday classes during the school year for children 3 to 9 and their parents. Emphasis is on hands-on activities.   There are Morning and Early Afternoon Science Clubs and After School Science Clubs.
Young Naturalists is for children 3 to 4 and their parents. Classes Fridays 9:15-10:45 a.m. and 12:45-2:15 p.m. $720 November to March.
Young Explorers Club is for children 4 to 5 and their parents. Wednesdays, 9:15-11:45 a.m. $1,575 October to June.
Young Scientists Circle is for children 5 to 7 and their parents. Tuesdays, 3:30-5 p.m. $795 October to June.
The Fellowship of Young Scientists is for children 7 to 9. Wednesdays, 3:30-5 p.m. $700 October to June.

The Alexander M. White Natural Science Center is a teaching exhibit on the ecology of the Greater City of New York, for children, teachers and the public. School programs are Monday through Fridays, at 10:15 a.m. and at 11:30 a.m. Special Education students are welcomed. Teachers should call the general reservation number for information on topics and to reserve a time.

The Discovery Room offers families and children ages 5 to 12 a hand-on, behind-the-scenes look at science. Admission is free with museum admission. To prevent overcrowding, entry is staggered and space may be limited.

ARCHDIOCESE OF NEW YORK

1011 First Ave.
New York, NY 10022

(212) 371-1000 Administrative

Joseph E. Panepinto, Executive Director of Youth Services
Languages Spoken: Spanish

Sites

1. ARCHDIOCESE OF NEW YORK
  1011 First Ave.
  New York, NY 10022

(212) 371-1000 Administrative

Joseph E. Panepinto, Executive Director of Youth Services

2. CARDINAL SPELLMAN CENTER
  137 East Second St.
  New York, NY 10009

(212) 677-6600 Administrative
(212) 995-8537 FAX

Thomas Rosati, Director

3. LT. JOSEPH P. KENNEDY, JR. MEMORIAL COMMUNITY CENTER
  34 West 134th St.
  New York, NY 10037

(212) 862-6401 Administrative
(212) 862-6421 FAX

David Dennis, Director

4. STATEN ISLAND CYO COMMUNITY CENTER
  120 Anderson Ave.
  Staten Island, NY 10302

(718) 420-1010 Administrative
(212) 273-8361 FAX

Fran Mitilieri, Director

5. CYO WEST BRONX COMMUNITY CENTER
  1527 Jesup Ave.
  Bronx, NY 10452

(718) 293-5934 Administrative
(718) 293-5866 FAX

Ted Staniecki, Director

Services

CYO
Arts and Crafts Instruction
Homework Help Programs
Sports, Individual
Sports, Team/Leagues
Tutoring

Ages: 6 to 12
Area Served: All Boroughs
Program Hours: Call for information
Program Capacity: Varies depending on program
Fees: Call for information
Medication Administered: No
Transportation Provided: No
Service Description: Recreational, educational, cultural and group work activities are offered to after school children. The following sports activities are also available through the CYO programs: basketball, golf, track, cheerleading,

<continued...>

softball and baseball. Children with special needs are considered on a case-by-case basis.
Sites: 1 2 3 4 5

ASIA SOCIETY

725 Park Ave.
New York, NY 10022

(212) 288-6400 Administrative
(212) 517-8315 FAX
(212) 327-9237 Education Department

www.asiasociety.org

Nancy Blume, Manager, Education Programs

Services

Museums

ASIAN PROFESSIONAL EXTENSION, INC.

120 Wall St., 3rd Fl.
New York, NY 10005

(212) 809-4391 Administrative
(212) 344-5636 FAX

www.apex-ny.org
apexny@earthlink.net

Sunny Kim, Executive Director
Languages Spoken: Chinese

Services

P.S. 1 READING PROGRAM
Creative Writing

Ages: 5 to12
Population Served: Underachiever
Area Served: All Boroughs
Program Hours: Every other Saturday in one of the public libraries
Staff/Child Ratio: 1:1
Fees: None
Medication Administered: No
Transportation Provided: No
Wheelchair Accessible: Yes
Service Description: Focuses on improving the reading abilities of elementary school students by creating a stimulating learning environment.

Homework Help Programs
Mentoring Programs

Ages: 13 to 18
Population Served: Underachiever
Area Served: All Boroughs
Program Hours: Call for information
Staff/Child Ratio: 1:1
Fees: None

Medication Administered: No
Transportation Provided: No
Wheelchair Accessible: No
Service Description: The APEX mentoring program addresses the personal, educational and social needs of high school and junior high school students through individual relationships with adult volunteers.

ASPHALT GREEN

555 E. 90th St.
New York, NY 10128-7803

(212) 369-8890 Administrative
(212) 996-4426 FAX

www.asphaltgreen.org

Carol Tweedy, Executive Director
Languages Spoken: Spanish

Services

Exercise Classes/Groups
Sports, Individual
Sports, Team/Leagues
Swimming

Ages: 18 months to 12 years
Area Served: All Boroughs
Wheelchair Accessible: Yes
Service Description: The Therapeutic Aquatics/Exercise Program, a year-round aquatics program for children 18 months to 12 years with physical disabilities, is designed to develop confidence in the water while swimming and doing exercises. Each child must be accompanied in the water by a parent or guardian. An interview and swim test required for all participants to ensure proper placement.
Contact: Hugo Skinner

ASPIRA OF NEW YORK

470 Seventh Ave., 3rd Fl.
New York, NY 10018

(212) 564-6880 Administrative
(212) 564-7152 FAX

Hector Gesualdo, Executive Director
Languages Spoken: Spanish

<continued...>

Sites

1. ASPIRA OF NEW YORK
2488 Grand Concourse, Rm. 424
Bronx, NY 10458

(718) 508-0013 Administrative
(718) 508-0017 FAX

www.aspira.org/ny.html

Alex Betancourt, Deputy Director

Services

Arts and Crafts Instruction
Homework Help Programs
Tutoring
Youth Development

Ages: All Ages
Program Hours: Monday - Friday: 3:30-6 p.m.
Fees: None
Service Description: Aspira provides after school services at the following schools located in the Bronx: Beacon School/JHS 139 and BEAM 10 P.S. 86X. Accommodations can be made for children with disabilities.
Contact: Alex Betancourt
Sites: 1

ASSOCIATION FOR CHILDREN WITH DOWN SYNDROME

4 Fern Pl.
Plainview, NY 11803

(516) 933-4700 Administrative
(516) 933-9524 FAX

www.acds.org
smuzio@optonline.net

Sebastian Muzio, Executive Director
Languages Spoken: Spanish

Services

Arts and Crafts Instruction
Child Care Centers
Dancing Instruction
Exercise Classes/Groups

Ages: 5 and up
Population Served: Autism, Developmental Disability, Down Syndrome, Speech/Language Disability
Program Hours: Monday - Friday: 3-6 p.m.
Transportation Provided: No
Wheelchair Accessible: Yes
Service Description: Provides a variety of after school recreational activities for children.
Contact: Karen Seltzer

ASSOCIATION FOR NEUROLOGICALLY IMPAIRED BRAIN INJURED CHILDREN, INC. (ANIBIC)

212-12 26th Ave.
Bayside, NY 11360

(718) 423-9550 Administrative
(718) 423-9838 FAX

Jeanne Parisi, Executive Director
Languages Spoken: Greek, Spanish

Sites

1. ASSOCIATION FOR NEUROLOGICALLY IMPAIRED BRAIN INJURED CHILDREN, INC. (ANIBIC)
212-12 26th Ave.
Bayside, NY 11360

(718) 423-9550 Administrative
(718) 423-9838 FAX

Jeanne Parisi, Executive Director

2. ASSOCIATION FOR NEUROLOGICALLY IMPAIRED BRAIN INJURED CHILDREN, INC. (ANIBIC)
30-56 Whitestone Expressway, #300
Flushing, NY 11354

(718) 661-9423 Administrative

Tara Wacshwender, Site Director

Services

Arts and Crafts Instruction
Music Instruction
Sports, Individual
Sports, Team/Leagues
Swimming

Ages: 5 to 17; weekend respite: 17 and up
Population Served: Asperger Syndrome, Attention Deficit Disorder (ADD/ADHD), Autism, Cerebral Palsy, Deaf/Hard of Hearing, Developmental Delay, Developmental Disability, Down Syndrome, Health Impairment, Learning Disability, Mental Retardation (mild-moderate), Neurological Disability, Seizure Disorder, Speech/Language Disability, Tourette Syndrome, Traumatic Brain Injury (TBI)
Area Served: All Boroughs
Program Hours: Weekend Respite: Saturday and Sunday: Noon-5 p.m. Call for information.
Fees: $13 per session
Wheelchair Accessible: Yes
Service Description: The recreation/socialization program provides direct comprehensive services to children and adults. A large variety of recreation, athletic and social programs help to build life and socialization skills. Individual programs are developed according to student's need. Reimbursement provided. A

<continued...>

weekend respite program is also available for those 17 and older. It provides an opportunity for young adults to meet new friends and participate in community events.
Sites: 1

TUTORING PROGRAM
Homework Help Programs
Tutoring

Ages: 5 to 22
Population Served: Asperger Syndrome, Attention Deficit Disorder (ADD/ADHD), Autism, Cerebral Palsy, Deaf/Hard of Hearing, Developmental Delay, Developmental Disability, Down Syndrome, Health Impairment, Learning Disability, Mental Retardation (mild-moderate), Neurological Disability, Seizure Disorder, Speech/Language Disability, Tourette Syndrome, Traumatic Brain Disorder
Area Served: All Boroughs
Fees: One hour session $18.00; 15 session committment
Medication Administered: No
Transportation Provided: No
Wheelchair Accessible: Yes
Sites: 1 2

ASSOCIATION FOR THE HELP OF RETARDED CHILDREN (AHRC)

200 Park Ave. South
New York, NY 10003

(212) 780-2500 Administrative
(212) 780-2732 FAX

www.ahrcnyc.org
sbstein@ahrcnyc.org

Michael Goldfarb, Executive Director
Languages Spoken: Chinese, Russian, Spanish

Sites

1. ASSOCIATION FOR THE HELP OF RETARDED CHILDREN (AHRC)
200 Park Ave. South
New York, NY 10003

(212) 780-2500 Administrative
(212) 780-2732 FAX

Courtney Sweeting, Director of Recreation Services

2. ASSOCIATION FOR THE HELP OF RETARDED CHILDREN (AHRC) - BROOKLYN BLUE FEATHER ELEMENTARY SCHOOL
477 Court St.
Brooklyn, NY 11231

(718) 834-0597 Administrative
(718) 834-0768 FAX

Carol Repole, Principal

Services

BRONX CHILDREN'S RECREATION
Art Therapy
Arts and Crafts Instruction
Cooking Classes
Music Instruction
Music Therapy
Recreational Activities

Ages: 6 to 12
Population Served: Mental Retardation (mild-moderate)
Area Served: Bronx
Program Hours: Saturdays and some Sundays: 10 a.m.-1 p.m.
Fees: Minimal to none
Transportation Provided: Yes
Service Description: Creative arts and music therapies, cooking classes, story time, outdoor activities and special seasonal events. Program takes place at the Samuel H. Young Post, 1530 Hutchinson River Parkway, Bronx New York 10466.
Sites: 1

STUDIO ARTS
Art Therapy
Arts and Crafts Instruction

Ages: 16 and up
Population Served: Developmental Disability, Mental Retardation (mild-moderate)
Area Served: All Boroughs
Program Hours: Fridays: 5-6:30 p.m.
Service Description: Drawing, painting, collage techniques and assorted art therapy.
Sites: 1

BROOKLYN AFTER SCHOOL FOR ELEMENTARY
Art Therapy
Arts and Crafts Instruction
Dance Therapy
Homework Help Programs
Music Therapy
Recreational Activities
Storytelling
Tutoring

Ages: 5 to 12
Area Served: Brooklyn
Program Hours: October - May; Tuesday, Wednesday, Thursday: 3-6 p.m.
Fees: Sliding scale
Transportation Provided: Yes, from after school site to home
Wheelchair Accessible: Yes
Service Description: An after school program for children with Mental Retardation/Developmental Delay, featuring creative arts therapy, music and dance therapy, recreational sports, trips in the community,

< continued... >

homework help and story time.
Sites: 2

BRONX DAY/EVENING RECREATION
Arts and Crafts Instruction
Cooking Classes
Dance Therapy
Field Trips/Excursions
Music Therapy
Recreational Activities
Sports, Individual

Ages: 16 and over
Population Served: Developmental Disability, Mental Retardation (mild-moderate)
Area Served: All Boroughs
Program Hours: Saturdays, 10 a.m.-2 p.m. (Day Program); 5:30-7:30 p.m. (Evening Program)
Fees: None
Transportation Provided: Yes (Day Program only)
Service Description: The Bronx Day Recreation provides creative arts therapy, music and dance therapy, cooking classes, sports and recreation, special seasonal events and monthly community outings. Participants in this program require extra supervision and do not travel independently. Priority is given to those not attending a day program. The Bronx Evening Recreation provides recreational sports activities, parties, discussions, art projects, dancing and community activities. Both programs are held at 1952 Mayflower Ave., Bronx, New York 10461.
Sites: 1

MANHATTAN SATURDAY RECREATION
Arts and Crafts Instruction
Cooking Classes
Dance Therapy
Field Trips/Excursions
Music Therapy

Ages: 6 to 12
Area Served: Manhattan
Fees: None
Service Description: Creative arts therapy, music and dance therapy, recreational sports, trips in the neighborhood and special seasonal events. Also provides a therapeutic recreation activities under close supervision and enriched staffing for children with challenging behaviors.
Sites: 1

BRONX TEEN AND YOUNG ADULT RECREATION
Arts and Crafts Instruction
Sports, Individual

Ages: 12 to 26
Population Served: Developmental Disability, Health Impairment, Mental Retardation (mild-moderate)
Area Served: Bronx
Program Hours: Saturdays and some Sundays, 10 a.m.-3 p.m.
Fees: None
Transportation Provided: Yes

Wheelchair Accessible: Yes
Service Description: Creative arts therapy, movement and dance therapy, adaptive sports, exercise time and special seasonal events. Priority is given to those not attending a day program during the week. Program takes place at 1500 Pelham Parkway South, Bronx.
Sites: 1

TEEN TRIPS IN THE COMMUNITY
Field Trips/Excursions

Ages: 13 to 19
Population Served: Developmental Disability, Mental Retardation (mild-moderate)
Area Served: All Boroughs
Fees: Minimal to none
Service Description: This program consists of one day trip per borough each month. Trips include Diner's club, movies, museums, Broadway and off-Broadway shows, motorcoach tours and other exciting places. Advanced signup is necessary and transportation is provided from designated pickup points in every borough.
Sites: 1

BOWLING PROGRAMS
Sports, Team/Leagues

Ages: 16 and over
Population Served: Developmental Disability, Mental Retardation (mild-moderate)
Area Served: All Boroughs
Fees: $3 to $5 for two games and shoe rental
Transportation Provided: No
Service Description: AHRC Bowling programs are open to members 16 and over. There is a program in every borough that takes place at the following times and locations:

BRONX
Gun Post Lanes
1215 Gun Hill Rd.
Saturday: 12:30 p.m.

BROOKLYN
Mark Lanes
423 88th St.
Saturday: Noon

MANHATTAN
Leisure Lanes
Port Authority Bus Terminal
42nd St. at Eighth Ave.
Saturday: 12:30 p.m.

QUEENS
Hollywood Lanes
99-23 Queens Blvd.
Rego Park
Saturday: 1 p.m.

< continued... >

STATEN ISLAND
Bowling on the Green
55 Mill Rd.
Sunday: 2 p.m.
Contact: Miriam Figueroa
Sites: 1

HUNTER COLLEGE AT THE NY LEAGUE
Tutoring

Ages: 16 and up
Population Served: Learning Disability
Area Served: All Boroughs
Program Hours: Wednesday: 5:30-7 p.m.
Fees: None
Transportation Provided: No
Wheelchair Accessible: Yes
Service Description: This class focuses on improving reading and basic math skills, history, geography and creative writing. Members must be reading at the minimum of a second grade level and will be tested prior to enrollment. Program takes place at the NY League Work Center, 200 Varick St., 7th Fl., New York.
Sites: 1

ASSOCIATION IN MANHATTAN FOR AUTISTIC CHILDREN, INC. (AMAC)

25 W. 17th St.
New York, NY 10011

(212) 645-5005 Administrative
(212) 645-0170 FAX

Frederica Blausten, Executive Director
Languages Spoken: Spanish

Services

Arts and Crafts Instruction
Exercise Classes/Groups
Homework Help Programs
Youth Development

Ages: 3 to 18
Population Served: Autism
Program Hours: Monday - Friday: 3-6 p.m., Saturday: 9 a.m.-4 p.m.
Fees: Call for information
Transportation Provided: Yes
Wheelchair Accessible: Yes
Service Description: Teaches leisure skills, social competencies and games to children who require supervision. Also offers homework assistance programs and physical fitness instruction.

Respite, Children's Out-of-Home

Ages: 7 to 21
Population Served: Autism
Program Hours: Call for information
Program Capacity: 12-14
Staff/Child Ratio: 1:2
Method of Payment: Sliding Scale
Transportation Provided: Yes
Service Description: Provides an overnight and weekend respite program for children and young adults.

ASSOCIATION TO BENEFIT CHILDREN

419 E. 86th St.
New York, NY 10028

(212) 831-1322 Administrative
(212) 426-9488 FAX

www.a-b-c.org
abc@a-b-c.org

Gretchen Buchenholtz, Executive Director
Languages Spoken: Spanish

Sites

1. ASSOCIATION TO BENEFIT CHILDREN - CASSIDY'S PLACE
419 E. 86th St.
New York, NY 10028

(212) 831-1322 Administrative
(212) 426-9488 FAX

www.a-b-c.org

Gretchen Buchenholtz, Executive Director

2. ASSOCIATION TO BENEFIT CHILDREN - ALL CHILDRENS HOUSE FAMILY CENTER/ THE GRAHAM SCHOOL
171 E. 121st St.
New York, NY 10035

(212) 996-2263 Administrative
(212) 996-3268 FAX

Elizabeth Mendez, Director

Services

Arts and Crafts Instruction
Exercise Classes/Groups
Storytelling

Ages: 4 and up
Area Served: All Boroughs
Program Hours: Monday - Friday: 3:30-6 p.m.
Program Capacity: 32
Staff/Child Ratio: 2:15
Fees: None
Medication Administered: No
Transportation Provided: No
Wheelchair Accessible: Yes

< continued... >

Service Description: Provides an after school program for mainstream and special needs children.
Contact: Missy Repko, Program Coordinator
Sites: 1

Respite, Children's Out-of-Home

Population Served: AIDS/HIV +, Asperger Syndrome, Asthma, Autism, Cerebral Palsy, Cystic Fibrosis, Deaf/Hard of Hearing, Developmental Delay, Developmental Disability, Down Syndrome, Emotional Disability, Health Impairment, Learning Disability, Mental Retardation (mild-moderate), Multiple Disability, Physical/Orthopedic Disability, Rare Disorder, Seizure Disorder, Speech/Language Disability, Spina Bifida, Traumatic Brain Injury (TBI), Underachiever
Area Served: All Boroughs
Medication Administered: No
Wheelchair Accessible: Yes, limited
Service Description: Provides services necessary to preserve and strengthen families in danger of being broken apart by overwhelming stresses of poverty. Services may include housing and case management, parent education, respite services, recreation and prevention programs.
Sites: 2

ASTOR HOME FOR CHILDREN

6339 Mill St.
PO Box 5005
Rhinebeck, NY 12572

(845) 876-4081 Administrative
(845) 876-2020 FAX

www.astorservices.org

Sister Logan Rose, Executive Director
Languages Spoken: American Sign Language, French, Spanish

Sites

1. ASTOR HOME FOR CHILDREN - ASTOR DAY TREATMENT - BRONX

4330 Byron Ave.
Bronx, NY 10466

(718) 324-7526 Administrative
(718) 994-8465 FAX

David Eckert, Ph.D., Director

Services

FAMILY SUPPORT PROGRAM
Respite, Children's Out-of-Home

Ages: Birth to 18
Population Served: Emotional Disability, Learning Disability
Area Served: Bronx, Hudson Valley

Program Hours: Call for information
Fees: Call for information
Medication Administered: No
Transportation Provided: No
Wheelchair Accessible: Yes
Service Description: Provides a range of support services to parents of children who are considered seriously emotionally disturbed. Services include weekly parent-support groups, educational seminars and respite care.
Contact: Parent Advocate, (718) 324-7526
Sites: 1

AUTISM FOUNDATION OF NEW YORK

1050 Forest Hill Road
Staten Island, NY 10314

(718) 370-8200 Administrative
(718) 370-8300 FAX

www.afny.org
aaog1@aol.com

Sandy Levine, Executive Director

Services

Dancing Instruction
Exercise Classes/Groups
Sports, Individual
Sports, Team/Leagues

Ages: All Ages
Population Served: Asperger Syndrome, Attention Deficit Disorder (ADD/ADHD), Autism, Developmental Disability, Neurological Disability, Pervasive Developmental Disorder (PDD/NOS)
Area Served: All Boroughs
Program Hours: Hours vary depending on program. Please call for further information.
Fees: Vary depending on program. Call for information.
Transportation Provided: No
Wheelchair Accessible: Yes
Service Description: The Autism Foundation of New York provides a variety of after school and weekend programs for children afflicted with Autism and Autism Spectrum disorders. Please contact the Foundation for a listing of programs, fees and dates.

BAIS AHARON - THE CREATIVE ACADEMICS AND REMEDIAL EDUCATION CENTER

6506-10 17th Ave.
Brooklyn, NY 11204

(718) 256-7760 Administrative
(718) 837-4225 FAX

Rabbi Chaim A. Stamm, Executive Director
Languages Spoken: Yiddish

Services

Tutoring

Ages: 6 to 18
Population Served: Attention Deficit Disorder (ADD/ADHD), Learning Disability, Speech/Language Disability
Area Served: All Boroughs
Program Hours: Call for information
Staff/Child Ratio: 1:1
Fees: Please call center for fees.
Medication Administered: No
Transportation Provided: No
Wheelchair Accessible: No
Service Description: Provides one-to-one tutoring.

BAIS EZRA

4510 16th Ave.
Brooklyn, NY 11204

(718) 851-6300 Intake
(718) 435-5533 Administrative

Services

Recreational Activities
Respite, Children's Out-of-Home

Ages: All Ages
Population Served: Developmental Disability
Area Served: Brooklyn, Nassau, Suffolk
Program Hours: Call for information
Program Capacity: Flexible
Staff/Child Ratio: 1:1
Fees: None
Medication Administered: No
Service Description: Able to serve the after school needs of children with developmental disabilities.

BALIN MANN ASSOCIATES

603 E. 23rd St.
Brooklyn, NY 11210

(718) 859-3367 Administrative

Amy Balin, Co-Director

Services

Remedial Education

Ages: 2 to adult
Population Served: Learning Disability, Dyslexia and all other related disabilities, Speech/Language Disability
Program Hours: Monday - Friday: hour-long sessions after school
Staff/Child Ratio: 1:1
Fees: Call for information.
Medication Administered: No
Transportation Provided: No
Wheelchair Accessible: No
Service Description: Provides speech-language therapy and educational therapy. Children with all language disorders are treated. Children are seen on an individual basis after school for hour-long sessions.

BALLET HISPANICO

167 W. 89th St.
New York, NY 10024

(212) 362-6710 Administrative
(212) 362-7809 FAX

www.ballethispanico.org
info@ballethispanico.org

Tina Ramírez, Artistic Director

Services

Dancing Instruction

Ages: 4 to 19
Area Served: All Boroughs
Program Hours: Hours and dates vary depending on program. Call for information.
Fees: Fees vary depending on program. Call for information.
Medication Administered: No
Transportation Provided: No
Service Description: Provides dancing instruction to children ages 4 to 19. Children with special needs are considered on a case-by-case basis.

BANK STREET COLLEGE OF EDUCATION - FAMILY CENTER

610 W. 112th St.
New York, NY 10025

(212) 979-0244 [236] Head Start
(212) 875-4547 Libarty Partnership Program FAX
(212) 875-4572 Home Based EI/Evaluation
(212) 875-4573 Preschool/Early Intervention
(212) 875-4566 FAX
(212) 875-4412 Child Care
(212) 875-4481 Liberty Partnership Program

Amy Flynn, Director
Languages Spoken: Spanish

Services

LIBERTY PARTNERSHIP PROGRAM AT BANK STREET COLLEGE
Arts and Crafts Instruction
Computer Classes
Homework Help Programs
Recreational Activities
Tutoring

Ages: 5th through 12th grade
Population Served: At Risk, Underachiever
Area Served: All Boroughs
Program Hours: Weekdays: 3:30-6:30 p.m., Saturday: 10 a.m.-12:30 p.m., Some school holidays, same hours.
Program Capacity: 230
Staff/Child Ratio: Classes of 15 or fewer
Fees: None
Medication Administered: No
Transportation Provided: No
Wheelchair Accessible: Yes
Service Description: Part of a state-wide comprehensive after school program. Provides a wide range of services to youth from disadvantaged areas and children at risk. In addition to youth programs, parent groups and advocacy are available.
Contact: Kara Knott, Interim Director

BARTOW-PELL MANSION MUSEUM CARRIAGE HOUSE AND GARDEN

895 Shore Road N.
Bronx, NY 10464

(718) 885-1461 Administrative

Mary Ellen Williamson, Executive Director

Services

Museums

BASKETBALL CITY

Pier 63 @ W. 23rd St.
New York, NY 10011

(212) 924-4040 Administrative
(212) 924-5550 FAX

www.basketballcity.com

Justin Leonard, Director of Youth Programs

Services

Sports, Team/Leagues

Ages: 6 to 16
Area Served: All Boroughs
Program Hours: Weekend programs: Saturday and Sunday: 10 a.m.-1 p.m.
Summer: Monday - Friday: 9 a.m.-4 p.m.
Program Capacity: Varies by program
Staff/Child Ratio: 1:5
Fees: Weekend programs: $190 per season
Summer camp: $300-325
Method of Payment: Cash, Check, Credit Card, Money Order
Medication Administered: No
Transportation Provided: No
Wheelchair Accessible: Yes
Service Description: Offers weekend programs during the school year and a summer camp. Provides instruction in the fundamentals of basketball and offers a chance to play as a team. Children with disabilities accepted on a case-by-case basis.

BAYSIDE YMCA

214-13 35th Ave.
Bayside, NY 11361

(718) 229-5972 Administrative
(718) 819-0058 FAX

www.ymcanyc.org
lfosco@ymcanyc.org

Laura Fosco, School Age Director

Services

Arts and Crafts Instruction
Homework Help Programs
Recreational Activities
Sports, Individual
Sports, Team/Leagues
Tutoring

Ages: 5 to 14
Program Hours: Monday - Friday: 3-6 p.m.
Fees: Call center for information
Method of Payment: Bank Draft, Cash, Credit Card, Personal Check
Medication Administered: No

< continued... >

Transportation Provided: Yes, from local schools
Service Description: Academic skills are encouraged through homework help and tutoring along with developing interpersonal relationships and self-esteem. Accommodations can be made for children with disabilities.
Contact: Laura Fosco, School-Age Director

BEDFORD HAITIAN COMMUNITY CENTER

1534 Bedford Ave.
Brooklyn, NY 11216

(718) 756-0600 Administrative
(718) 771-6597 FAX

Joseph Dormeus, MSW, Executive Director
Languages Spoken: French, Haitian Creole

Services

Arts and Crafts Instruction
Exercise Classes/Groups
Homework Help Programs
Tutoring

Ages: 6 to 12
Population Served: AIDS/HIV+, Autism, Cerebral Palsy, Developmental Delay, Developmental Disability, Down Syndrome, Mental Retardation (mild-moderate), Mental Retardation (severe-profound), Pervasive Developmental Disorder (PDD/NOS)
Area Served: Brooklyn
Program Hours: Monday - Friday: 3-6 p.m.
Fees: None
Medication Administered: No
Transportation Provided: No
Wheelchair Accessible: Yes

BEDFORD STUYVESANT COMMUNITY MENTAL HEALTH CENTER

1406 Fulton St.
Brooklyn, NY 11216

(718) 443-1742 Administrative
(718) 636-1520 FAX

Ophie A. Franklin, Executive Director
Languages Spoken: French, Haitian Creole, Spanish

Sites

1. BEDFORD STUYVESANT COMMUNITY MENTAL HEALTH CENTER - FAMILY SUPPORT PROGRAM
340 Halsey St.
Brooklyn, NY 11216

(718) 919-8269 Administrative
(718) 571-4564 FAX
(718) 443-1742 After school recreation

Edeline Fleury, Manager, Family Support Services

Services

Recreational Activities

Ages: 6 and up
Population Served: AIDS/HIV+, Attention Deficit Disorder (ADD/ADHD), Developmental Delay, Developmental Disability, Emotional Disability, Juvenile Offender, Learning Disability, Mental Retardation (mild-moderate)
Area Served: Brooklyn
Fees: Call for information
Wheelchair Accessible: No
Service Description: Offers an after school program and recreational activities. A Saturday recreation program is available.
Sites: 1

BEDFORD STUYVESANT YMCA

1121 Bedford Ave.
Brooklyn, NY 11216

(718) 789-1497 Administrative

Services

Arts and Crafts Instruction
Exercise Classes/Groups
Homework Help Programs
Sports, Individual
Sports, Team/Leagues

Ages: 2 to 12
Program Hours: Monday - Friday: 3-6 p.m.
Fees: Call center for information
Method of Payment: Bankdraft, Cash, Credit Card or Personal Check
Medication Administered: No
Service Description: This program helps school-aged children grow in spirit, mind and body. This is accomplished through homework help, teamwork during sports and skills building. Accommodations can be made for children with special needs.
Contact: Sandra Perch

BEEKMAN SCHOOL

220 E. 50th St.
New York, NY 10022

(212) 755-6666 Administrative
(212) 888-6085 FAX

www.beekmanschool.org

George Higgins, Headmaster

<continued...>

Services

THE TUTORING SCHOOL
Computer Classes
Creative Writing
English as a Second Language
Exercise Classes/Groups
Homework Help Programs
Tutoring

Ages: 14 to 18
Population Served: Attention Deficit Disorder (ADD/ADHD)
Area Served: All Boroughs, New Jersey, Long Island, Westchester
Program Hours: Monday - Friday (hours are flexible)
Program Capacity: 80
Staff/Child Ratio: 1:3
Fees: Hourly or by semester; Call school for detailed information.
Method of Payment: Check
Medication Administered: No
Transportation Provided: No
Wheelchair Accessible: No
Service Description: After school tutoring for high school students. At-home instruction can also be arranged. Provides a 3-week mini session in June and a 6-week summer school program from July to mid-August.
Contact: Lisa Chasin, Director of The Tutoring School

BELLPORT AREA COMMUNITY ACTION COMMITTEE

1685 Montauk Highway
Bellport, NY 11713

(631) 286-3107 Administrative
(631) 776-7671 FAX

Mary Ann Ragona, Executive Director
Languages Spoken: Spanish

Services

Arts and Crafts Instruction
Child Care Centers
Homework Help Programs
Sports, Team/Leagues

Ages: 5 to 12
Population Served: Developmental Delay, Developmental Disability, Learning Disability, Mental Retardation (mild-moderate), Mental Retardation (severe-profound), Multiple Disability, Neurological Disability, Speech/Language Disability
Program Hours: Monday - Friday: 3:30-6 p.m.
Fees: None
Transportation Provided: Yes
Service Description: Located at two sites, the program provides services to youth and families, including counseling, substance abuse counseling and tutoring, teen support services, after school child care, peer leadership training and family support for

developmentally disabled persons at the Boys & Girls Club of the Bellport area and the A.S.C. Program at Bellport High School.

BELVEDERE CASTLE IN CENTRAL PARK

The Arsenal, 830 Fifth Ave.
New York, NY 10021

(212) 772-0210 Administrative
(212) 772-0214 FAX

www.centralparknyc.org
stewardship@centralparknyc.org

Randi Ballan, Community Service Program

Services

Museums
Parks/Recreation Areas

Ages: 5 and up
Area Served: All boroughs
Program Hours: 10a.m. - 5p.m.
Wheelchair Accessible: Yes
Service Description: Available to all children during opening hours. The Youth Core is a program for high school students (14 to 18) who do restoration work.

BETH ELOHIM

274 Garfield Pl.
Brooklyn, NY 11215

(718) 768-3814 Administrative
(718) 768-7414 FAX

Bobbie Finkelstein, Executive Director

Services

Acting Instruction
Arts and Crafts Instruction
Computer Classes
Dancing Instruction
Homework Help Programs
Music Instruction
Sports, Individual
Sports, Team/Leagues
Storytelling
Swimming

Ages: 5 to 10
Population Served: Learning Disability, Speech/Language Disability
Program Hours: Monday - Friday: 3-6 p.m.
Program Capacity: 140 children/day
Staff/Child Ratio: 1:6 (five and six year olds), 1:8 (seven to ten year olds)
Fees: Per trimester: $780 for 5 days, $670 for 4 days, $560 for 3 days, $435 for 2 days, $255 for 1 day

< continued... >

Method of Payment: Cash, Check, Credit Card
Medication Administered: Yes
Transportation Provided: No
Wheelchair Accessible: No
Service Description: Congregation Beth Elohim's After School Center offers children a wide variety of instructional classes and recreational activities in a safe and caring environment. The program encourages each child to develop at his or her own pace and to express themselves and their creativity in a relaxed and enjoyable atmosphere. Classes include team sports, gymnastics, swimming, cooking, drama, art, dance, computers and chess.

BETH HANDLER ASSOCIATES

350 Central Park West
New York, NY 10025

(212) 316-3237 Administrative
(212) 316-0051 FAX

Beth Handler

Services

Remedial Education
Study Skills Assistance

Ages: 6 and up
Population Served: Attention Deficit Hyperactive Disorder (ADD/ADHD), Learning Disability
Area Served: All Boroughs
Program Hours: Call for information
Fees: Call for information.
Medication Administered: No
Transportation Provided: No
Wheelchair Accessible: Yes

BIG APPLE CIRCUS

505 Eighth Ave., 19th Fl.
New York, NY 10018

(800) 922-3772 Customer Service
(212) 268-2500 Administrative
(212) 268-3163 FAX

www.bigapplecircus.org

Gary Dunning, Executive Director

Services

CIRCUS OF THE SENSES
Theater Performances

Ages: Birth to 17
Population Served: Deaf/Hard of Hearing, Visual Disability/Blind
Area Served: All Boroughs
Program Hours: Performance takes place the first Thursday in December at 11 a.m.

Fees: Complimentary tickets
Medication Administered: No
Transportation Provided: No
Wheelchair Accessible: Yes
Service Description: Circus of the Senses is a special production of the Big Apple Circus designed to meet the needs of children who are blind or vision impaired and/or deaf or hearing impaired.

BIG APPLE GAMES

General Office, IS 318
101 Walton St.
Brooklyn, NY 11206

(718) 782-0589 Administrative
(718) 384-7867 FAX

Alan Fierstein, Director

Services

Sports, Individual
Sports, Team/Leagues

Ages: 9 to 21
Program Hours: Call for information
Fees: Call for information
Service Description: The summer sports program has sites throughout the city in public schools. They include children with disabilities on an individual basis.

BIG BROTHERS/BIG SISTERS OF NEW YORK CITY, INC.

223 E. 30th St.
New York, NY 10016

(212) 686-2042 Administrative
(212) 779-1221 FAX

www.bigsnyc.org

Alan Luks, Director
Languages Spoken: French, Spanish

Services

CENTER FOR TRAINING AND FAMILY SERVICES
Mentoring Programs

Population Served: Emotional Disability
Area Served: All Boroughs
Service Description: One-to-one matching of a child from single-parent families and a carefully screened adult volunteer. The volunteer provides guidance, support and role modeling through friendship. Volunteers and youth meet bi-weekly for four hours, participating in various social, recreational and educational activities. There is

<continued...>

a career focus with the teen matches. All youth are evaluated on an individual basis.

BIG SISTER EDUCATIONAL ACTION AND SERVICE CENTER

117-08 Merrick Blvd.
Jamaica, NY 11434

(718) 723-1119 Administrative
(718) 723-1123 FAX

Virginia LaMarr, Executive Director

Services

English as a Second Language
Homework Help Programs
Test Preparation
Tutoring

Ages: 7 and up
Population Served: Underachiever
Area Served: Queens
Program Hours: Monday - Friday: 3:30-5 p.m., Saturday: 9 a.m.-12 p.m. Adults can attend Monday - Friday: 8:30 a.m.-3 p.m.
Program Capacity: 150
Staff/Child Ratio: 1:3
Fees: None
Medication Administered: No
Transportation Provided: No
Wheelchair Accessible: No
Service Description: Provides academic enhancement programs for children and adults.

BLOOMINGDALE SCHOOL OF MUSIC

323 W. 108th St.
New York, NY 10025

(212) 663-6021 Administrative
(212) 932-9429 FAX

www.bloomingdalemusic.org
registrar@bloomingdalemusic.org

Lawrence Davis, Executive Director

Services

Music Instruction

Ages: 6 months and up
Area Served: All Boroughs
Program Hours: Weekdays: 9 a.m.-9 p.m. ; Saturdays: 9 a.m.-5 p.m.; Sundays: 11 a.m.- 6 p.m. Call for details and appointments.
Staff/Child Ratio: 1:1
Fees: Vary from program to program, financial aid available.
Method of Payment: Cash, Checks, Money Orders, Visa, MasterCard, Discover and Debit Cards

Medication Administered: No
Transportation Provided: No
Wheelchair Accessible: Yes
Service Description: There is something for everyone at Bloomingdale. For the student just starting out, there is a highly experienced faculty, patient, supportive and well acquainted with the challenges that beginning students face. For the advanced student, there are exciting new performing opportunities through the advanced student recitals, the concerto competition, the performance competition and over 15 chamber music ensembles. For the busy adult student, there is the new "season ticket" program for private lessons and chamber music, which allows for a more flexible schedule. Children with disabilities considered on a case-by-case basis.

BOOKER T. WASHINGTON LEARNING CENTER

325 E. 101st St.
New York, NY 10029

(212) 427-0404 Learning Center
(212) 831-5557 FAX

Rev. Leroy Ricksy, Director
Languages Spoken: Spanish

Services

Computer Classes
Homework Help Programs
Tutoring

Ages: 6 to 13
Area Served: All Boroughs
Program Hours: Monday - Friday: 3-5:45 p.m.
Program Capacity: 36
Staff/Child Ratio: 1:8
Fees: Sliding Scale
Medication Administered: No
Transportation Provided: No
Wheelchair Accessible: No
Service Description: Provides after school programs for all school age children. Children with special needs are considered on a case-by-case basis.
Contact: Kim Wright, Program Coordinator

BOSTON SECOR COMMUNITY CENTER

3540 Bivona St.
Bronx, NY 10475

(718) 671-1040 Administrative
(718) 671-0879 FAX

Gloria Carty, Director
Languages Spoken: French, Spanish

< continued... >

Services

Arts and Crafts Instruction
Computer Classes
Field Trips/Excursions
Homework Help Programs
Sports, Team/Leagues
Tutoring

Ages: 6 to 19
Area Served: Bronx
Program Hours: Monday - Friday: 3-6 p.m.
Fees: None
Medication Administered: No
Transportation Provided: No
Service Description: Provides an after school program which offers a variety of activities for children. Children with special needs are considered on a case-by-case basis.

BOY SCOUTS OF AMERICA - GREATER NEW YORK COUNCIL

350 Fifth Ave., 4th Fl.
New York, NY 10018

(212) 242-1100 Administrative
(212) 242-3630 FAX

www.bsa-gnyc.org
info@bsa-gnyc.org

Anthony Cardiello, Director of Children's Programs

Services

SCOUTING FOR THE HANDICAPPED
Youth Development

Ages: 6 to 20
Population Served: Autism, Cerebral Palsy, Developmental Disability, Emotional Disability, Mental Retardation (mild-moderate), Mental Retardation (severe-profound), Pervasive Developmental Disorder (PDD/NOS), Visual Disability/Blind
Area Served: All Boroughs
Wheelchair Accessible: Yes
Service Description: Scouting programs offer recreation, socialization, trips, lessons on the environment, character development and remedial programs. Scouting activities are also available for boys with special needs. Children in special education programs in New York public schools are eligible for in-school program.
Contact: Dave Gibbs, (212) 651-2910

BOYS AND GIRLS CLUBS OF AMERICA

3 W. 35th St., 9th Fl.
New York, NY 10001

(800) 854-2582 Toll Free
(212) 351-5480 Administrative
(212) 351-5493 FAX

www.bgca.org

Jim Schwab, Regional Vice President

Services

Arts and Crafts Instruction
Homework Help Programs
Recreational Activities
Tutoring
Youth Development

Ages: 6 to 12
Area Served: Nationwide
Program Hours: Call for information
Fees: Call for information
Medication Administered: No
Transportation Provided: No
Wheelchair Accessible: Yes
Service Description: Offers a comprehensive homework help and tutoring program. Power Hour is designed to raise the academic proficiency of Club members. Children with disabilities considered on a case-by-case basis.

BRONX LOCATIONS

GLORIA WISE ACTIVITIES COMMITTEE
Boys & Girls Clubs
950 Baychester Avenue
Bronx, NY 10475-1703
718-379-2830
Mr. Charles Rosen, Executive Director

GLORIA WISE YOUTH ACTIVITIES COMMITTEE
Boys & Girls Club
Beacon Unit
3710 Barnes Avenue
Bronx, NY 10467
718-654-5881
Ms. Egeria Bennett, Unit Director

GLORIA WISE YOUTH ACTIVITIES COMMITTEE
Boys & Girls Club
Promoting Self-Esteem After School Program
4140 Hutchinson River Parkway
Bronx, NY 10475
718-379-2830
Dr. Robert Barbo, Unit Director

KIPS BAY BOYS & GIRLS CLUB, INC.
1930 Randall Avenue
Bronx, NY 10473
718-893-8600
Mr. Daniel Quintero, Executive Director

< continued... >

KIPS BAY BOYS & GIRLS CLUB, INC.
I.S. 158 Extension
700 Home Street
Bronx, NY 10456-5435
718-542-1155
Mr. Derek Harrison, Site Supervisor

KIPS BAY BOYS & GIRLS CLUB, INC.
P.S. 47 Extension
1794 East 172nd Street
Bronx, NY 10472-1936
718-822-8455
Ms. Vivian Vasquez, Site Supervisor

KIPS BAY BOYS & GIRLS CLUB, INC.
P.S. 102 Extension
1827 Archer Street
Bronx, NY 10460-6203
718-792-4003
Mr. Terrence Rice, Site Supervisor

MADISON SQUARE BOYS & GIRLS CLUB
Columbus Club House
543 East 189th Street
Bronx, NY 10458-5927
718-733-5500
Mr. Deryl Edmead-Guzman, Unit Director

MADISON SQUARE BOYS & GIRLS CLUB
Hoe Avenue Building
1665 Hoe Avenue
Bronx, NY 10460-5304
718-328-3900
Mr. Cedric Dew, Unit Director

PATHWAYS FOR YOUTH BOYS & GIRLS CLUB
625 Castle Hill Avenue
Bronx, NY 10473
718-828-4518
Mr. Neil Berger, Executive Director

PATHWAYS FOR YOUTH BOYS & GIRLS CLUB
Beacon Center, I.S. 74 Unit
730 Bryant Avenue
Bronx, NY 10474
718-542-6850
Mr. Victor Carrion, Director

PATHWAYS FOR YOUTH BOYS & GIRLS CLUB
Beacon Center, I.S. 148 Unit
3630 Third Avenue, Room 227
Bronx, NY 10456
718-293-5454
Yolando Cotto-James, Director

BROOKLYN LOCATIONS

CAREY GARDENS BOYS & GIRLS CLUB
2315 Surf Avenue
Brooklyn, NY 11224-2112

718-996-3170
Mr. Samuel Moore, Program Director

FLATBUSH BOYS & GIRLS CLUB
2245 Bedford Avenue
Brooklyn, NY 11226-4003
718-462-6100
Mr. Ronald Skeete, Program Director

GENESIS HOMES
330 Hinsdale Avenue
Brooklyn, NY 11207
718-385-7353
Ms. Donna Dickerson

HELP 1 PLAZA
515 Blake Avenue
Brooklyn, NY 11207
718-385-7353
Ms. Donna Dickerson

NAVY YARD BOYS CLUB, INC.
240 Nassau Street
Brooklyn, NY 11201
718-625-4295
Mr. Gary Branch, Unit Director

MANHATTAN LOCATIONS

THE CHILDREN'S AID SOCIETY
105 East 22nd Street
New York, NY 10010-5413
212-949-4917
Mr. Philip Coltoff, Executive Director

DUNLEVY MILBANK BOYS & GIRLS CLUB
14-32 West 118th Street
New York, NY 10026-1904
212-996-1716
Mr. Randy Cameron, Unit Director

DYCKMAN CENTER - BOYS & GIRLS CLUB
3782 Tenth Avenue
New York, NY 10034-1862
212-567-8782
Ms. Rosa C. Agosto, Administrative Director

EAST HARLEM BOYS & GIRLS CLUB
130 East 101st Street
New York, NY 10029
212-348-2343
Ms. Carmen LaLuz Rivera, Director

FREDERICK DOUGLASS BOYS & GIRLS CLUB
885 Columbus Avenue
New York, NY 10025-4531
212-865-6337
Ms. Gloria Daniels, Unit Director

GENESIS - RFK
113 East 13th Street

< continued... >

New York, NY 10003
212-979-0244
Debra Welsch

GREENWICH VILLAGE BOYS & GIRLS CLUB
219 Sullivan Street
New York, NY 10012-1301
212-254-3074
Ms. Risa Young, Unit Director

THE HARRIMAN CLUBHOUSE
287 East 10th Street
New York, NY 10009-4816
212-533-2550
Mr. Habib Ullah, Unit Director

I.S. 90
21 Jumel Place
New York, NY 10032
212-927-8314
Ms. Augustina Gonzalez, Site Director

THE JEFFERSON PARK CLUBHOUSE
321 East 111th Street
New York, NY 10029-3003
212-677-2661
Mr. José Vasquez, Unit Director

M.L. WILSON BOYS & GIRLS CLUB OF HARLEM, INC.
425 West 144th Street
New York, NY 10031-5209
212-283-6770
Ms. Lanette Smith, Executive Director

MADISON SQUARE BOYS & GIRLS CLUB, INC.
350 Fifth Avenue, Suite 912
New York, NY 10118
212-760-9600
Mr. Anthony F. Bandelato, Executive Director
Mr. Antonio Fort, Program Director

THE MILLIKEN CLUBHOUSE
135 Pitt Street
New York, NY 10002-1833
212-677-2929
Mr. Jamie Sanchez, Unit Director

P.S. 5 - WASHINGTON HEIGHTS
Boys & Girls Club
3703 10th Avenue
New York, NY 10034-1860
212-567-5787
Ms. Lissette Brooks, Unit Director

RHINELANDER BOYS & GIRLS CLUB
356 East 88th Street
New York, NY 10028-4904
212-876-0500
Ms. Denise Taylor, Unit Director

SALOME URENA COMMUNITY SCHOOL - I.S. 218
Boys & Girls Club

4600 Broadway
New York, NY 10040-2102
212-569-2880
Mr. Richard Negron, Unit Director

22nd STREET CLUB HOUSE
380 Second Avenue
New York, NY 10010
212-477-2200
Ms. Debra Welsch

QUEENS LOCATIONS

FAR ROCKAWAY CLUBHOUSE
426 beach 40th Street
Far Rockaway, NY
718-471-5453
Mr. Luke Melton

FLUSHING CLUB HOUSE
133-01 41st Road
Flushing, NY 11355-3631
718-886-5454
Mr. Ron Britt, Unit Director

SOUTH QUEENS BOYS & GIRLS CLUB
110-04 Atlantic Avenue
Richmond Hill, NY 11419
718-441-6050
Mr. Leo Compton, Executive Director

VARIETY BOYS & GIRLS CLUB OF QUEENS, INC.
21-12 30th Road
Long Island City, NY 11102-3331
718-728-0946
Mr. Dayan Maharaj, Executive Director

STATEN ISLAND LOCATION

GOODHUE BOYS & GIRLS CLUB
304 Prospect Avenue
New Brighton, SI 10301-2115
718-447-2630 Ms. Ilene Pappert, Unit Director

BOYS AND GIRLS HARBOR

1 E. 104th St.
New York, NY 10029

(212) 427-2244 [582] Administrative
(212) 427-2334 FAX

www.boysharbor.org

Hans Hegaman, President/CEO
Languages Spoken: Spanish

<continued...>

Services

Acting Instruction
Arts and Crafts Instruction
Computer Classes
Dancing Instruction
English as a Second Language
Equestrian Therapy
Exercise Classes/Groups
Field Trips/Excursions
Homework Help Programs
Mentoring Programs
Music Instruction
Sports, Individual
Sports, Team/Leagues
Storytelling
Swimming
Tutoring
Youth Development

Ages: 6 to 12
Area Served: New York
Program Hours: Monday - Friday: 3-6 p.m.
Fees: Call for information
Medication Administered: No
Transportation Provided: No
Wheelchair Accessible: Yes
Service Description: Provides after school programs that offer a variety of recreational and academic activities for children. Children with special needs are considered on a case-by-case basis.

Child Care Centers

Ages: 6 months to 13
Program Hours: Call for information
Transportation Provided: No
Wheelchair Accessible: Yes
Contact: Bernadette Wallace, Assistant Executive Director, (212) 427-2244 ext. 596

BRIDGEWOOD TUTORING SERVICE

40-16 Morgan St.
Little Neck, NY 11362

(718) 229-8563 Administrative

Paul Bridgewood

Services

Tutoring

Ages: Grades 9 - 12
Area Served: Queens
Program Hours: Monday - Friday: 3:30-8 p.m. Saturday and Sunday: 9 a.m.-8 p.m.
Staff/Child Ratio: 1:1
Fees: $50.00 per hour.
Medication Administered: No
Transportation Provided: No
Service Description: Provides in-home tutoring,

specializing in math and all the sciences. Tutors for the SAT, Advanced Placement, and Regents and pre-Regents examinations. Children with disabilities considered on a case-by-case basis.

BRONX COMMUNITY COLLEGE

University Ave. and W. 181st St.
Bronx, NY 10453

(718) 289-5171 Administrative
(718) 289-5170 Administrative
(718) 289-6018 FAX

www.bcc.cuny.edu

Languages Spoken: Spanish

Services

Tutoring

Ages: 6 to 14
Area Served: All Boroughs
Program Hours: Weekends (Call for exact times)
Fees: $70
Medication Administered: No
Transportation Provided: No
Wheelchair Accessible: Yes
Service Description: Reading and math weekend programs. Children with special needs considered on a case-by-case basis.

BRONX DEVELOPMENTAL CENTER

2400 Halsey St.
Bronx, NY 10461

(718) 430-0755 Respite
(718) 430-0700 General Information

Fran Sullivan, Director
Languages Spoken: Spanish

Services

Respite, Children's Out-of-Home

Ages: 4.9 to 18
Population Served: Autism
Area Served: Bronx
Program Hours: Saturdays: 10 a.m.-4 p.m.
Fees: None
Medication Administered: No
Transportation Provided: Yes
Service Description: Saturday respite program for children with autism and other behavior issues. An after school program is available for children who attend a 6:1:1 school program at PS 176X.

BRONX HOUSE JEWISH COMMUNITY CENTER

990 Pelham Parkway S.
Bronx, NY 10461

(718) 792-1800 Administrative
(718) 792-6802 FAX

Sharon Truenhut, Executive Director
Languages Spoken: Russian

Services

Arts and Crafts Instruction
Dancing Instruction
Homework Help Programs
Music Instruction
Sports, Team/Leagues
Swimming

Ages: 6 to 12
Area Served: Bronx
Program Hours: Monday - Friday: 3-6 p.m.
Fees: Call center for information
Medication Administered: No
Transportation Provided: No
Wheelchair Accessible: No
Service Description: Provides after school program which offers a variety of activities for children. Children with special needs are considered on a case-by-case basis.

BRONX MUSEUM OF THE ARTS

1040 Grand Concourse
Bronx, NY 10456

(718) 681-6000 Administrative
(718) 681-6181 FAX

bxmaedu@earthlink.net

Eadhon Hall, Director of Education
Languages Spoken: Spanish

Services

Museums

BRONX ORGANIZATION FOR AUTISTIC CITIZENS

P.S. 176 @ 178, 750 Baychester Ave.
Bronx, NY 10475

(718) 671-9796 Administrative

Emmanuel Hunter, Executive Director

Services

Respite, Children's Out-of-Home

Ages: 5 to 21
Population Served: Autism, Developmental Disability
Area Served: Bronx
Program Hours: Tuesday - Thursday: 2:30-5:15 p.m.
Service Description: A recreation, socialization and out-of-home respite program for children with Autism.

BRONX ORGANIZATION FOR THE LEARNING DISABLED (BOLD)

770 Beck St.
Bronx, NY 10455

(718) 589-7379 Administrative
(718) 589-3322 FAX

Michael Egan, Executive Director
Languages Spoken: Spanish

Services

Arts and Crafts Instruction
Homework Help Programs
Sports, Individual
Sports, Team/Leagues

Ages: 6 to 15; 15 to 17
Population Served: At-Risk, Learning Disability
Area Served: Bronx
Program Hours: Monday - Friday: 3-6 p.m. and Saturdays: 1-5 p.m.
Fees: None
Medication Administered: No
Transportation Provided: No
Service Description: An after school program for at-risk teens. A Saturday program is also available for children ages 6 to 15, from 1-5 p.m.. The program is held at P.S. 89 and P.S. 980 in the Bronx.

BRONX RIVER ART CENTER AND GALLERY

1087 E. Tremont Ave.
Bronx, NY 10460

(718) 589-5819 Administrative

www.bronxriverart.org
gnathan@bronxriverart.org

Gail Nathan, Executive Director
Languages Spoken: Spanish

< continued... >

Services

Arts and Crafts Instruction

Ages: 9 to 19
Area Served: All Boroughs
Program Hours: Monday - Friday: 4-6 p.m.
Fees: Please call for registration information
Medication Administered: No
Transportation Provided: No
Service Description: Offers a variety of art classes. Children with special needs are considered on a case-by-case basis.

BRONX YMCA

2 Castle Hill Ave.
Bronx, NY 10473

(718) 792-9736 Administrative

Gerry Arrighi, John Catto

Sites

1. BRONX YMCA
2 Castle Hill Ave.
Bronx, NY 10473

(718) 792-9736 Administrative

2. BRONX YMCA - JACOBI SPORTS CENTER
Pelham Parkway and Eastchester Road
Bronx, NY 10461

(718) 792-9717 Administrative

Services

HOLIDAY CAMP
Arts and Crafts Instruction
Youth Development

Ages: 2 to 12
Area Served: Bronx
Program Hours: Holiday Camp takes place during winter recess in February and Easter vacation.
Fees: 9 a.m.- 4 p.m., $80; 7:30 a.m.-6 p.m., $105; Annual registration fee: $50.
Method of Payment: Cash, Credit Card (American Express, MasterCard or Visa), Money Order
Medication Administered: No
Transportation Provided: No
Service Description: Participants will work with and enjoy learning experiences relating to health, values, science explorations and educational enrichment. Children will enjoy the company of their friends and also learn to build new relationships. They will be in a safe, supervised and comfortable environment. Children with special needs are considered on a case-by-case basis.
Sites: 1

Arts and Crafts Instruction
Homework Help Programs
Sports, Individual
Sports, Team/Leagues
Tutoring

Ages: 2 to 12
Area Served: Bronx
Program Hours: Monday - Friday: 3-6 p.m.
Fees: Call for information.
Medication Administered: No
Transportation Provided: No
Service Description: The philosophy of the YMCA is that children need time to relax after the end of the school day. The program provides opportunities to participate in values sessions, informal games, sports, arts and crafts, have a snack, receive homework assistance, and socialize and maintain meaningful friendships. Children with special needs are considered on a case-by-case basis. The YMCA provides services at the following Bronx schools: P.S. 71, 3040 Roberts Avenue; P.S. 76, 900 Adee Avenue; P.S. 97, 1375 Mace Avenue; P.S. 105, 725 Brady Avenue; P.S. 106, 2120 St. Raymond Avenue; P.S. 108, 1166 Neill Avenue
Sites: 1

JUNIOR YANKEES BASEBALL PROGRAM
Exercise Classes/Groups
Sports, Team/Leagues

Ages: 5 to 8
Area Served: Bronx
Program Hours: Time varies depending on team schedule. Please call for further information.
Fees: $50, program fee; $50 annual registration fee.
Method of Payment: Cash, Credit Card (American Express, MasterCard, Visa), Money Order
Medication Administered: No
Transportation Provided: No
Wheelchair Accessible: No
Service Description: There are three divisions to this program: The Pee Wee Division, The Tee Ball Division and The Minors Division. All programs are designed to teach baseball skills in a positive environment. All participants will receive instruction in all aspects of the game with a comprehensive fitness program component. All participants are guaranteed to play and will receive a uniform and an award. Children with special needs are considered on a case-by-case basis.
Sites: 1

DISABLED SUMMER YOUTH SWIM PROGRAM
Recreational Activities
Swimming

Ages: 5 to 21
Population Served: Developmental Disability,

<continued...>

Physical/Orthopedic Disability
Area Served: Bronx
Program Hours: Call for information
Fees: None
Service Description: Provides swimming instruction, adaptive aquatic and other recreational activities. Includes transportation.
Sites: 2

BROOKLYN ARTS EXCHANGE

421 5th Ave.
Brooklyn, NY 11215

(718) 832-0018 Administrative
(718) 832-9189 FAX

Marya Warshaw, Executive Director

Services

Dancing Instruction

Ages: 3 to 15
Program Hours: Call for information
Fees: 12-weeks/1-hour sessions $108
Method of Payment: Scholarship, Sliding Scale
Medication Administered: No
Transportation Provided: No
Service Description: Classes are offered in modern and creative dance and multi-arts for developing motor skills, timing and the creative process. Children with mild/moderate disabilities are mainstreamed on the basis of an interview. Some scholarships and parental work exchange available. Summer full-day camp available; no transportation.

BROOKLYN BOTANIC GARDEN

1000 Washington Ave.
Brooklyn, NY 11225

(718) 623-7200 Administrative
(718) 623-7220 Tours

www.bbg.org

Ted Macklin, Children's Programs

Services

Parks/Recreation Areas

Ages: All Ages
Population Served: All Disabilities
Area Served: All Boroughs
Program Hours: Call for information
Fees: Adults (16 and up): $3, Children (under 16): Free
Wheelchair Accessible: Yes
Service Description: Botanic garden offering guided tours and classes. Many of the educational programs can be adapted for special education.

BROOKLYN BUREAU OF COMMUNITY SERVICE

285 Schermerhorn St.
Brooklyn, NY 11217

(718) 310-5600 Administrative
(718) 855-1517 FAX

www.bbcs.org

Donna Santarsiero, Executive Director
Languages Spoken: Haitian Creole, Spanish

Sites

1. BROOKLYN BUREAU OF COMMUNITY SERVICE

285 Schermerhorn St.
Brooklyn, NY 11217

(718) 875-0710 Administrative
(718) 855-1517 FAX

www.bbcs.org

Donna Santarsiero, Executive Director

2. BROOKLYN BUREAU OF COMMUNITY SERVICE - BEDFORD STUYVESANT FAMILY CENTER
20 New York Ave.
Brooklyn, NY 11216

(718) 622-9400 Administrative

Irwin Lubell, Director

Services

AFTERSCHOOL LITERACY PROGRAM
Homework Help Programs
Tutoring

Ages: 6 to 10
Program Hours: Monday - Friday: 3-7 p.m.
Fees: None
Wheelchair Accessible: Yes
Service Description: After school programs can accommodate children with disabilities.
Contact: Claire Longo
Sites: 1 2

BROOKLYN CENTER FOR THE URBAN ENVIRONMENT (BCUE)

The Tennis House
Prospect Park
Brooklyn, NY 11215

(718) 788-8500 Administrative

<continued...>

Services

Arts and Crafts Instruction
Recreational Activities
Sports, Individual
Sports, Team/Leagues

Ages: 5 to 12
Area Served: Brooklyn
Program Hours: Call for information
Fees: Fees vary, depending on program. Call for information.
Medication Administered: No
Transportation Provided: No
Service Description: Brooklyn Center for the Urban Environment offers a variety of after school programs for children. Chess Mates - Children learn how to play this challenging game under the guidance of a chess instructor; Ceramics - Children can explore their creativity through clay; UpBeat Art: Playing with Color - Using illustrations, fruits, vegetables, animals and masks to trigger their imagination, this class provides a rainbow of projects that explore and enhance the natural talent and creativity of young children; The Science of Tennis - This class will build upon the tennis skills of children who have taken the BCUE beginner tennis program or who have had other prior instruction; Roller Hockey - Children use their hockey skills to develop teamwork and good sportsmanship; Hot Wheels: Scientific Biking - Children enjoy safe bike riding in Prospect Park; Advanced In-Line Skating and In-Line Skating for Beginners - Two separate programs where children are coached in this new sport and advance their skills. Children with special needs are accepted on a case-by-case basis.
Contact: Jessica Scanell, After School Program Assistant

BROOKLYN CENTRAL YMCA

218 Hicks St.
Brooklyn, NY 11201

(718) 522-6000 Administrative

Sandra Perch, Contact

Services

Arts and Crafts Instruction
Exercise Classes/Groups
Homework Help Programs
Sports, Individual
Sports, Team/Leagues
Tutoring

Ages: 4 to 10
Program Hours: Monday - Friday: 3-6 p.m.
Fees: $47/week (non-members), $37/week (members)
Method of Payment: Scholarships available
Medication Administered: No
Transportation Provided: No
Wheelchair Accessible: No
Service Description: Academic skills are encouraged

through homework help and tutoring along with developing interpersonal relationships and self-esteem. Accommodations can be made for children with disabilities.

BROOKLYN CHILDREN'S MUSEUM

145 Brooklyn Ave.
Brooklyn, NY 11213

(718) 735-4400 Administrative
(718) 604-7442 FAX
(718) 735-4402 TDD

www.bchildmus.org

Carol Enseki, Director
Languages Spoken: Spanish

Services

SPECIAL NEEDS FAMILY PROGRAM
Arts and Crafts Instruction
Storytelling

Ages: 3 to 14
Population Served: Autism, Cerebral Palsy, Deaf-Blind, Deaf/Hard of Hearing, Developmental Delay, Developmental Disability, Diabetes, Down Syndrome, Emotional Disability, Gifted, Learning Disability, Mental Retardation (mild-moderate), Multiple Disability, Neurological Disability, Physical/Orthopedic Disability, Sickle Cell Anemia, Speech/Language Disability, Spina Bifida, Tourette Syndrome, Underachiever, Visual Disability/Blind
Area Served: All Boroughs
Program Hours: The workshops are offered every other month: October, December, February, April and June.
Program Capacity: 25 maximum
Staff/Child Ratio: One teacher per class. There should be one adult per every two children, depending upon the severity of the disability.
Fees: $4, suggested admission, and an additional $3 per person
Method of Payment: Cash or Check
Medication Administered: No
Transportation Provided: No
Wheelchair Accessible: No
Service Description: Family workshops explore special themes based on cultural artifacts and natural science specimens.
Contact: Hana Elwell, Special Needs Coordinator

SPECIAL NEEDS OUTREACH PROGRAM
Arts and Crafts Instruction
Music Instruction
Storytelling

Ages: 3 to 14
Population Served: Autism, Cerebral Palsy,

< continued... >

Deaf-Blind, Deaf/Hard of Hearing, Developmental Delay, Developmental Disability, Diabetes, Down Syndrome, Emotional Disability, Gifted, Learning Disability, Mental Retardation (mild-moderate), Multiple Disability, Neurological Disability, Physical/Orthopedic Disability, Sickle Cell Anemia, Speech/Language Disability, Spina Bifida, Tourette Syndrome, Underachiever, Visual Disability/Blind
Area Served: All Boroughs
Program Hours: Call for information
Program Capacity: 15 maximum
Staff/Child Ratio: One teacher per class visit. Depending upon the severity of child's disability, there should be at least one adult per every two students.
Fees: Package includes Portable Collection suitcase: $200/class, Non-package - $35/class
Method of Payment: 50% deposit is required before visit. Checks or Purchase Orders are accepted.
Medication Administered: No
Transportation Provided: No
Wheelchair Accessible: Yes
Service Description: The Outreach Program begins in the classroom as a package deal. The instructors may bring live animals or cultural artifacts to the classroom with a hands-on activity. The same instructor will facilitate your visit to the museum for one of the following school group adventures: Face to Face - Explores diversity and appreciation of differences between cultures. Native America - Teaches how some Native American groups depend on their environments. Sounds Like Fun - Explores the science of sound through hands-on activities and music. Natural Wonders - Explores what living things depend on to live and grow. Global Communities - Examines cultural objects from around the world. Our Bodies Our Bones - Explores the skeletal forms of humans and animals.
Contact: Hana Elwell, Special Needs Coordinator

AFTER SCHOOL ADVENTURES
Arts and Crafts Instruction

Ages: 5 to 12
Program Hours: Monday - Friday: 3-6 p.m.
Program Capacity: 30 students/group
Fees: $3.00/child
Wheelchair Accessible: Yes
Service Description: Organized after-school groups from Brooklyn school districts are invited to participate in the After School Adventures Program. This program offers visits to the exhibitions, hands on entertaining and instructional workshops. Programs can be adapted to meet the needs of children with disabilities.
Contact: Education Department

Museums

BROOKLYN COLLEGE

Bedford Ave. and Ave. H
Brooklyn, NY 11210

(718) 951-5000 Administrative
(718) 951-4543 Administrative
(718) 951-4111 Preparatory Center for the Performing Arts

www.bcprepcenter.org

Services

PREPARATORY CENTER FOR THE PERFORMING ARTS
Acting Instruction
Dancing Instruction
Music Instruction

Ages: 4 to 18
Area Served: All Boroughs
Program Hours: Vary with programs. Most programs are on Saturdays. All programs are for the full academic year (27 or 29 lessons, depending on program).
Program Capacity: 300
Staff/Child Ratio: 1:1 individual instruction (music programs); 1:5 or 1:12 group instruction
Fees: Vary with program
Method of Payment: Check or money order. Payment is for the full year. A four-payment plan is available.
Medication Administered: No
Transportation Provided: No
Wheelchair Accessible: Yes (except administrative office)
Service Description: Offers a very wide range of programs in music, theater arts and dance. In the music program both private and group lessons are available. We offer a Suzuki Method for Violin program (parents must attend). Other instuments offered include piano, violin, viola, cello, flute oboe, clarinet, saxophone, basson, french horn, trumpet, trombone, tuba, guitar and harp. Voice lessons, music theory and composition are offered for children, 12 and up. The Dance program offers Creative Movement (ages 4-7), Ballet and Modern Dance (ages 6-18), and Tap, Jazz and Theatre Dance (ages 9-18). The Theater programs include Beginners, Please (ages 6-9), Early Stages (ages 9-13) and Act Now (ages 9-18).

BROOKLYN CONSERVATORY OF MUSIC

58 Seventh Ave.
Brooklyn, NY 11217-3608

(718) 622-3300 Administrative
(718) 622-3957 FAX

www.brooklynconservatory.com

Rick Frank, Director
Languages Spoken: Spanish

Sites

1. BROOKLYN CONSERVATORY OF MUSIC
58 Seventh Ave.
Brooklyn, NY 11217-3608

(718) 622-3300 Administrative

www.brooklynconservatory.com

2. BROOKLYN CONSERVATORY OF MUSIC - QUEENS
42-76 Main St. at Blossom Ave.
Flushing, NY 11355

(718) 461-8910 Administrative

Services

SONGS, SOUNDS, LEAPS AND BOUNDS PROGRAM
Music Instruction

Ages: 18 months to Adult
Area Served: Brooklyn, Queens
Service Description: The Conservatory offers programs for children from the age of 18 months. School-age children are generally ready to begin private instruction. Private instruction is available in most instruments and voice. For a modest additional fee, children can also round out their education with group classes in music skills or by participating in one of the many childrens' choruses, ensembles or classes that are offered. Children with disabilities are considered on a case-by-case basis.
Sites: 1 2

BROOKLYN GYMNASTICS CENTER

1635 Bath Ave.
Brooklyn, NY 11214

(718) 232-6444 Administrative
(718) 232-3805 FAX

www.brooklyngymnastics.com
bgcadmin@brooklyngymnastics.com

Peter Hristov, Director
Languages Spoken: Russian, Spanish

Services

Arts and Crafts Instruction
Dancing Instruction
Recreational Activities
Sports, Individual
Sports, Team/Leagues

Ages: 1 and up
Area Served: Brooklyn
Program Hours: Vary, Monday - Saturday
Staff/Child Ratio: 1:8
Fees: Please call center for information.
Method of Payment: Cash, Check, Credit Card
Medication Administered: No
Transportation Provided: No
Wheelchair Accessible: No
Service Description: Provides gymnastics classes, dance and art classes.

BROOKLYN HISTORICAL SOCIETY (THE)

128 Pierrepont St.
Brooklyn, NY 11201

(718) 222-4111 Administrative
(718) 222-3794 FAX

Rebecca Krucoff, Education Director

Services

BROOKLYN AT PLAY
Exercise Classes/Groups
Recreational Activities

Ages: 5 to 12
Program Hours: Classes are one hour and fifteen minutes long. Call for exact days and time.
Program Capacity: 20
Fees: $95
Medication Administered: No
Transportation Provided: No
Wheelchair Accessible: Yes
Service Description: Jacob's Ladder, Cup and Ball and Potsie are games that have been played by Brooklyn's children over the past four centuries. Children are given the opportunity to "travel back in time" and try their hands at games of the past while discovering Brooklyn's ever changing history. Children with disabilities are considered on a case-by-case basis.

THEN & NOW
Museums
Storytelling

Ages: 5 to 12
Program Hours: Classes are one hour and fifteen minutes long. Call for exact days and time.

<continued...>

Program Capacity: 20 children
Fees: $95/child
Medication Administered: No
Transportation Provided: No
Wheelchair Accessible: Yes
Service Description: Artifacts from the Brooklyn Historical Society collection are a link to the past in this interactive workshop. Students will have the opportunity to touch and learn about unfamiliar objects from Brooklyn's past and consider what life may have been like 20, 50 or 100 years ago. Children with disabilities are considered on a case-by-case basis.

BROOKLYN LEARNING CENTER

Medical Arts Bldg., 3rd Fl.
142 Joralemon St.
Brooklyn, NY 11201

(718) 935-0400 Administrative

margolislearning@juno.com

Joan Margolis, Director
Languages Spoken: French, Spanish, German

Services

Tutoring

Ages: 5 to Adult
Area Served: All Boroughs
Program Hours: Monday - Friday: 11:30 a.m.-7:30 p.m., Saturday: 10 a.m.-5 p.m.
Staff/Child Ratio: 1:1
Fees: $70 per hour
Method of Payment: Check or cash
Medication Administered: No
Transportation Provided: No
Wheelchair Accessible: Yes (limited)
Service Description: Provides tutoring services and can accommodate children with special needs. An Learning Disabilities specialist is available.

BROOKLYN MUSEUM OF ART (THE)

200 Eastern Parkway
Brooklyn, NY 11238

(718) 638-5000 [230] Administrative
(718) 783-6501 FAX
(718) 399-8440 TTY

www.brooklynart.org

Arnold Lehman, Executive Director

Services

Museums

BROOKLYN PUBLIC LIBRARY - THE CHILD'S PLACE FOR CHILDREN WITH SPECIAL NEEDS

2065 Flatbush Ave.
Brooklyn, NY 11234

(718) 253-4948 Administrative
(718) 252-1520 FAX
(718) 252-1039 TDD

www.brooklynpubliclibrary.org

Carrie Banks, Librarian
Languages Spoken: American Sign Language, French, Spanish, Hebrew

Sites

1. BROOKLYN PUBLIC LIBRARY - THE CHILD'S PLACE FOR CHILDREN WITH SPECIAL NEEDS - FLATLANDS BRANCH

2065 Flatbush Ave. (at Ave. P)
Brooklyn, NY 11234

(718) 253-4948 Administrative
(718) 252-1520 FAX

www.brooklynpubliclibrary.org

Carrie Banks, Librarian

2. BROOKLYN PUBLIC LIBRARY - THE CHILD'S PLACE FOR CHILDREN WITH SPECIAL NEEDS - GREENPOINT BRANCH

107 Norman Ave.
Brooklyn, NY 11222

(718) 349-8504 Administrative

www.brooklynpubliclibrary.org

Denise Lattimore

3. BROOKLYN PUBLIC LIBRARY - THE CHILD'S PLACE FOR CHILDREN WITH SPECIAL NEEDS - RED HOOK BRANCH

7 Wolcott St. (at Dwight St.)
Brooklyn, NY 11231

(718) 935-0203 Administrative

www.brooklynpubliclibrary.org

Dejah Lynch, Librarian

Services

AFTER SCHOOL STORIES
Arts and Crafts Instruction
Storytelling

Ages: 5 to 12
Area Served: Brooklyn
Program Hours: Days and hours vary from site to site. Please call your local library for details.

<continued...>

Program Capacity: 12
Staff/Child Ratio: 1 (plus parents):12
Fees: None
Medication Administered: Parents may administer on site
Transportation Provided: No
Wheelchair Accessible: Yes
Service Description: A fun-filled hour of stories, music and crafts for children with and without special needs.
Sites: 1 2 3

OUR GARDEN CLUB
Arts and Crafts Instruction
Storytelling

Ages: 5 to 12
Program Hours: Friday: 4:30-5:30 p.m., July and August. Monthly April - October
Program Capacity: 12
Staff/Child Ratio: 1:12
Fees: None
Medication Administered: Parents may administer on site.
Transportation Provided: No
Wheelchair Accessible: Yes
Service Description: Children hear stories and sing songs about gardening. Then they work in the fully accessible garden. Craft projects and plants are taken home.
Sites: 1 3

Recreational Activities

Ages: Birth to 9
Sites: 3

BROOKLYN SCHOOL FOR SPECIAL CHILDREN

376 Bay 44th St.
Brooklyn, NY 11214

(718) 946-9700 Administrative
(718) 714-0197 FAX

Teresa Del Priore, Director of Education

Services

Homework Help Programs

Ages: Birth to 6
Population Served: Autism, Cerebral Palsy, Deaf/Hard of Hearing, Developmental Delay, Developmental Disability, Down Syndrome, Emotional Disability, Health Impairment, Learning Disability, Mental Retardation (mild-moderate), Mental Retardation (severe-profound), Multiple Disability, Neurological Disability, Physical/Orthopedic Disability, Seizure Disorder, Speech/Language Disability, Spina Bifida, Visual Disability/Blind
Area Served: Brooklyn
Program Hours: Monday - Friday: 3-6 p.m.
Fees: Call school for information

Medication Administered: No
Wheelchair Accessible: Yes

BROOKLYN SERVICES FOR AUTISTIC CITIZENS, INC.

1420 E. 68th St.
Brooklyn, NY 11234

(718) 236-9057 Administrative

Terri Sciametta, President

Services

Respite, Children's Out-of-Home

Ages: 6 to 20
Population Served: Autism, Developmental Disability
Area Served: Brooklyn
Program Hours: Saturdays, hours vary. Call for information.
Staff/Child Ratio: 1:2
Transportation Provided: No
Wheelchair Accessible: No
Service Description: Offers recreation, socialization, and academic programs as appropriate, held on Saturdays for children with autism. Physical education, arts and crafts, music and trips are conducted in a 1:2 staff to child setting.

BROOKWOOD CHILD CARE

25 Washington St.
Brooklyn, NY 11201

(718) 596-5555 Administrative
(718) 596-7564 FAX

Fatima Goldman, Executive Director
Languages Spoken: Haitian Creole, Spanish

Services

FAMILY DAY CARE
Child Care Centers

Ages: 2 months to 13
Population Served: Allergies, Asthma, Attention Deficit Disorder (ADD/ADHD), Learning Disability, Speech/Language Disability
Area Served: Brooklyn (Bedford Stuyvesant, Fort Green, Crown Heights, Park Slope, Bushwick, East New York))
Program Hours: Monday - Friday: 8 a.m.-6 p.m.
Program Capacity: 165
Staff/Child Ratio: 1:5
Fees: Sliding Scale, determined by ACD
Medication Administered: No
Transportation Provided: No

< continued... >

Wheelchair Accessible: No
Service Description: The Family Day Care program of this multiservice center provides day care in licensed homes. Staff is not trained for working with severe disabilties, but children with disabilities who do not need special care are included.
Contact: Joan Reid, (718) 596-5555, ext. 554

BROWNSTONE SCHOOL AND DAY CARE CENTER

128 W. 80th St.
New York, NY 10024

(212) 874-1341 Administrative
(212) 875-1013 FAX

Christina Huang, Director
Languages Spoken: Chinese, Haitian Creole, Spanish

Services

Acting Instruction
Arts and Crafts Instruction
Cooking Classes
Homework Help Programs
Sports, Individual
Sports, Team/Leagues

Ages: 5 to 8
Population Served: Learning Disability, Underachiever
Area Served: All Boroughs
Program Hours: Monday - Friday: 3:30-5:45 p.m.
Program Capacity: 36
Staff/Child Ratio: 1:10
Fees: Call for information
Medication Administered: No
Transportation Provided: No
Wheelchair Accessible: No
Service Description: Provides after school programs that offer a variety of activities.

CAMBRIA CENTER FOR THE GIFTED CHILD

233-10 Linden Blvd.
Cambria Heights, NY 11411

(718) 341-1991 Administrative
(718) 341-2395 FAX

Sheree Palmer, Director
Languages Spoken: French, Spanish

Services

Music Instruction

Ages: 6 to 13
Population Served: Gifted
Area Served: Queens
Program Hours: Monday - Friday: 3-6 p.m.
Program Capacity: Flexible

Staff/Child Ratio: 1:1
Fees: $60 per month
Method of Payment: Cash, Check
Medication Administered: Yes
Transportation Provided: No
Wheelchair Accessible: No
Service Description: Lessons are one hour per week. Studens must have access to instrument to practice. Piano includes group lessons in theory. Violin, viola, cello and drums also offered. Students with disabilities are considered on a case-by-case basis.
Contact: Yvonne Reid, Director, Day and After School Music

CARDINAL MCCLOSKEY SERVICES

2 Holland Ave.
White Plains, NY 10603

(914) 997-8000 Administrative
(914) 997-2166 FAX

Marjorie McLouglin, Director
Languages Spoken: Arabic, French, Spanish

Sites

1. CARDINAL MCCLOSKEY SERVICES - NEW YORK CITY

349 E. 149th St. 8th Fl.
Bronx, NY 10459

(718) 402-0081 Day Care
(718) 993-7700 Foster Care

Patricia Eberle, Administrative Director, Day Care

2. CARDINAL MCCLOSKEY SERVICES - GROUP DAY CARE

889 E. 180th St.
Bronx, NY 10460

(718) 220-3355 Administrative
(718) 220-0649 FAX

Dalia Marcano, Director

Services

Arts and Crafts Instruction
Child Care Centers
Recreational Activities

Ages: 6 to 10
Area Served: Bronx
Program Hours: Monday - Friday: 8 a.m.-6 p.m.
Program Capacity: 110
Staff/Child Ratio: 3:30
Fees: Sliding scale, determined by ACD
Medication Administered: No
Transportation Provided: No
Wheelchair Accessible: No
Service Description: Day care center provides a variety of after school activities. Children with

<continued...>

special needs are considered on a case-by-case basis.
Sites: 2

Child Care Resource and Referral

Ages: 6 weeks to 12 years
Area Served: Bronx
Program Hours: Monday - Friday: 8 a.m.-6 p.m.
Program Capacity: 800
Fees: Sliding scale, determined by ACD
Wheelchair Accessible: No
Service Description: This site provides referrals to contracted child care providers. Children are cared for in registered or licensed individual homes. Children with disabilties are considered on a case-by-case basis.
Sites: 1

CARIBBEAN AND AMERICAN FAMILY SERVICES, INC.

1035 E. 214th St.
Bronx, NY 10469

(718) 405-0623 Administrative
(718) 654-3641 FAX

Hugh Beckford, Executive Director

Services

Acting Instruction
Arts and Crafts Instruction
Homework Help Programs

Ages: 5 to 12
Program Hours: Monday - Friday: 3-6 p.m.
Fees: None
Medication Administered: No
Transportation Provided: No
Wheelchair Accessible: Yes
Service Description: After school programs offered to school age children. Accommodations can be made for children with disabilities, depending on the severity of the disability. Call for information.

CAROL'S EDUCARE CHILD CARE CENTER, INC.

113-15 Springfield Blvd.
Queens Village, NY 11429

(718) 740-2557 Administrative
(718) 464-6565 FAX

Jennifer Green, Director

Services

Child Care Centers
Homework Help Programs
Recreational Activities

Ages: 2 to 10
Area Served: All boroughs
Program Hours: Monday - Friday: 7 a.m.-5:30 p.m. (After School 3-5 p.m.)
Summer: 7 a.m.-5:30 p.m.
Program Capacity: 25
Staff/Child Ratio: Child care: 2:15 or 20, depending on age. After school: 1:10
Fees: After School: $300 per month
Summer Program; $425 per month
Method of Payment: Cash or Money Order
Medication Administered: No
Transportation Provided: No
Wheelchair Accessible: No
Service Description: After school program provides homework help. After students do homework, there are snacks and playtime. Summer program has a variety of recreational activities. Children with disabilities are considered on a case-by-case basis.

CARVER COMMUNITY CENTER

55 E. 102nd St.
New York, NY 10029

(212) 289-8722 After School Program
(212) 289-2708 Administrative
(212) 360-1947 FAX

Diana Ayala, Director
Languages Spoken: Spanish

Services

Arts and Crafts Instruction
Computer Classes
Homework Help Programs
Tutoring

Ages: 6 to 12
Population Served: Attention Deficit Disorder (ADD/ADHD), Emotional Disability, Learning Disability, Speech/Language Disability, Underachiever
Area Served: Bronx, Manhattan
Program Hours: Monday - Friday: 3:15-6:15 p.m.
Program Capacity: 44
Staff/Child Ratio: 1:5
Fees: None
Medication Administered: Yes
Transportation Provided: No
Wheelchair Accessible: Yes
Service Description: After school programs offered to school age children.
Contact: Robert Pratt, After School Coordinator

CASITA MARIA

928 Simpson St.
Bronx, NY 10459

(718) 589-2230 Administrative
(718) 589-7414 Social Services
(718) 589-5714 FAX

www.unhny.org/unh/mem-casita.html
casitamaria@gateway.net

Gladys Padro-Soler, Executive Director
Languages Spoken: Spanish

Services

Arts and Crafts Instruction
Homework Help Programs
Tutoring

Ages: 6 to 15
Program Hours: Monday - Friday: 3-6 p.m.
Fees: None
Medication Administered: No
Transportation Provided: No
Wheelchair Accessible: No
Service Description: Education remains the focal point of Casita Maria's efforts. Through its center for education, children, teens and adults enjoy many different educational programs. Children are counseled individually by a certified counselor, as the need arises. Children with special needs are considered on a case-by-case basis.
Contact: Laura Young, Senior Coordinator; Marta Rivera, Director of Youth Services

CASTLE CLINTON NATIONAL MONUMENT

Battery Park
New York, NY 10004

(212) 344-7220 Administrative
(212) 825-6874 FAX

www.nps.org

Joseph Avery, Superintendent
Languages Spoken: Spanish

Services

Museums

CASTLE HILL COMMUNITY CENTER

625 Castle Hill Ave.
Bronx, NY 10473

(718) 828-4518 Administrative
(718) 824-9579 FAX

José Rodríguez, Director
Languages Spoken: Spanish

Sites

1. CASTLE HILL COMMUNITY CENTER
625 Castle Hill Ave.
Bronx, NY 10473

(718) 828-4518 Administrative
(718) 824-9579 FAX

José Rodríguez, Director

2. CASTLE HILL COMMUNITY CENTER - M.S. 131
885 Bolton Ave., Rm. 260
Bronx, NY 10473

(718) 991-7490 Administrative
(718) 328-6705 FAX

Eva López

Services

Acting Instruction
Arts and Crafts Instruction
Computer Classes
Exercise Classes/Groups
Music Instruction
Recreational Activities
Sports, Team/Leagues

Ages: 6 to 12
Population Served: Attention Deficit Disorder (ADD/ADHD)
Area Served: Bronx
Program Hours: Monday - Friday: 3-6 p.m.
Fees: None
Medication Administered: No
Transportation Provided: No
Service Description: An after school program that offers a variety of programs and activities for school age children. Children with special needs are considered on a case-by-case basis.
Sites: 1 2

CATALPA YMCA

Catalpa Ave. and 64th St.
Ridgewood, NY 11227

(718) 821-6271 Administrative

www.ymca.org
catalpay@ymca.org

Lester J. Bates, Executive Director

Services

Arts and Crafts Instruction
Computer Classes
Exercise Classes/Groups
Homework Help Programs
Sports, Individual
Sports, Team/Leagues
Tutoring

< continued... >

Ages: 6 to 11
Area Served: Queens
Program Hours: Monday - Friday: 3-6 p.m. (September - June)
Fees: $269/month
Method of Payment: Cash, Check, Money Order
Medication Administered: No
Transportation Provided: No
Wheelchair Accessible: No
Service Description: Children receive homework help from caring staff, participate in quiet and active games, and learn about health and fitness. Children with special needs are accepted on a case-by-case basis.

CATHOLIC BIG BROTHERS OF NEW YORK

45 E. 20th St.
New York, NY 10003

(212) 477-2250 Administrative
(212) 471-2739 FAX

www.cbbnyc.org
cbbnyc@aol.com

JoAnne Celler, Program Director
Languages Spoken: Spanish

Services

THE CORE MATCH PROGRAM
Mentoring Programs

Ages: 7 to 14
Program Hours: 3 - 4 times per month on weekends. Call for exact dates and times.
Staff/Child Ratio: 1:1
Fees: Please call center for information
Medication Administered: No
Transportation Provided: No
Service Description: Volunteers are matched one-to-one with a child. They pick up and return the child to his/her home. "Bigs" engage their "littles" in a wide variety of recreational, social, educational and cultural activities. Children with disabilities must be evaluated before they are accepted.

CATHOLIC BIG SISTERS

220 A East 4th St., 3rd Fl.
New York, NY 10009

(212) 475-3291 Administrative
(212) 475-0280 FAX

www.catholicbigsisters.org

Emily Forham, Executive Director
Languages Spoken: Spanish

Services

Mentoring Programs

Ages: 8 to 17
Area Served: Manhattan
Program Hours: 2 outings per month
Program Capacity: Depends on the number of volunteers available.
Staff/Child Ratio: 1:1
Fees: None
Medication Administered: No
Transportation Provided: No
Wheelchair Accessible: Yes
Service Description: This program consists of three partners, the volunteer ("Big Sister"), the child and the parents. All three agree to at least two outings each month, frequent telephone contact, and that the match will last for at least a year. All outings are scheduled on weekends or school holidays. Children with disabilities are considered on a case-by-case basis.

CATHOLIC GUARDIAN SOCIETY

1011 First Ave.
New York, NY 10022

(212) 371-1000 Administrative
(212) 758-5892 FAX

John Frein, Executive Director

Services

PLANNED WEEKEND RESPITE
Respite, Children's Out-of-Home

Ages: 5 and up
Population Served: Developmental Disabilties
Area Served: Manhattan
Program Hours: Friday: 6 p.m. - Sunday: 6 p.m.
Program Capacity: 2 individuals per weekend
Wheelchair Accessible: No
Contact: Juno Greeves, Program Coordinator

CENTER FOR FAMILY SUPPORT, INC. (THE)

333 Seventh Ave., 9th Fl.
New York, NY 10001

(212) 629-7939 Administrative
(212) 239-2211 FAX

Steven Vernikoff, Executive Director
Languages Spoken: Spanish

< continued... >

Sites

1. CENTER FOR FAMILY SUPPORT, INC. (THE) - WILLOWBROOK ROAD
930 Willowbrook Rd.
Staten Island, NY 10314

(718) 983-5418 Administrative

Susan Bunkowski, Special Education Teacher

Services

Homework Help Programs
Tutoring

Ages: 5 to 12
Program Hours: Wednesday: 3-5:30 p.m.
Program Capacity: 8
Staff/Child Ratio: 2:1
Fees: None
Medication Administered: No
Transportation Provided: Yes
Wheelchair Accessible: Yes
Service Description: Provides after school services that can accommodate children with disabilities.
Contact: Nancy Lampidelli, Supervisor of After School Program
Sites: 1

CENTRAL FAMILY LIFE CENTER

59 Wright St.
Staten Island, NY 10304

(718) 273-8414 Administrative
(718) 981-3740 FAX

Dr. Calvin Rice, Executive Director

Services

Respite, Children's Out-of-Home

Ages: 6 and up
Population Served: Autism, Developmental Disability
Area Served: Staten Island
Program Hours: Saturday: 9 a.m.-5:30 p.m. If family can provide their own transportation, child may stay until 9 p.m.
Program Capacity: 15
Staff/Child Ratio: 1:4
Fees: None (for respite program)
Medication Administered: Yes
Transportation Provided: Yes
Wheelchair Accessible: Yes
Service Description: The Saturday respite program provides recreational activities, such as trips to movies and amusement areas, and dinner out. Breakfast, lunch and dinner are provided.
Contact: Millie Pitchford

CENTRAL PARK - CHARLES A. DANA DISCOVERY CENTER

36 W. 110th St.
New York, NY 10026

(212) 860-1370 Administrative
(212) 860-1378 FAX

www.centralparknyc.org

Barbara Nowak, Director

Services

Nature Centers/Walks
Parks/Recreation Areas
Recreational Activities

Ages: 6 and up
Area Served: All Boroughs
Program Hours: Call for information
Fees: None
Medication Administered: No
Transportation Provided: No
Wheelchair Accessible: Yes
Service Description: Provides a variety of workshops and weekend programs for children.

CENTRAL PARK WILDLIFE CENTER

830 Fifth Ave.
New York, NY 10021

(212) 439-6538 Education Department
(212) 861-6030 Administrative

www.wcs.org/zoos/wildlifecenters/centralpark/

April Rivkin

Services

KEEPING UP WITH KEEPERS
Nature Centers/Walks
Zoos/Wildlife Parks

Ages: 6 and up
Program Hours: Saturday: 1-2:30 p.m.
Fees: $30/member, $35/non-member, (fee is for Keeping Up with Keepers program)
Method of Payment: Check, Credit Card, Money Order
Medication Administered: No
Transportation Provided: No
Wheelchair Accessible: Yes
Service Description: Keeping Up with Keepers allows the participant to experience the zoo from a whole new perspective. Go behind the scenes to find out how the keepers work with animals. Children with disabilities are considered on a case-by-case basis.

CENTRAL QUEENS YM-YWHA

67-09 108th St.
Forest Hills, NY 11375

(718) 268-5011 Administrative
(718) 793-0515 FAX

www.members.aol.com/cqueensy

Bob Friedman, Director
Languages Spoken: Hebrew

Services

Arts and Crafts Instruction
Homework Help Programs
Recreational Activities
Sports, Team/Leagues

Ages: 7 and up
Area Served: Queens
Program Hours: Monday - Thursday: 3:15-6:15 p.m.
Program Capacity: 110
Staff/Child Ratio: 1:8
Fees: Call for information
Medication Administered: No
Transportation Provided: Yes, offered from select Queens schools.
Wheelchair Accessible: No
Service Description: A mainstream community after school program. It includes art, sports, homework help and other recreational activities. Children can also enroll in specialty classes offered at the Y. Children with special needs may attend the after school program, contingent upon the therapeutic diagnosis of the child.

CERTIFIED TUTORING SERVICE

777 Foster Ave.
Brooklyn, NY 11230

(800) 218-8867 Toll Free
(718) 434-0944 Administrative

Tom O'Brien, Director

Services

Tutoring

Ages: Grades K to 12
Population Served: Emotional Disability, Learning Disability
Area Served: All Boroughs, Nassau, New Jersey, Suffolk, Westchester
Staff/Child Ratio: 1:1
Service Description: Provides in-home tutoring. Willing to work with students with emotional and learning difficulties.

CHAI LIFELINE

151 W. 30th St., 3rd Fl.
New York, NY 10001

(718) 465-1300 Administrative
(212) 465-0949 FAX

www.chailifeline.org
info@chailifeline.org

Rabbi Simcah Scholar, Executive Vice President
Languages Spoken: Hebrew, Yiddish

Services

Arts and Crafts Instruction
Field Trips/Excursions

Ages: 4 to 21
Population Served: AIDS/HIV +, Asthma, Cancer, Cardiac Disorder, Cerebral Palsy, Cystic Fibrosis, Deaf-Blind, Deaf/Hard of Hearing, Diabetes, Health Impairment, Multiple Disability, Neurological Disability, Physical/Orthopedic Disability, Rare Disorder, Seizure Disorder, Sickle Cell Anemia, Spina Bifida, Technology Supported, Tourette Syndrome, Traumatic Brain Injury (TBI), Visual Disability/Blind
Area Served: All Boroughs
Program Hours: Call for information
Staff/Child Ratio: Depending on need
Fees: None
Medication Administered: No
Transportation Provided: Yes
Wheelchair Accessible: Yes
Service Description: Programs include events such as fishing and trips to amusement parks. There are also overnight programs during holiday season for the siblings of medically ill children.

CHAMA CHILD DEVELOPMENT CENTER

218 W. 147th St.
New York, NY 10039

(212) 368-4710 Administrative
(212) 926-4810 FAX

Tampie Watson, Executive Director
Languages Spoken: French, Spanish, Various African Dialects

Services

Arts and Crafts Instruction
Music Instruction
Recreational Activities

Ages: 6 to 12
Population Served: Autism, Developmental Delay, Developmental Disability, Down Syndrome, Learning Disability, Mental Retardation (mild-moderate), Mental Retardation (severe-profound)

< continued... >

Area Served: Manhattan
Program Hours: Monday - Thursday: 3-6 p.m.
Program Capacity: 30
Staff/Child Ratio: 1:5
Fees: None
Medication Administered: No
Transportation Provided: Yes
Wheelchair Accessible: No
Service Description: Provides after school programs for children with special needs, focusing primarily on children with developmental disabilities.
Contact: Ms. Collins, Intake Coordinator

CHELSEA PIERS - PIER 62

23rd St. and the Hudson River
New York, NY 10011

(212) 336-6666 Administrative
(212) 336-6000 Administrative
(212) 336-6500 After School Program

www.chelseapiers.com

Services

Sports, Individual
Sports, Team/Leagues

Ages: 18 months to 13 years
Area Served: All boroughs
Program Hours: Classes are 1-1.5 hours. Classes offered Monday - Friday and on weekends. Call for information. Summer program also offered.
Staff/Child Ratio: 1:7
Fees: Depends on age and length of class. Call for information.
Method of Payment: Cash or credit card
Medication Administered: No
Transportation Provided: No. Transportation is provided for summer program only.
Wheelchair Accessible: No
Service Description: The after school program offers gymnastics (ages 18 months to 13 years), soccer (ages 3 to 12 years) and rock climbing (ages 4 to 12 years). Children with disabilities are considered on a case-by-case basis.
Contact: Gymnastics: Peter Gorman
Soccor: Ari Tillman
Rock Climbing: Cory Ismaili

CHILD CARE COUNCIL OF NASSAU COUNTY, INC.

925 Hempstead Turnpike, Suite 400
Franklin Square, NY 11010

(516) 358-9250 Administrative
(516) 358-9287 FAX

www.childcarenassau.org
cccnassau@earthlink.net

Jan Barbieri, Executive Director
Languages Spoken: Spanish

Services

Child Care Resource and Referral

Service Description: Provides information and referral services to parents seeking childcare services for children with or without special needs.

CHILD CARE COUNCIL OF SUFFOLK

60 Calvert Ave.
Commack, NY 11725

(631) 462-0303 Administrative
(631) 462-1617 FAX

www.childcaresuffolk.org
resourcereferral@childcaresuffolk.org

Janet Walerstein, Executive Director
Languages Spoken: Italian, Spanish

Services

Child Care Resource and Referral

Service Description: Provides information and referral services to parents seeking childcare services for children with or without special needs.

CHILD CARE COUNCIL OF WESTCHESTER

470 Mamaroneck Ave., Suite 302
White Plains, NY 10605

(914) 761-3456 Administrative
(914) 761-1957 FAX

www.childcare-experts.org/cccw/ccwhp.html
cccwny@aol.com

Languages Spoken: Spanish

< continued... >

Services

Child Care Resource and Referral

Service Description: Provides information and referral services to parents seeking childcare services for children with or without special needs.

CHILD CARE, INC.

275 Seventh Ave., 15th Fl.
New York, NY 10001

(212) 929-7604 Administrative
(212) 929-5785 FAX

ccinyc@aol.com

Nancy Kolben, Executive Director
Languages Spoken: Spanish

Services

Child Care Resource and Referral

Service Description: Provides information and referral services to parents seeking childcare services for children with or without special needs.

CHILD DEVELOPMENT SUPPORT CORPORATION

352-358 Classon Ave.
Brooklyn, NY 11238

(718) 398-6370 Help Line
(718) 398-2050 Administrative
(718) 398-6883 FAX

Freddie Hamilton, Executive Director
Languages Spoken: French, Haitian Creole, Spanish

Sites

1. CHILD DEVELOPMENT SUPPORT CORPORATION

352-358 Classon Ave.
Brooklyn, NY 11238

(718) 230-0056 Administrative
(718) 398-2050 Administrative
(718) 230-0112 FAX
(718) 398-6883 FAX

Freddie Hamilton, Executive Director

2. CHILD DEVELOPMENT SUPPORT CORPORATION- DAY CARE SERVICES

1213 Fulton St.
Brooklyn, NY 11216

(718) 398-6738 Administrative
(718) 398-6182 FAX

Letisha Wadsworth, Director of Day Care Services

Services

Arts and Crafts Instruction
Exercise Classes/Groups
Homework Help Programs
Tutoring

Ages: 14 to 21
Area Served: Brooklyn
Program Hours: Monday - Friday: 3-6 p.m.
Fees: None
Medication Administered: No
Transportation Provided: No
Wheelchair Accessible: Yes
Service Description: Provides after school programs for teenagers. Children with disabilities considered on a case-by-case basis.
Contact: Anita Grant, Head, Youth Department
Austin Green, Youth Counselor
Sites: 1

DAY CARE SERVICES
Child Care Resource and Referral

Sites: 2

CHILDREN AND ADULTS WITH ATTENTION DEFICIT DISORDERS (CHADD)

8181 Professional Place, Suite 201
Landover, FL 20785

(800) 233-4050 Administrative
(301) 306-7090 FAX

www.chadd.org
national@chadd.org

E. Clarke Ross, Chief Executive Officer

Sites

1. CHILDREN AND ADULTS WITH ATTENTION DEFICIT DISORDERS - NEW YORK CITY

PO Box 133
New York, NY 10024-0133

(212) 721-0007 Administrative
(212) 721-0074 FAX

Hal Meyer, Chapter Director

Services

Social Skills Training

Ages: Birth to 22
Population Served: Attention Deficit Disorder (ADD/ADHD)
Area Served: All Boroughs
Program Hours: Monday - Friday: 9-11:30 a.m.
Fees: Call for information
Medication Administered: No

<continued...>

Transportation Provided: No
Wheelchair Accessible: Yes
Service Description: Provides socialization training for children, study and organizational skills, and individual case management.
Sites: 1

CHILDREN'S AID SOCIETY

105 E. 22nd St.
New York, NY 10010

(212) 949-4800 Administrative
(212) 460-5941 FAX
(212) 949-4930 Head Start

www.childrensaidsociety.org

Philip Coltoff, Executive Director
Languages Spoken: Sign Language, Spanish

Sites

1. CHILDREN'S AID SOCIETY - DUNLEVY MILBANK CHILDREN'S CENTER

14-32 W. 118th St.
New York, NY 10026

(212) 996-1716 Information
(212) 369-8339 Medical Clinic

2. CHILDREN'S AID SOCIETY - FREDERICK DOUGLAS CHILDREN'S CENTER

885 Columbus Ave.
New York, NY 10025

(212) 865-6337 Information / Head Start
(212) 864-7771 FAX
(212) 222-8790 Mental Health Clinic

3. CHILDREN'S AID SOCIETY - GOODHUE CHILDREN'S CENTER

304 Prospect Ave.
Staten Island, NY 10301

(718) 447-2630 Administrative
(718) 981-3827 FAX

4. CHILDREN'S AID SOCIETY - RHINELANDER CHILDREN'S CENTER

350 E. 88th St.
New York, NY 10128

(212) 876-0500 Administrative (V/TDD)
(212) 876-9718 FAX

Charlotte Prinze, Director

5. CHILDREN'S AID SOCIETY - DREW HAMILTON COMMUNITY CENTER

220 West 143rd St.
New York, NY 10030

(212) 281-6118 Administrative

6. CHILDREN'S AID SOCIETY - GREENWICH CHILDREN'S CENTER

209-219 Sullivan St.
New York, NY 10012

(212) 254-3074 Administrative

7. CHILDREN'S AID SOCIETY - TAFT LEARNING CENTER

1724 Madison Ave.
New York, NY 10029

(212) 831-0556 Administrative

Services

Computer Classes
Exercise Classes/Groups
Homework Help Programs
Sports, Individual
Sports, Team/Leagues
Tutoring

Ages: 3 to 11
Population Served: All Disabilities
Area Served: All Boroughs
Program Hours: Monday - Friday: 3-6 p.m.
Fees: None
Medication Administered: No
Service Description: The after school programs provide educational, arts, recreation, socialization and leadership activities in a nurturing environment. The aim is to help youngsters improve interpersonal communications skills, self-esteem and teamwork, enhance academic skills, explore their interests and expand their world view.
Sites: 1 2 3 4 5 6 7

RHINELANDER SATURDAY PROGRAM FOR DEAF AND HARD OF HEARING
Recreational Activities

Ages: 5 to 19
Population Served: Deaf/Hard of Hearing
Area Served: All Boroughs
Program Hours: Saturday: 10 a.m.-3 p.m. (2 Saturdays per month, September through July)
Staff/Child Ratio: 3:7
Fees: None
Medication Administered: Call for information
Transportation Provided: No
Wheelchair Accessible: Yes
Service Description: The program is divided by age group. Each group has a group leader,

< continued... >

assistant and aid.
Contact: Dara Robinson, nbb61010@aol.com
Sites: 4

CHILDREN'S MUSEUM OF MANHATTAN (CMOM)

212 W. 83rd St.
New York, NY 10024

(212) 721-1223 [241] Administrative
(212) 721-1127 FAX

www.cmom.org

Jennifer Kozel, Director of School and Outreach Programs
Languages Spoken: Spanish

<u>Services</u>

Acting Instruction
Arts and Crafts Instruction
Computer Classes
Music Instruction
Storytelling

Ages: 4 to 12
Area Served: All Boroughs
Program Hours: Monday - Friday: 3:45-5 p.m.
Fees: $300/10 sessions, (for special after school programs)
Method of Payment: Check, Credit Card
Medication Administered: No
Transportation Provided: No
Wheelchair Accessible: Yes
Service Description: The Children's Museum of Manhattan offers a variety of after school programs. In Really Gross Biology, children take a closer look at CMOM's Body Odyssey exhibition. They make mucus, burps and scabs to investigate why the body produces this stuff. In Art-n-Orbit, children create motorized helicopters and spinning robots. In Water Play, children explore the properties of water through a series of experiments (These are just some of the courses offered by the museum). Photography and T.V. production workshops are also offered.

Museums

CHILDREN'S MUSEUM OF THE ARTS

182 Lafayette St.
New York, NY 10013-3276

(212) 274-0986 Administrative
(212) 274-1776 FAX

www.cmany.org
info@cmany.org

Elizabeth Reiss, Executive Director

<u>Services</u>

Arts and Crafts Instruction
Music Instruction

Ages: 2 to 10
Program Hours: Classes are from 4-5 p.m., with supervised "free time" from 3-4 p.m. and 5-5:30 p.m.
Staff/Child Ratio: 1:8
Fees: Call for information
Medication Administered: No
Wheelchair Accessible: Yes
Service Description: Children will make paints, stretch canvases, work with plaster and clay, try their hands at a pottery wheel, and learn how to create music. Wednesday: 5-7-year olds (beginners), Thursday: 8-year olds and up (advanced), Friday: 5-7-year olds (intermediate)

Museums

CHILDREN'S ZOO AT FLUSHING MEADOW CORONA PARK

53-51 111 St.
Flushing, NY 11368

(718) 271-1500 Administrative
(718) 271-4441 FAX
(718) 271-7361 Education Department

Robin Stalton, Executive Director

<u>Services</u>

Arts and Crafts Instruction
Nature Centers/Walks
Parks/Recreation Areas
Zoos/Wildlife Parks

Ages: 2 to 12
Program Hours: Weekends and holidays: 1-4 p.m.
Fees: Check with zoo
Medication Administered: No
Transportation Provided: No
Wheelchair Accessible: Yes
Service Description: The Education Center will have arts and crafts and other activities on weekends and all public holidays. Most activities are free with zoo admission. Look for signs at zoo entrance.

CHINATOWN YMCA

100 Hester St.
New York, NY 10002

(212) 219-8393 Administrative

Henry Mui, CWA, Director Family Suppport Program
Languages Spoken: Chinese, Spanish

<u>Services</u>

Arts and Crafts Instruction
Computer Classes
Exercise Classes/Groups
Homework Help Programs
Recreational Activities
Remedial Education
Sports, Individual
Sports, Team/Leagues

Ages: 6 to 11 (Y After School Program)
12 to 18 (Beacon Program)
Area Served: All boroughs
Program Hours: Monday - Friday: 3-7 p.m.
Fees: Nominal fee for Y After School programs. None
for Beacon. Please call for information.
Method of Payment: Scholarship, Payment Plan
Wheelchair Accessible: Yes
Service Description: There are two programs at the
Chinatown Y: the After School Program and the Beacon
Program. Activities are very similar. For the Y After
School program; children who attend P.S. 1, P.S. 2, P.S.
42, P.S. 124, P.S. 126, P.S. 130 or Saint James and
Saint Joseph, will be escorted by a counselor to the
Chinatown YMCA. No transportation or escorts are
provided for the Beacon Program. There are also
summer day camps, one for children 5 to 11, that runs
from 9 a.m-6 p.m., Monday - Friday and one for children
12 to 17 that runs 10 a.m-4 p.m., Monday - Thursday.
Call for more information.
Contact: Nika Yau, Director of Child Care: After School
Glenn MacAfee, Beacon Program

CHINESE-AMERICAN PLANNING COUNCIL

150 Elizabeth St.
Manhattan, 10012

(212) 941-0920 Administrative
(212) 966-8581 FAX

David Chen, Executive Director
Languages Spoken: Chinese (Cantonese, Mandarian),
Korean

<u>Sites</u>

**1. CHINESE-AMERICAN PLANNING COUNCIL -
CENTRAL ADMINISTRATION**
150 Elizabeth St.
New York, NY 10012

(212) 941-0920 Administrative
(212) 966-8581 FAX

David Chen, Executive Director

2. CHINESE-AMERICAN PLANNING COUNCIL
365 Broadway, 1st Fl.
New York, NY 10013-3906

(212) 941-0030 Administrative
(212) 226-5351 FAX

www.asianweb.net/news

Yim King Tsui, Director

<u>Services</u>

Child Care Resource and Referral
Sites: 1 2

CHURCH AVENUE MERCHANTS
BLOCK ASSOCIATION (CAMBA)

1720 Church Ave., 2nd Fl.
Brooklyn, NY 11226

(718) 287-2600 Administrative
(718) 287-2645 Administrative
(718) 287-0857 FAX

www.camba.org
Loreliel@.camba.org

Joanne M. Oplustil, Executive Director
Languages Spoken: Chinese, Haitian Creole,
Croatian, Farsi, Filipino, Russian, Spanish

<u>Sites</u>

**1. CHURCH AVENUE MERCHANTS BLOCK
ASSOCIATION (CAMBA)**
P.S. 269
1957 Nostrand Ave.
Brooklyn, NY 11210

(718) 462-0435 Administrative
(718) 462-0554 FAX

Brian Corrigan/ Lee Motayne, Beacon Directors

<continued...>

2. CHURCH AVENUE MERCHANTS BLOCK ASSOCIATION (CAMBA)
700 Cortelyou Road
Brooklyn, NY 11218

(718) 856-2341 Administrative
(718) 693-7433 FAX

www.camba.org
dkreiss@earthlink.net

Daniel Kreiss, Director

3. CHURCH AVENUE MERCHANTS BLOCK ASSOCIATION (CAMBA)
15 Snyder Avenue
Brooklyn, NY 11226

(718) 469-8064 Administrative
(718) 469-8063 FAX

www.camba.org

Rohan Jeremiah, Director

4. CHURCH AVENUE MERCHANTS BLOCK ASSOCIATION (CAMBA)
790 East New York Ave.
Brooklyn, NY 11203

(718) 493-8920 Administrative
(718) 467-3549 FAX

www.camba.org
nadia6710@yahoo.com

Nadia Bryan, Director

Services

ONE WORLD AFTERSCHOOL PROGRAM
Acting Instruction
Arts and Crafts Instruction
Computer Classes
Creative Writing
Dancing Instruction
Homework Help Programs
Music Instruction
Sports, Team/Leagues
Storytelling

Ages: 11 to 14
Population Served: Asthma, Attention Deficit Disorder (ADD/ADHD), Developmental Delay, Emotional Disability, Gifted, Learning Disability, Speech/Language Disability, Underachiever
Area Served: Brooklyn
Program Hours: Monday - Friday: 2:45-5:45 p.m.
Program Capacity: 200
Staff/Child Ratio: 1:15
Fees: None
Medication Administered: No
Transportation Provided: No
Wheelchair Accessible: Yes
Service Description: The One World After School Program serves 200 students at I.S. 62. The program is a collaboration between CAMBA, Inc. and I.S. 62. One

World provides homework help, project-based activities that encourage students to explore their own heritage, technology classes, weekly conflict resolution classes and workshops in the arts. CAMBA after school programs are open to all students, including students with special needs.
Contact: Christie Hodgkins, Director of After School Services, CAMBA, Inc.
Sites: 2

RENAISSANCE AFTER SCHOOL PROGRAM
Acting Instruction
Arts and Crafts Instruction
Creative Writing
Dancing Instruction
Field Trips/Excursions
Music Instruction
Sports, Team/Leagues

Ages: 11 to 15
Population Served: Asthma, Attention Deficit Disorder (ADD/ADHD), Developmental Delay, Emotional Disability, Gifted, Learning Disability, Underachiever
Area Served: Brooklyn
Program Hours: Monday - Friday: 3-6 p.m.
Program Capacity: 175
Staff/Child Ratio: 1:15
Fees: None
Medication Administered: No
Transportation Provided: No
Wheelchair Accessible: Yes
Service Description: The Renaissance After School Program serves 175 students at M.S. 391. A collaboration between CAMBA, Inc. and M.S. 391, Renaissance offers homework assistance, rites of passage classes, and clubs that include drumming, step, photography, science, art and football. CAMBA after school programs are open to all students, including those with special needs.
Contact: Christie Hodgkins, Director of After School Services, CAMBA, Inc.
Sites: 4

KIDS CONNECT AFTER SCHOOL PROGRAM
Acting Instruction
Arts and Crafts Instruction
Creative Writing
Dancing Instruction
Homework Help Programs
Music Instruction
Storytelling

Ages: 5 to 12
Population Served: Asthma, Attention Deficit Disorder (ADD/ADHD), Developmental Delay, Developmental Disability, Emotional Disability, Gifted, Learning Disability, Speech/Language Disability, Underachiever
Area Served: Brooklyn
Program Hours: Monday - Friday: 3-6 p.m.
Program Capacity: 275

<continued...>

Staff/Child Ratio: 1:10
Fees: None
Medication Administered: No
Transportation Provided: Yes, transportation can be provided through district office requests.
Wheelchair Accessible: No
Service Description: The Kids Connect After School Program serves 275 students at P.S. 109. A collaboration between CAMBA, Inc. and P.S. 109, Kids Connect offers homework help, weekly conflict resolution classes, literacy and math enrichment, visual arts and drama workshops, community service, family night events. Kids Connect earned a CitiGroup Success Fund award for facilitating the successful inclusion of children with special needs into the after school program.
Contact: Christie Hodgkins, Director of After School Services, CAMBA, Inc.
Sites: 3

BEACON 269
Arts and Crafts Instruction
Computer Classes
Creative Writing
Dancing Instruction
English as a Second Language
Field Trips/Excursions
Homework Help Programs
Sports, Team/Leagues
Storytelling

Ages: 10 to 21
Population Served: Underachiever
Area Served: Brooklyn
Program Hours: Monday - Friday: 2-10 p.m., Saturday: 12-10 p.m.
Program Capacity: 1,700 students per calendar year
Fees: None
Medication Administered: No
Transportation Provided: No
Wheelchair Accessible: Yes
Service Description: Young people and adults are invited to enroll in a variety of programs in a safe and controlled environment. Programs are geared toward enriching the lives of participants. Schedules of activities are revised as needed throughout the year to meet the needs of community residents who rely on our services. Interested parties are encouraged to call for updated information.
Sites: 1

CHURCH OF ST. MARK - SCHOOL DISTRICT 17

134 President St.
Brooklyn, NY 11213

(718) 756-6607 Administrative

Arts and Crafts Instruction
Homework Help Programs
Recreational Activities
Remedial Education
Tutoring

Ages: 3 to 11
Population Served: Deaf/Hard of Hearing, Learning Disability, Underachiever
Area Served: Brooklyn
Program Hours: Monday - Friday: 3-6 p.m.
Fees: $75 per week
Method of Payment: Cash, Check, Money Order
Medication Administered: No
Transportation Provided: No
Wheelchair Accessible: No
Service Description: Provides an after school program where children receive homework help and can also engage in recreational activities. One on one tutoring is available if needed.
Contact: Iyonne Forbes, Director

CHURCHILL SCHOOL AND CENTER, INC. (THE)

301 E. 29th St.
New York, NY 10016

(212) 722-0610 Administrative
(212) 722-1387 FAX

www.churchillcenter.org
mkessler@churchillschool.com

Marsha Kessler, Director

Services

ENHANCING SOCIAL SKILLS DEVELOPMENT
Social Skills Training

Ages: 5 and up
Population Served: Attention Deficit Disorder (ADD/ADHD), Developmental Disability, Learning Disability, Speech/Language Disability
Area Served: NYC Metro Area
Program Hours: Call for information
Staff/Child Ratio: 2:7
Fees: Call for information
Transportation Provided: No
Wheelchair Accessible: Yes
Service Description: An after school program for children with learning disabilities or attention deficit hyperactivity disorder. The goal for each participant is to acquire and practice social skills needed to successfully interact with peers, handle new social situations, talk to teachers and adults and interact with family.

<continued...>

Tutoring

Ages: 6 to 10
Population Served: Learning Disability, Underachiever
Area Served: All Boroughs
Program Hours: 2 afternoons: 4-5 p.m., 5-6 p.m. Call for more information.
Program Capacity: 36
Staff/Child Ratio: 1:6
Fees: None
Medication Administered: No
Transportation Provided: No
Wheelchair Accessible: Yes
Service Description: After school reading clinic using an Orton-Gillingham reading approach.

CITIZENS ADVICE BUREAU (CAB)

2054 Morris Ave.
Bronx, NY 10453

(718) 365-0910 Administrative
(718) 365-0697 FAX

Carolyn McLaughlin, Executive Director
Languages Spoken: Spanish

Sites

1. CITIZENS ADVICE BUREAU (CAB)

1130 Grand Concourse Ave.
Bronx, NY 10456

(718) 293-0727 Administrative

Jean Tibets, Program Coordinator

Services

Acting Instruction
Computer Classes
Exercise Classes/Groups
Homework Help Programs
Swimming
Tutoring

Ages: 6 to 12
Area Served: Bronx
Program Hours: Monday - Friday: 3-6 p.m.
Program Capacity: 70
Staff/Child Ratio: 1:2
Fees: $260/month
Method of Payment: Scholarships available
Medication Administered: No
Transportation Provided: No
Wheelchair Accessible: Yes
Service Description: Provides after school activities for children ages 6 to 12. Children with special needs are considered on a case-by-case basis.
Contact: Gwen, Registrar
Sites: 1

CITIZENS CARE DAY CARE CENTER

2322 Third Ave.
New York, NY 10035

(212) 427-6766 Administrative
(212) 423-0894 FAX

Alfred Sloan, Director
Languages Spoken: Spanish

Services

CITIZENS CARE DAY CARE CENTER II
Acting Instruction
Arts and Crafts Instruction
Child Care Centers
Computer Classes
Creative Writing
Dancing Instruction
Exercise Classes/Groups
Field Trips/Excursions
Homework Help Programs
Music Instruction
Sports, Individual
Sports, Team/Leagues
Storytelling

Ages: 5 to 12
Population Served: Asthma, Attention Deficit Disorder (ADD/ADHD), Developmental Delay, Emotional Disability, Gifted, Health Impairment, Learning Disability, Mental Retardation (mild-moderate), Multiple Disability, Physical/Orthopedic Disability, Speech/Language Disability, Underachiever
Area Served: All Boroughs
Program Hours: Monday - Friday: 8 a.m.-6 p.m.
Program Capacity: All day (8 a.m - 6 p.m.): 75, After School (2-6 p.m.) 57
Staff/Child Ratio: Varies
Fees: $80/week
Method of Payment: Cash or Money Orders only
Medication Administered: Yes, Community Health Worker on site
Transportation Provided: No
Wheelchair Accessible: Yes
Service Description: A program that provides all day services for preschool children and after school services for those in school.

CITY LIGHTS PROGRAM, INC.

P.O. Box 121
Belle Harbor, NY 11694

(718) 474-7834 Administrative
city_lights_program@msn.com

Dr. Gil Skyer, Executive Director

< continued... >

Services

Field Trips/Excursions
Recreational Activities
Storytelling

Ages: 16 to Adult
Population Served: Asperger Syndrome, Attention Deficit Disorder (ADD/ADHD), Developmental Delay, Developmental Disability, Emotional Disability, Gifted, Learning Disability, Mental Retardation (mild-moderate), Neurological Disability, Tourette Syndrome, Traumatic Brain Injury, Underachiever
Area Served: All Boroughs
Program Hours: Weekends, call for exact times
Staff/Child Ratio: 1:8
Fees: $350 per year plus activity fee
Medication Administered: No
Transportation Provided: Yes
Wheelchair Accessible: No
Service Description: Recreation and socialization for teens and young adults with learning disabilities and adjustment difficulties. Participants meet one or two Sunday afternoons per month for activities such as concerts, disco parties, theatre, sports events, trips to dude ranches, etc. Groups are arranged according to age and abilities.

CLAREMONT NEIGHBORHOOD CENTER

489 E. 169th St.
Bronx, NY 10456

(718) 588-1000 Administrative
(718) 681-0736 FAX
(718) 588-2283 After School Program

Rachel Spivey, Executive Director
Languages Spoken: Spanish

Services

Homework Help Programs
Recreational Activities
Sports, Individual
Sports, Team/Leagues
Tutoring

Ages: 5 to 13
Population Served: Learning Disability, Underachiever
Area Served: Bronx, Manhattan
Program Hours: Monday - Friday: 2:30-6:30 p.m.
Program Capacity: 110
Staff/Child Ratio: 3:30
Fees: $45 per month
Method of Payment: Cash, Money Order
Medication Administered: No
Transportation Provided: Yes from neighborhood schools. Children are picked up and walked to Center.
Wheelchair Accessible: No
Service Description: A Partners in Reading program is available where small groups of young children get reading help and exercises for reading, writing and more.

There is a Saturday program that includes dance, drama, karate, and Boy, Girl and Cub Scouts. Children with special needs can be accommodated on a case-by-case basis.
Contact: Michael Williams, Program Coordinator
Leonard Heard

CLOISTERS (THE)

Fort Tryon Park
New York, NY 10040

(212) 923-3700 Administrative
(212) 795-3640 FAX

www.metmuseum.org

Peter Barnet, Executive Director

Services

Museums

CLUSTER, INC.

20 S. Broadway, Suite 501
Yonkers, NY 10701

(914) 963-6440 Administrative
(914) 963-4566 FAX

Clifford Schneider, President

Services

Arts and Crafts Instruction
Exercise Classes/Groups
Homework Help Programs
Storytelling
Tutoring

Ages: 6 to 13
Area Served: Bronx, Yonkers
Program Hours: Monday - Friday: 4-6 p.m.
Program Capacity: 50
Staff/Child Ratio: 1:8/10
Fees: None
Medication Administered: No
Transportation Provided: No
Wheelchair Accessible: Yes
Service Description: Provides after school programs where children can participate in a variety of activities, among them are conflict resolution, arts and crafts, homework help and the Harry Potter book club. Children with disabilities are considered on a case-by-case basis.

COLONY-SOUTH BROOKLYN HOUSES, INC.

297 Dean St.
Brooklyn, NY 11217

(718) 625-3810 Administrative
(718) 875-8719 FAX

Balaguru Cacarla, Executive Director
Languages Spoken: Spanish

Services

Homework Help Programs
Social Skills Training
Tutoring

Ages: 4 to 16
Population Served: At Risk
Area Served: Bronx
Program Hours: Saturday during the school year.
Program Capacity: 75
Staff/Child Ratio: 1:15
Fees: None
Transportation Provided: Children are picked up at schools and shelters in the Board of Education District 19.
Wheelchair Accessible: Yes
Service Description: Provides a socialization program to help at risk children and youth. Some tutoring and homework help is available.
Contact: Robert Santiego

COLUMBIA UNIVERSITY

4101 Lewisohn Hall, 2970 Broadway
New York, NY 10027-9829

(800) 895-1169 Administrative

www.columbia.edu/cu/gs/
gs-admit@columbia.edu

Sites

1. COLUMBIA UNIVERSITY - CENTER FOR EDUCATIONAL AND PSYCHOLOGICAL SERVICES

667 Thorndike Hall, Box 91
505 W. 120th St.
New York, NY 10027

(212) 678-3262 Administrative
(212) 678-4034 FAX

Denilia Rosa, Director

2. COLUMBIA UNIVERSITY - TUTORING AND TRANSLATING AGENCY

2960 Broadway, MC 5727
New York, NY 10027

(212) 854-4888 Administrative

Kathleen O'Connor, Executive Director

Services

Remedial Education

Ages: All Ages
Population Served: Learning Disability
Area Served: All Boroughs
Fees: $35 per hour
Method of Payment: Cash, Check, Credit Card, Money Order
Medication Administered: No
Service Description: Provides individual tutoring. In-home tutoring available.
Sites: 1 2

COLUMBIA UNIVERSITY - TEACHER'S COLLEGE - EDUCATIONAL AND PSYCHOLOGICAL SERVICES

525 W. 120th St.
New York, NY 10027

(212) 678-3262 Administrative
(212) 678-8105 FAX

Dinelia Rosa, Ph.D., Director
Languages Spoken: Spanish

Services

Tutoring

Ages: 8 and up
Population Served: Asthma, Attention Deficit Disorder (ADD/ADHD), Developmental Delay, Diabetes, Emotional Disability, Gifted, Learning Disability, Mental Retardation (mild-moderate), Speech/Language Disability, Underachiever
Area Served: All Boroughs, New Jersey
Wheelchair Accessible: Yes
Service Description: Offers educational and psychological services to children. Services are offered by doctoral students in training practicum under close supervision of licensed educators and psychologists.

COMMITTEE FOR HISPANIC CHILDREN AND FAMILIES, INC.

140 W. 22nd St., Suite 301
New York, NY 10011

(212) 206-1090 Administrative
(212) 206-8093 FAX

Elba Montalvo, Executive Director
Languages Spoken: Spanish

< continued... >

<u>Services</u>

Child Care Resource and Referral

COMMUNITY ASSOCIATION FOR PROGRESSIVE DOMINICANS

2268 Amsterdam Ave.
New York, NY 10033

(212) 740-3866 Administrative
(212) 740-1543 FAX

Jose Jacoeo, Executive Director
Languages Spoken: Spanish

<u>Services</u>

Arts and Crafts Instruction
Computer Classes
Homework Help Programs
Tutoring

Ages: 5 to 13
Area Served: Manhattan
Program Hours: Monday - Friday: 3-6 p.m.
Fees: Call for information
Medication Administered: No
Transportation Provided: No
Wheelchair Accessible: Yes
Service Description: Provides after school activities for children. Children with special needs are accepted on a case-by-case basis.

COMMUNITY OPPORTUNITIES AND DEVELOPMENT AGENCY (CODA)

564 Thomas S. Boyland St.
Brooklyn, NY 11212

(718) 345-4779 Administrative
(718) 345-4700 FAX

Dr. Emil D. Deloache, Executive Director
Languages Spoken: Haitian Creole, Spanish

<u>Services</u>

Homework Help Programs
Recreational Activities
Tutoring

Ages: 6 to 21
Population Served: Asthma, Attention Deficit Disorder (ADD/ADHD), Autism, Deaf/Hard of Hearing, Developmental Delay, Developmental Disability, Diabetes, Health Impairment, Learning Disability, Mental Retardation (mild-moderate), Mental Retardation (severe-profound), Speech/Language Disability
Area Served: Brooklyn (Ocean Hill, Brownsville, East Flatbush, Crown Heights, Bedford Stuyvesant)

Program Hours: Monday - Friday: 3-7 p.m.
Fees: Call for information
Transportation Provided: Yes
Service Description: Assistance with homework, math and reading tutoring, therapeutic recreation, weekly communication workshop, full course dinner and mainstream recreation are offered.

COMMUNITY SERVICE COUNCIL OF GREATER HARLEM, INC.

207 W. 133rd St.
New York, NY 10030

(212) 926-0281 Administrative
(212) 862-6119 FAX

Joan Brown, Director

<u>Services</u>

Arts and Crafts Instruction
Child Care Centers
Computer Classes
Exercise Classes/Groups
Field Trips/Excursions
Homework Help Programs
Music Instruction
Sports, Individual
Sports, Team/Leagues
Tutoring

Ages: 2.6 to 12
Population Served: Attention Deficit Disorder (ADD/ADHD), Emotional Disability, Learning Disability, Physical/Orthopedic Disability, Underachiever
Area Served: Manhattan
Program Hours: Monday - Friday: 3-6 p.m. All day during the summer.
Program Capacity: 20 per class
Staff/Child Ratio: 2:20
Fees: Sliding Scale
Medication Administered: Yes
Transportation Provided: No
Wheelchair Accessible: Yes
Service Description: Provides an after school program that offers a variety of activities for children.

COMMUNITY UNITED METHODIST CHURCH

81-10 35th Ave.
Jackson Heights, NY 11372

(718) 446-0559 Administrative
(718) 458-7893 FAX

www.jacksonhghtsumchurch.org

Karen Ellefsen, Principal

< continued... >

Services

Exercise Classes/Groups
Homework Help Programs
Sports, Individual
Sports, Team/Leagues
Tutoring

Ages: 4 to 14
Program Hours: Monday - Friday: 3-6:30 p.m.
Fees: $100, summer. No fees for after school program.
Service Description: The After School Achievement Club works on homework guidance and small group tutoring. When homework is completed, students are able to choose from a variety of activities, sports, games and an original big screen movie. Children with special needs are considered on a case-by-case basis.

CONCORD FAMILY SERVICES

1221 Bedford Ave.
Brooklyn, NY 11215

(718) 398-3499 Administrative
(718) 638-3016 FAX

Lelar E. Floyd, Executive Director
Languages Spoken: Spanish

Services

Arts and Crafts Instruction
Computer Classes
Field Trips/Excursions
Homework Help Programs
Tutoring

Ages: 6 to 20
Population Served: Dyslexia, Emotional Disability, Learning Disability, Underachiever
Area Served: Brooklyn
Program Hours: Monday - Friday: 3:30-5:30 p.m.
Program Capacity: 40
Staff/Child Ratio: 1:10
Fees: $15 per hour for tutoring
Method of Payment: Cash, Checks, Money Orders
Medication Administered: Yes
Transportation Provided: No
Wheelchair Accessible: Yes
Service Description: Offers an after school program that provides a variety of activities, primarily for children in foster care.

CONCOURSE HOUSE

2751 Grand Concourse
Bronx, NY 10468

(718) 584-4400 Administrative
(718) 584-4724 FAX

chousebx@aol.com

Manuela Schaudt, Executive director
Languages Spoken: Spanish

Services

Arts and Crafts Instruction
Child Care Centers
Computer Classes
Mentoring Programs
Music Instruction
Storytelling
Tutoring

Ages: Birth to 9
Population Served: Homeless Women and Children
Program Hours: Day care: 8 a.m.-6 p.m., After school: 3-8 p.m.
Program Capacity: 75 to 85 resident children, 24 neighborhood children
Staff/Child Ratio: 1:2/3
Fees: Sliding Scale
Method of Payment: Money Orders
Medication Administered: No
Transportation Provided: No
Wheelchair Accessible: Yes
Service Description: Concourse House has on-site child care for residents of the shelter, as well as pre-school for low income families in the neighborhood. We provide after school services for school-age children that includes tutoring assistance and literacy assistance.

COOPER-HEWITT NATIONAL DESIGN MUSEUM

2 E. 91st St.
New York, NY 10028

(212) 849-8380 Youth Education
(212) 849-8400 Administrative

www.si.edu/ndm

Andrew Svedlor, Educational DE

Services

Museums

CRAFT STUDENTS LEAGUE OF THE YWCA OF NEW YORK

610 Lexington Ave.
New York, NY 10022

Margaret Ann Murphy

Services

Recreational Activities

Ages: 13 to 21
Area Served: All Boroughs
Program Hours: Sunday: 12-3 p.m.
Fees: None
Medication Administered: No
Transportation Provided: Yes
Wheelchair Accessible: Yes
Service Description: Provides a networking program for teens and young adults. Teens and young adults with special needs are considered on a case-by-case basis.

CREATIVE MUSIC THERAPY STUDIO

20 W. 20th St., Suite 803
New York, NY 10011

(212) 414-5407 Administrative

Ann Turry, Co-director

Services

Music Therapy

Ages: 2 and up
Population Served: All Disabilities
Area Served: All Boroughs
Program Hours: Call for information
Fees: Individual: $65 per session, session is 30 minutes long. Group: $35 per session, session is 40 minutes long.
Method of Payment: Cash, Check
Medication Administered: No
Transportation Provided: No
Wheelchair Accessible: Yes
Service Description: Provides individual and group sessions.

CROSS ISLAND YMCA

238-10 Hillside Ave.
Bellerose, NY 11426

(718) 479-0505 Administrative
(718) 468-9568 FAX

www.ymcanyc.org
crossisland@ymcanyc.org

Jean Dattner, Senior Program Director
Languages Spoken: Spanish

Services

Arts and Crafts Instruction
Homework Help Programs
Recreational Activities
Sports, Individual
Sports, Team/Leagues
Swimming

Ages: 3 to 12
Area Served: Queens
Program Hours: Monday - Friday: 3-6 p.m.
Fees: Fees vary for member and non-members of YMCA. Please call for information
Method of Payment: ATM Cards, Cash, Checks, Credit Cards, Money Orders
Medication Administered: No
Transportation Provided: Yes
Service Description: Provides a safe and convenient alternative to meet the needs of working parents. Off-site programs are offered at P.S. 18 and P.S. 133. Children with disabilities considered on a case-by-case basis.

CROWN HEIGHTS SERVICE CENTER, INC.

1193 Dean St., 2nd Fl.
Brooklyn, NY 11216

(718) 774-9800 Administrative
(212) 774-0231 FAX

Jessie Hamilton, Executive Director

Services

Acting Instruction
Arts and Crafts Instruction
Computer Classes
Homework Help Programs
Mentoring Programs
Tutoring

Ages: 8 to 18
Population Served: AIDS/HIV +, Emotional Disability, Juvenile Offender, Sickle Cell Anemia, Substance Abuse, Substance Exposed
Program Hours: Monday - Friday: 3-6 p.m.
Program Capacity: 45
Staff/Child Ratio: 1:7
Fees: None
Medication Administered: No
Transportation Provided: No
Wheelchair Accessible: No

DAIRY IN CENTRAL PARK (THE)

830 Fifth Ave., (65th St. south of the Mall)
New York, NY 10021

(212) 794-6564 The Dairy Visitor Center

Services

Nature Centers/Walks
Parks/Recreation Areas

DAY CARE COUNCIL OF NEW YORK, INC.

10 E. 34th St., 6th Fl.
New York, NY 10016

(212) 213-2423 Administrative
(212) 213-2650 FAX

dccny@compuserve.com

Andrea Anthony, Executive Director
Languages Spoken: Haitian Creole, Spanish

Sites

1. DAY CARE COUNCIL OF NEW YORK, INC.
10 E. 34th St., 6th Fl.
New York, NY 10016

(212) 213-2423 Administrative
(212) 213-2650 FAX

Andrea Anthony, Executive Director

2. DAY CARE COUNCIL OF NEW YORK, INC. - BROOKLYN
204 Parkside Ave.
Brooklyn, NY 11225

(718) 282-4500 Administrative
(718) 282-5511 FAX

Lisa Caswell, Director

3. DAY CARE COUNCIL OF NEW YORK, INC. - JAMES E. HALL FAMILY DAY CARE NETWORK
94-20 Guy Brewer Blvd., Rm. 2F01E
Jamaica, NY 11452

(718) 262-2247 Administrative

Indra Moore, Coordinator

Services

Child Care Resource and Referral
Service Description: Provides information and referral services to parents seeking childcare services for children with or without special needs.
Sites: 1 2 3

DEF DANCE JAM WORKSHOP

215 W. 114th St.
New York, NY 10025

(212) 694-0477 Administrative/TDD

www.defdancejam.org
info@defdancejam.org

Aziza, Director
Languages Spoken: Sign Language

Services

Acting Instruction
Arts and Crafts Instruction
Creative Writing
Dancing Instruction
Exercise Classes/Groups
Homework Help Programs
Mentoring Programs
Music Instruction
Music Performances
Storytelling
Theater Performances

Ages: 9 to 25
Population Served: All Disabilities, Deaf/Hard of Hearing
Area Served: All Boroughs
Program Hours: Monday and Tuesday: 4-8 p.m.
Program Capacity: 45-50
Staff/Child Ratio: 1:5
Fees: Call for information
Transportation Provided: Yes
Wheelchair Accessible: Yes
Service Description: An intergenerational performing arts and academic program with youth, adult and elder members who are deaf, hearing and physically or developmentally challenged. Through education, workshops, awareness-building, community service, and performances, the Def Dance Jam Workshop seeks to empower its members artistically, academically and culturally.

DEPARTMENT OF PARKS AND RECREATION OF NEW YORK CITY

Central Park
The Arsenal
New York, NY 10021

(212) 360-3456 Events Hot Line
(212) 360-8111 Administrative
(718) 699-4129 Administrative

www.nyc.gov/parks

Emily Brennan, Director of Central Recreation

<continued...>

Services

Acting Instruction
Arts and Crafts Instruction
Homework Help Programs
Parks/Recreation Areas
Sports, Individual
Sports, Team/Leagues

Ages: 6 to 13
Population Served: All Disabilities
Program Hours: Monday - Friday: 3-6 p.m.
Fees: None
Transportation Provided: No
Service Description: The Department of Parks and Recreation offers after school programs in 32 recreation centers citywide. All parks' after school programs offer educational and recreational activities for children. Programs can accommodate children with disabilities. Parks Enhanced After School Programs feature instruction by talented teachers in the fields of literacy, performing arts, visual arts and much more.

BRONX

St. Mary's Pool
450 St. Ann's Ave.
Bronx, NY 10455
(718) 402-5157

St. James Golden Age Center
2530 Jerome Ave.
Bronx, NY 10468
(718) 822-4271

BROOKLYN

Sunset Recreation Center
7th Ave. & 43rd St.
Brooklyn, NY 11232
(718) 965-6533

Brownsville Recreation Center
1555 Linden Blvd.
Brooklyn, NY 11212
(718) 485-4633

St. John's Recreation Center
1251 Prospect Place
Brooklyn, NY 11213
(718) 771-2787

Herbert Von King Recreation Center
670 Lafayette Ave.
Brooklyn, NY 11216
(718) 622-2082

MANHATTAN

Jackie Robinson Recreation Center
West 146th St. & Bradhurst Ave.
New York, NY 10039

(212) 234-9607

Thomas Jefferson Pool
2180 First Ave.
New York, NY 10029
(212) 860-1383

J. Hood Wright Senior Center
173 Fort Washington Ave.
New York, NY 10032
(212) 927-1514

Carmine Recreation Center
1 Clarkson St.
New York, NY 10014
(212) 242-5228

Hamilton Fish Recreation Center
128 Pitt St.
New York, NY 10002
(212) 387-7688

Hansborough Recreation Center
35 W. 134th St.
New York, NY 10037
(212) 234-9603

New York Alfred E. Smith Recreation Center
80 Catherine St.
New York, NY 10038
(212) 285-0300

Pelham Fritz Recreation Center
18 West 122nd St.
New York, NY 10027
(212) 860-1380

QUEENS

Lost Battalion Hall Recreation Center
93-29 Queens Blvd.
Flushing, NY 11374
(718) 263-1163

Sorrentino Recreation Center
1848 Cornaga Ave.
Far Rockaway, NY 11691
(718) 471-4818

STATEN ISLAND

Jennifer Schweiger Playground
Jules Drive, Elson Court and Regis Drive
(program is held within the building
located in the park)
Staten Island, NY 10314
(718) 477-5471

DIAL-A-TEACHER

260 Park Ave. S.
New York, NY 10010

(212) 598-9205 Homework Help
(212) 529-6218 FAX
(212) 777-8499 TDD

Languages Spoken: Chinese, French, Greek, Haitian Creole, Hebrew, Italian, Korean, Russian, Spanish

Services

Homework Help Programs

Area Served: All Boroughs
Program Hours: Monday - Thursday: 4-7 p.m.
Service Description: An after school telephone service where students can receive teacher assistance with homework, and parents can receive professional advice on how they can more effectively help their children at home with school work. Services are offered throughout the school year. Conferences and workshops on a variety of topics for parents are also offered.

DIGITAL CLUBHOUSE

55 Broad St., Lower Level
New York, NY 10004

(212) 269-4284 Administrative
(212) 269-4287 FAX

www.digiclub.org
dapp@hotmail.com

Marty Kraussman, Executive Director

Services

DIGITALLY ABLED PRODUCERS PROGRAM
Computer Classes
Mentoring Programs

Ages: 12 to 16
Population Served: Cerebral Palsy, Deaf/Hard of Hearing, Developmental Disability, Down Syndrome, Health Impairment, Mental Retardation (mild-moderate), Multiple Disability, Neurological Disability, Physical/Orthopedic Disability, Rare Disorder, Speech/Language Disability, Spina Bifida, Technology Supported
Area Served: Manhattan
Program Hours: Saturday (during school year); Tuesday - Thursday (summer); Lab is open, Monday - Friday: Noon-6 p.m.
Fees: None
Medication Administered: No
Transportation Provided: No
Wheelchair Accessible: Yes
Service Description: The Digitally Abled Producers Program (DAPP) is a youth leadership development program that teaches students advanced digital technology tools to enable them to become successful

civic entrepreneurs and leaders in the 21st century.
Contact: Kawi Mailutha, Program Coordinator

DISCOVERY PROGRAMS, INC.

251 West 100th St.
New York, NY 10025

(212) 749-8717 Administrative

Lisa Stark, Executive Director

Services

Exercise Classes/Groups
Recreational Activities
Sports, Individual
Sports, Team/Leagues

Ages: 6 months - 7 years
Area Served: All Boroughs
Program Hours: Monday - Friday: 3-5:30 p.m.
Program Capacity: 300
Staff/Child Ratio: 2:8-12
Fees: Vary depending on classes. Please call for further information.
Medication Administered: No
Transportation Provided: No
Wheelchair Accessible: Yes
Service Description: Provides a variety of after school recreational and athletic activities. Please call for fees and classes available. Children with special needs can be accommodated.
Contact: John Diaz, Administrator

DOME PROJECT, INC. (THE)

486 Amsterdam Ave.
New York, NY 10024

(212) 724-1780 Administrative
(212) 724-6982 FAX

Joel Flax, Executive Director
Languages Spoken: Spanish

Services

THE ACADEMIC TUTORING PROGRAM
Homework Help Programs
Mentoring Programs
Tutoring

Ages: 10 to 20
Area Served: All Boroughs
Program Hours: 1.5 hours per week
Staff/Child Ratio: 1:1
Fees: Call for information
Medication Administered: No
Transportation Provided: No
Wheelchair Accessible: Yes
Service Description: The Academic Tutoring and Mentoring program uses educational

<continued...>

consultants who help volunteer tutors create rigorous individualized lesson plans for each student. Children with special needs considered on a case-by-case basis.

PARTNER'S PROGRAM
Mentoring Programs

Ages: 12 to 18
Area Served: Manhattan
Program Hours: 2 times/month 2-3 hours
Staff/Child Ratio: 1:1
Medication Administered: No
Transportation Provided: No
Service Description: The Partner's Program is a girls only mentoring program for girls ages 12 - 18. Each girl in the group is paired with the same adult partner for 8 months. The adults in the group are thought of as partners instead of mentors, because each person in the group has something to teach the other. Children with disabilities considered on a case-by-case basis.
Contact: Hilary Kopple, Girl's Program Coordinator

DOOR (THE) - A CENTER OF ALTERNATIVES

555 Broome St.
New York, NY 10013

(212) 941-9090 Administrative
(212) 941-0714 FAX

www.door.org

Michael Zisser, Executive Director
Languages Spoken: Chinese, Spanish

Services

Arts and Crafts Instruction
Recreational Activities
Social Skills Training

Ages: 12 to 21
Population Served: All Disabilities
Area Served: All Boroughs
Program Hours: Hours vary depending on program. Call for information
Fees: Call for information
Medication Administered: No
Transportation Provided: No
Wheelchair Accessible: Yes
Service Description: A multi-service agency providing youth services and addressing important unmet legal needs. Offers counseling, recreation, arts, education and job programs, case management, crisis intervention, advocacy and medical services. The Door also provides civil legal services to young people throughout New York City in the areas of family law, public benefits, immigration, housing, consumer affairs, education and civil rights.

DOUGLASTON AFTER SCHOOL CENTER

41-14 240th St.
Douglaston, NY 11363

(718) 631-8874 Administrative

Cecilia V. LaRock

Services

Acting Instruction
Cooking Classes
Dancing Instruction
Music Instruction
Recreational Activities
Storytelling

Ages: 5 to 14
Population Served: Autism, Cerebral Palsy, Developmental Disability, Down Syndrome, Health Impairment, Mental Retardation (mild-moderate), Multiple Disability, Neurological Disability, Physical/Orthopedic Disability, Seizure Disorder, Speech/Language Disability
Program Hours: Monday - Friday: 3-5:30 p.m.
Fees: $585
Medication Administered: No
Transportation Provided: No
Wheelchair Accessible: Yes
Service Description: This after school program integrates children with and without special needs. Children with mental retardation and/or physical disability qualify. Activities include drama, music, poetry, cooking, dance, yoga and storytelling. Children from the neighborhood work alongside children who have physical and developmental disabilities.

DR. WHITE COMMUNITY CENTER

200 Gold St.
Brooklyn, NY 11201

(718) 875-8801 Administrative
(718) 875-6347 FAX

jamiekogan@hotmail.com

Languages Spoken: Spanish

Services

Acting Instruction
Arts and Crafts Instruction
Computer Classes
Dancing Instruction
Field Trips/Excursions
Homework Help Programs
Music Instruction
Social Skills Training

Ages: 6 to 15
Population Served: Attention Deficit Disorder (ADD/ADHD), Emotional Disability, Gifted,

< continued... >

Juvenile Offender, Underachiever
Area Served: Brooklyn
Program Hours: Monday - Friday: 3:30-6 p.m.
Program Capacity: 60 children
Staff/Child Ratio: 2:25
Fees: $10 per semester, $20 per school year
Method of Payment: Cash or Check
Medication Administered: No
Transportation Provided: Teachers will pick up students who attend P.S. 67, P.S. 307, P.S. 287 from their respective schools.
Wheelchair Accessible: Yes
Service Description: Children increase their social and academic skills through literacy activities, creative outlets (i.e., dance, drawing and drama) and community projects. The program provides particular assistance to children who may be experiencing difficulties in behavior and academics. Case management services, as well as individual and family therapy, are available to children, and their families enrolled in the program.
Contact: Jaime Kogan, Program Coordinator

DREAM CATCHERS - THERAPEUTIC RIDING

155 W. 70th St., #110
New York, NY 10023

(212) 799-1792 Administrative
(212) 799-1792 FAX

www.dcriders.org
info@dcriders.com

Denise Colón, President and Founder

Services

Equestrian Therapy

Ages: 5 and up
Population Served: Asperger Syndrome, Attention Deficit Disorder (ADD/ADHD), Autism, Cerebral Palsy, Deaf/Hard of Hearing, Developmental Delay, Developmental Disability, Down Syndrome, Emotional Disability, Learning Disability, Mental Retardation (mild-moderate), Multiple Disability, Neurological Disability, Pervasive Developmental Disorder, Physical/Orthopedic Disability (some restrictions), Seizure Disorder, Speech/Language Disability, Traumatic Brain Injury (some restrictions)
Children of all disabilities are encouraged to apply for an evaluation
Area Served: Bronx, Manhattan, Westchester
Program Hours: Friday: 4-6 p.m., Saturday: 9:30-11:30 a.m. , Monday: 4-5:30 p.m.
Program Capacity: Limited enrollment
Fees: $200 per series of 8 riding lessons
Method of Payment: Limited number of scholarships available
Medication Administered: No
Transportation Provided: No
Wheelchair Accessible: Yes
Service Description: The goal of the program is to enrich the lives of persons with disabilities through the use of equine-assisted therapy. Games, props and exercises help riders achieve a sense of joy and accomplishment. Therapeutic riding is known to have a positive effect on balance and mobility, as well as self-confidence, self-esteem and spirituality. The movement of the horse, and the connection between horse and rider can enhance the overall functioning of an individual struggling with a disability.

DYCKMAN FARM HOUSE MUSEUM

4881 Broadway
New York, NY 10034

(212) 304-9422 Administrative
(212) 304-3635 FAX

www.dyckman.org
dyckmanfhm@worldnet.att.net

Allyson Bowen, Director
Languages Spoken: Spanish

Services

LIFE ON THE FARM
Museums

Ages: 3 and up
Population Served: Developmental Delay, Developmental Disability, Down Syndrome, Emotional Disability, Gifted, Mental Retardation (mild-moderate), Mental Retardation (severe-profound), Visual Disability/Blind
Area Served: All Boroughs, Westchester, New Jersey (north)
Program Hours: Reservations are required, and tours are generally scheduled at 10 a.m. and 12 p.m., Tuesday - Friday. Programs are usually 90 minutes in length, but can be tailored to fit the specific needs of your group.
Program Capacity: 30 participants
Staff/Child Ratio: 1:10
Fees: $1 - basic tours, $2 - craft activities
Method of Payment: Cash
Medication Administered: No
Transportation Provided: No
Wheelchair Accessible: No
Service Description: Includes a tour of the museum and opportunities to handle 19th century artifacts and handspin wool into yarn. Students explore the house and grounds with a museum educator looking for evidence of the way people lived before modern technology. An up-close look at the farmhouse kitchen, including the tools and equipment used in open-hearth cooking, provides students with a sense of how people prepared food before stoves and refrigerators were invented. In the final segment of the program, students learn to spin wool by hand while observing wheel-spinning and

<continued...>

weaving demonstrations.
Contact: Katie Beltramo, Education Director

EAST HARLEM BLOCK SCHOOLS, INC.

94 E. 111th St.
New York, NY 10029

(212) 722-6350 Administrative
(212) 722-5283 FAX

Dianne Morales, Executive Director
Languages Spoken: Spanish

Services

Arts and Crafts Instruction
Homework Help Programs
Tutoring

Ages: 3 to 18
Area Served: Manhattan
Program Hours: Monday - Friday: 3-6 p.m.
Fees: None
Medication Administered: No
Transportation Provided: No
Wheelchair Accessible: Yes
Service Description: Provides an after school program which accepts children with special needs on a case-by-case basis.

EAST HARLEM COUNCIL FOR COMMUNITY IMPROVEMENT

413 E. 120th St.
New York, NY 10035

(212) 410-7707 Administrative
(212) 828-4653 FAX

www.bway.net/~ehcci
ehcci@el.net

Raul Rodríguez, Executive Director
Languages Spoken: Spanish

Sites

1. EAST HARLEM COUNCIL FOR COMMUNITY IMPROVEMENT - EL FARO BEACON COMMUNITY CENTER

2351 First Ave., Rm. 153/154
New York, NY 10035

(212) 410-4227 Administrative
(212) 410-4885 FAX

Santos Negron, Director

Services

Recreational Activities
Respite, Children's Out-of-Home

Ages: 6 and up
Population Served: Developmental Disability
Area Served: Manhattan
Program Hours: Call for information
Fees: Call for information
Medication Administered: No
Transportation Provided: No
Wheelchair Accessible: Yes
Service Description: A multiservice center that provides Saturday out-of-home respite, recreation and socialization for young people with developmental disabilities and opportunities for more independent living through the establishment of community residences for adults.
Sites: 1

EAST HARLEM COUNCIL FOR HUMAN SERVICES, INC.

2253 Third Ave., 2nd Fl.
New York, NY 10035

(212) 427-8876 Day Care Program
(212) 289-6650 Administrative
(212) 427-1592 FAX
(212) 427-9011 Head Start
(212) 824-1978 Family Day Care

Josephine Lopez, Executive Director
Languages Spoken: Spanish

Services

EHCHS FAMILY DAY CARE PROGRAM
Child Care Resource and Referral

Ages: 2 months to 12
Area Served: Manhattan
Program Hours: Monday - Friday: 8 a.m.-6 p.m.
Fees: ACD determines fees
Medication Administered: No
Transportation Provided: No
Wheelchair Accessible: No
Service Description: Provides referrals to child care centers, both full day and part time (for mainstream and special needs school age children).

EAST HARLEM TUTORIAL PROGRAM, INC.

2050 Second Ave.
New York, NY 10029

(212) 831-0650 Administrative
(212) 289-7367 FAX

www.east-harlem.com

Carmen Vega-Rivera, Executive Director
Languages Spoken: Spanish

Services

Acting Instruction
Computer Classes
Dancing Instruction
Field Trips/Excursions
Homework Help Programs
Music Instruction
Storytelling
Swimming
Test Preparation
Tutoring

Ages: 6 to 19
Population Served: Asthma, Attention Deficit Disorder (ADD/ADHD), Learning Disability, Underachiever
Area Served: All Boroughs
Program Hours: Monday - Friday: 3:30-5:30 p.m., 6-7 p.m. Saturday 10 a.m.-12 (during school year); Monday - Friday 8:30 a.m.-4 p.m., 9 a.m.-5 p.m. (summer). Summer tutoring program from 1-5 p.m.
Fees: Call for information
Medication Administered: No
Transportation Provided: No
Wheelchair Accessible: No
Service Description: Provides educational assistance through tutoring, creative arts and other programs designed to help children reach their potential. The summer program combines academics and creative arts. Activities include bookmaking, photography, visual art, computer, puppetry, theatre, poetry/creative writing, storytelling, game-making and other activities, plus swimming once a week at a state park. Students work on projects for presentation at the end of the summer. There are frequent field trips related to the special projects. For junior counselors (20 teenagers training to become counselors) there is a series of interviews with famous figures which culminates in a newsletter at the end of the summer. A parent Workshop Series is also offered on various topics of interest.

EAST SIDE CREATIVE ARTS STUDIO

317 E. 89th St.
New York, NY 10028

(212) 369-9492 Administrative

David Herman, Director

Services

Music Therapy

Ages: All Ages
Area Served: All Boroughs
Program Hours: Call for information
Fees: Call for information
Medication Administered: No
Transportation Provided: No
Wheelchair Accessible: Yes
Service Description: Provides individual music therapy sessions. Individual instruction in piano and guitar are also provided.

EAST SIDE HOUSE SETTLEMENT

337 Alexander Ave.
Bronx, NY 10454

(718) 665-5250 Administrative
(718) 292-3037 FAX

Julius Bennett, Director
Languages Spoken: Spanish

Services

Arts and Crafts Instruction
Child Care Centers
Homework Help Programs
Social Skills Training

Ages: 5 to 12
Population Served: Developmental Disability, Learning Disability
Area Served: Bronx
Program Hours: Monday - Friday: 3-6 p.m.
Fees: Please call for information.
Method of Payment: Sliding Scale
Medication Administered: No
Transportation Provided: No
Wheelchair Accessible: Yes
Service Description: Through the after school program, the East Side House Settlement implements comprehensive programs in a safe environment that emphasizes independence, exposes youngsters to the arts, improves youngster's socialization and communication skills.
Contact: Margaret Watson, Director of After School Services

EASTERN DISTRICT YMCA

125 Humboldt St.
Brooklyn, NY 11206

(718) 782-8300 Administrative

Services

Arts and Crafts Instruction
Computer Classes
Exercise Classes/Groups
Homework Help Programs
Recreational Activities
Sports, Individual
Sports, Team/Leagues
Tutoring

Ages: 5 to 12
Area Served: Brooklyn
Program Hours: Monday - Friday: 3-6 p.m.
Fees: Call for fees
Medication Administered: No
Transportation Provided: No
Wheelchair Accessible: No
Service Description: A mainstream after school program that offers a variety of recreational and educational programs. Children with disabilities are considered on a case-by-case basis.

EDEN II PROGRAMS

150 Granite Ave.
Staten Island, NY 10303

(718) 816-1422 Administrative
(718) 816-1428 FAX

www.eden2.org

Joanne Gerenser, MA, Executive Director

Services

Respite, Children's Out-of-Home
Tutoring

Ages: 3 and up
Population Served: Asperger Syndrome, Autism, Pervasive Developmental Disorder (PDD/NOS)
Area Served: New York State
Fees: Call for information
Wheelchair Accessible: Yes
Service Description: Provides specialized community based programs and other opportunities, with the goal of achieving the highest possible quality of life.

EIHAB HUMAN SERVICES, INC.

222-40 96th Ave.
Queens Village, NY 11429

(718) 465-8833 Administrative
(718) 465-9217 FAX

Fatma Abboud, Executive Director
Languages Spoken: Arabic, Haitian Creole, Russian, Spanish

Services

Arts and Crafts Instruction
Exercise Classes/Groups
Field Trips/Excursions
Homework Help Programs
Recreational Activities

Ages: 5 to 12
Population Served: Autism, Mental Retardation (mild/moderate)
Area Served: Brooklyn
Program Hours: Monday, Tuesday, Wednesday: 2:30-5:30 p.m.
Program Capacity: 40
Staff/Child Ratio: 1:2 (low functioning), 1:4 (high functioning)
Fees: None
Medication Administered: No
Transportation Provided: Yes
Wheelchair Accessible: No
Service Description: After school program for children predominantly with Mental Retardation or Autism. Provides homework assistance, recreational activities, exercise, arts and crafts, enrichment and occasional field trips.
Contact: Khadija or Cynthia, Program Directors (718) 451-2700

EL FARO BEACON COMMUNITY CENTER

2351 First Ave., Rm 153/154
New York, NY 10035

(212) 410-4227 Administrative
(212) 410-4885 FAX

Santos Negrón, Director
Languages Spoken: Spanish

Services

Arts and Crafts Instruction
Exercise Classes/Groups
Homework Help Programs
Respite, Children's Out-of-Home
Sports, Individual
Sports, Team/Leagues
Swimming

Ages: 8 to 21

< continued... >

Population Served: All Disabilities, Autism, Cerebral Palsy, Developmental Delay, Developmental Disability, Down Syndrome, Emotional Disability, Learning Disability, Mental Retardation (mild-moderate), Mental Retardation (severe-profound), Multiple Disability
Program Hours: Monday - Wednesday: 3-7 p.m., Saturday: 9 a.m.-4 p.m.
Program Capacity: 30
Staff/Child Ratio: 1:4 or 5
Fees: None
Medication Administered: No
Transportation Provided: Yes
Wheelchair Accessible: Yes
Contact: Cheryl Punter, Program Manager

EL MUSEO DEL BARRIO

1230 Fifth Ave.
New York, NY 10029

(212) 831-7272 Administrative

Languages Spoken: Spanish

Services

Museums

Ages: 5 and up
Area Served: All Boroughs, New Jersey, Connecticut
Program Hours: Wednesday - Sunday: 11 a.m.-5 p.m.
Program Capacity: 30
Staff/Child Ratio: 1:10
Fees: Guided Tours: 30 Students - $60; 30 Adults - $75
Medication Administered: No
Transportation Provided: No
Wheelchair Accessible: Yes
Service Description: The guided tours of El Museo del Barrio's galleries introduce visitors to El Museo's history, mission and exhibitions. One particular exhibition is given a special "Focus Tour," through which education staff, artists, educators, docents and interns incorporate contemporary approaches to art education during the guided tour. The guide discusses relevant art-making techniques, specific artists and related art history. The house educator works with artist educators, docents and interns to develop themes for the guided tours, with assistance from the Curatorial Staff. One-hour Guided tours are offered for visiting groups and may be designed in collaboration with educators who have specific goals or objectives for their visit to El Museo. The art on view often becomes a point of departure of discussions about El Barrio, Spanish Harlem, Puerto Rico and Latin America, in general, and the roles of Puerto Ricans and Latinos in the United States.

ELMCOR AFTER SCHOOL PROGRAM

32-02 Junction Blvd.
E. Elmhurst, NY 11369

(718) 446-8010 Administrative

David Mitchell, Executive Director

Services

Recreational Activities
Tutoring

Ages: 7 to 18
Area Served: Queens
Program Hours: Monday and Wednesday: 3:45-5:45 p.m.; Saturday, 9 a.m.-12 p.m.
Fees: Please call for information.
Medication Administered: No
Transportation Provided: No
Wheelchair Accessible: Yes
Service Description: After school recreation and tutoring program. Children with special needs are considered on a case-by-case basis.

EMPIRE LEARNING SERVICES OF MANHATTAN

141 E. 55th St.
New York, NY 10022

(718) 622-6878 Administrative
(718) 622-4759 FAX

Dr. Bonnie Nuzum, President

Services

Homework Help Programs
Study Skills Assistance
Test Preparation
Tutoring

Ages: 4 to 12
Population Served: Learning Disability
Area Served: Brooklyn, Manhattan
Program Hours: Call for information
Fees: Please call for information.
Medication Administered: No
Transportation Provided: No
Wheelchair Accessible: No
Service Description: Services include individual tutoring in reading, math, writing and specific subject areas; test preparation for middle school, high school and college entrance exams; and homework help (for individual students or small groups) to give students the skills they need to organize and successfully complete homework assignments.

EMPIRE STATE GAMES FOR THE PHYSICALLY CHALLENGED

350 New Campus Drive
Brockport, NY 14420--299

(716) 395-5620 Administrative

www.empirestategames.org

Susan Maxwell, Games Coordinator
Languages Spoken: Sign Language

Services

Sports, Individual
Sports, Team/Leagues

Ages: 5 to 21
Population Served: Arthritis, Cerebral Palsy, Deaf/Hard of Hearing, Dwarfism, Muscular Dystrophy, Physical/Orthopedic Disability, Visual Disability/Blind
Area Served: All Boroughs
Program Hours: Schedule changes yearly. Call for information.
Fees: None
Wheelchair Accessible: Yes
Service Description: The Games for the Physically Challenged offers competition in a variety of adapted sports plus fitness and training workshops for young people with physical challenges.

EMPOWERMENT INSTITUTE FOR MENTALLY RETARDED OF GREATER NEW YORK, INC.

192-05 Linden Blvd.
St. Albans, NY 11412

(718) 977-0072 Administrative
(718) 977-0076 FAX

Ms. Rowser, Executive Director

Services

Respite, Children's Out-of-Home

Ages: All Ages
Population Served: Developmental Disability, Mental Retardation (mild-moderate), Mental Retardation (severe-profound)
Area Served: Queens
Program Hours: Call for information
Fees: Call for information
Method of Payment: Medicaid
Wheelchair Accessible: Yes

ENACT (EDUCATIONAL NETWORK OF ARTISTS IN CREATIVE THEATRE)

80 Eighth Ave., Suite 1102
New York, NY 10011

(212) 741-6591 Administrative
(212) 741-6594 FAX

www.enact.org
enact@rcn.com

Diana Feldman, Executive Director
Languages Spoken: Spanish

Services

Acting Instruction
Drama Therapy

Ages: 6 and up
Population Served: Attention Deficit Disorder (ADD/ADHD), At-Risk, Autism, Developmental Delay, Developmental Disability, Down Syndrome, Emotional Disability, Learning Disability, Mental Retardation (mild-moderate), Mental Retardation (severe-profound), Speech/Language Disability
Area Served: All Boroughs
Fees: Call for information
Service Description: A professional drama-in-education company which offers participatory creative drama workshops and drama therapy programs to students, educators and community organizations, including creative drama for children with developmental and emotional disabilities. The programs are held mainly in schools, but special arrangements can be made for outside sites.

EPILEPSY INSTITUTE (THE)

257 Park Ave. S., Suite 302
New York, NY 10010

(212) 677-8550 Administrative
(212) 677-5825 FAX

Pamela Conford, Executive Director
Languages Spoken: Spanish

Services

Recreational Activities

Ages: 18 and up
Population Served: Epilepsy, Seizure Disorder
Area Served: All Boroughs, Westchester
Program Hours: Weekends. Call for information.
Fees: Call for information
Method of Payment: Payment Plan, Sliding Scale
Wheelchair Accessible: Yes
Service Description: Provides information and

<continued...>

many services to persons with epilepsy, their families and the community on Epilepsy from childhood through adulthood. Recreational activities are also offered on weekends; call for further information.

EVELYN DOUGLIN CENTER FOR SERVING PEOPLE IN NEED, INC.

241 37th St., Suite 604
Brooklyn, NY 11232

(718) 965-1998 Administrative
(718) 451-4359 FAX

Seibert R. Phillips, Executive Director

Sites

1. EVELYN DOUGLIN CENTER FOR SERVING PEOPLE IN NEED, INC.

241 37th St., Suite 604
Brooklyn, NY 11232

(718) 451-4346 Administrative
(718) 451-4359 FAX

Charles Archer, Site Director

2. PHILIP PETER SHORIN DAY HABILITATION

3505-09 Ave. S
Brooklyn, NY 11234

(718) 787-1772 Administrative
(718) 787-1850 FAX

Services

Art Therapy
Arts and Crafts Instruction
Music Therapy

Ages: 5 to 17
Population Served: All Disabilities (Children must be eligible for OMRDD services).
Area Served: Brooklyn
Program Hours: Monday, Tuesday, Wednesday: 3-6 p.m.
Program Capacity: 35
Staff/Child Ratio: 1:2
Fees: None
Medication Administered: Yes
Transportation Provided: Yes
Wheelchair Accessible: Yes
Service Description: Provides after school services for children ages 5 to 17. The program offers domestic ADL skills training, as well as many other programs and activities for children with special needs.
Sites: 1

SATURDAY RECREATION PROGRAM
Arts and Crafts Instruction
Music Instruction
Storytelling

Ages: 5 to 16
Population Served: Developmental Disability, Mental Retardation (mild-moderate), Mental Retardation (severe-profound),
Area Served: Brooklyn
Program Hours: Saturdays: 10 a.m.-3 p.m.
Fees: Call for information
Transportation Provided: Yes
Service Description: Brooklyn-based, Saturday recreation program for ambulatory children with mental retardation or developmental disabilities.
Sites: 1

PROJECT FUN
Arts and Crafts Instruction
Field Trips/Excursions
Recreational Activities
Storytelling

Ages: 11 to 17
Population Served: Developmental Disability, Mental Retardation (mild-moderate), Mental Retardation (severe-profound)
Area Served: Brooklyn
Program Hours: Monday, Tuesday and Wednesday: 3-6 p.m.
Transportation Provided: Yes
Service Description: After school recreation program for ambulatory children with mental retardation or developmental disabilities. Program provides a licensed recreation therapist, in-house recreational activities and community outings.
Contact: Dan Greenberg
Sites: 2

FAMILIES FIRST, INC.

250 Baltic St.
Brooklyn, NY 11201

(718) 237-1862 Administrative
(718) 260-9402 FAX

www.familiesfirstbrooklyn.org

Linda Blyer, Executive Director

Services

Arts and Crafts Instruction
Exercise Classes/Groups
Music Instruction

Ages: Birth to 7
Population Served: Deaf/Hard of Hearing, Learning Disability, Visual Disability/Blind
Area Served: All Boroughs
Program Hours: Monday - Friday: 3-6 p.m.

< continued... >

Program Capacity: 6 to 10 per class
Staff/Child Ratio: 1:1 (plus parents)
Fees: Call for information
Medication Administered: No
Transportation Provided: No
Wheelchair Accessible: No
Service Description: Provides after school programs for mainstream as well as special needs children. Spanish and French classes are offered, but membership is required in order to attend these classes.

FAMILY DYNAMICS, INC.

613-619 Throop Ave.
Brooklyn, NY 11216

(718) 919-1226 Administrative
(718) 919-2017 FAX

Marlene Christian, Program Director
Languages Spoken: Spanish

Services

Arts and Crafts Instruction
Computer Classes
Creative Writing
Homework Help Programs
Music Instruction
Tutoring

Ages: 10 to 18
Area Served: Brooklyn (Bedford Stuyvesant community)
Program Hours: Monday - Friday: 2-6 p.m.
Program Capacity: 25
Staff/Child Ratio: 1:5
Fees: None
Medication Administered: No
Transportation Provided: No, but car fare is provided.
Wheelchair Accessible: Yes
Service Description: Provides an after school program for children/teenagers between the ages of 10 and 18. Children with special needs are considered on a case-by-case basis.

FAMILY LEARNING CENTER, INC.

78-03 Queens Blvd.
Elmhurst, NY 11373

(718) 520-6940 Administrative
(718) 692-7040 Administrative

Languages Spoken: Spanish

Services

Homework Help Programs
Remedial Education
Test Preparation

Ages: 5 to 18
Population Served: Developmental Delay,

Speech/Language Disability
Area Served: Queens
Program Hours: Call for information.
Fees: Call for information.
Service Description: Provides homework help, test preparation, and remedial education.

FEATHERBED LANE YOUTH CENTER, INC.

1640 Grand Ave.
Bronx, NY 10453

(718) 731-8660 Administrative
(718) 731-8660 FAX

Dr. Gregory Gustavson, Director
Languages Spoken: Spanish

Services

Arts and Crafts Instruction
Computer Classes
Field Trips/Excursions
Sports, Individual
Sports, Team/Leagues
Tutoring

Ages: 6 to 14
Area Served: Brooklyn
Program Hours: Monday - Friday: 3:30-6 p.m.
Program Capacity: Depends on the number of staff available.
Staff/Child Ratio: 1:10
Fees: None
Medication Administered: No
Transportation Provided: No
Wheelchair Accessible: No
Service Description: An after school program that runs from September to June. Children with disabilities considered on a case-by-case basis.

FLATBUSH YMCA

1401 Flatbush Ave.
Brooklyn, NY 11210

(718) 469-8100 Administrative
(718) 284-5537 FAX

www.ymcanyc.org

Michael Keller, Executive Director

Services

Homework Help Programs
Recreational Activities
Sports, Team/Leagues

Ages: 7 to 15
Program Hours: Tuesday - Thursday: 4-6 p.m.
Saturday: 11 a.m.-1 p.m.

<continued...>

Fees: Call for information
Medication Administered: No
Transportation Provided: Yes
Service Description: This program helps school aged children grow in spirit, mind and body. This is accomplished through homework help, team work during sports and skills building. Can accommodate children with disabilities.
Contact: Yvonne Richards, Director of After School Program

FLUSHING CLUB HOUSE

133-01 41st Road
Flushing, NY 11355

(718) 886-5454 Administrative
(718) 886-4179 FAX

Ron Britt, Unit Director

Services

Arts and Crafts Instruction
Homework Help Programs

Ages: 6 to 18
Area Served: Manhattan, Queens
Program Hours: Monday - Friday: 3-9 p.m.
Program Capacity: 200-300
Fees: Dependant on child's age.
Medication Administered: Yes
Transportation Provided: No
Wheelchair Accessible: Yes
Service Description: After school and recreation program providing assistant with homework and arts and crafts instruction. Children with special needs are considered on a case-by-case basis.

FLUSHING YMCA

138-46 Northern Blvd
Flushing, NY 11354

(718) 961-6880 Administrative
(718) 445-8392 FAX

www.ymcanyc.org

Languages Spoken: Korean

Services

Arts and Crafts Instruction
Recreational Activities
Sports, Team/Leagues

Ages: 5 to 14
Program Hours: The After School program operates Monday - Friday: 3-6 p.m. The Holiday programs are held on Martin Luther King Jr. Day, Mid Winter Recess, Spring Recess, Brooklyn Queens Day, Yom Kippur, Columbus Day, Veteran's Day, National Election Day, Winter

Recess: 7:30 a.m.-7 p.m. The Half Day programs operate on half-days: 12-7 p.m.
Fees: Call YMCA for information.
Medication Administered: No
Transportation Provided: No
Service Description: The Flushing YMCA offers holiday, half-day and after school programs for children in kindergarten - eighth grade. The after school program corresponds with the Board of Education calendar and is designed for working parents seeking quality child care. The program provides a safe, enjoyable and relaxing environment for your child. Children with disabilities will be accommodated on a case-by-case basis.

FLYING WHEELS TRAVEL

143 W. Bridge St.
PO Box 382
Owatonna, MN 55060-0382

(507) 451-5005 Administrative
(507) 451-1685 FAX

www.flyingwheelstravel.com
thq@ll.net

Barbara Jacobson, President

Services

Travel

Ages: All ages
Population Served: All Disabilities
Service Description: Customized, independent travel arranged for people with disabilities.

FOREST HILLS COMMUNITY HOUSE

108-25 62nd Drive
Forest Hills, NY 11375

(718) 592-5757 Administrative
(718) 592-2933 FAX

www.fhch.org
dcastro@fhch.org

Luis Harris, Director
Languages Spoken: Spanish

Services

Arts and Crafts Instruction
Computer Classes
Homework Help Programs
Recreational Activities
Remedial Education

Ages: 2 to 21
Population Served: Emotional Disability (mild), Learning Disability (mild)

< continued... >

Program Hours: Monday - Friday: 3:30-5:30 p.m.
Fees: Call center for information.
Method of Payment: Sliding Scale
Medication Administered: No
Transportation Provided: Yes
Wheelchair Accessible: Yes
Service Description: Forest Hills Community House provides activities for children, including homework help, recreation, arts and crafts, computer and literacy activities.

FRAUNCES TAVERN MUSEUM

54 Pearl St.
New York, NY 10004

(212) 425-1778 [19] Administrative
(212) 509-3467 FAX

www.frauncestavernmuseum.org
publicity@frauncestavernmuseum.org

Dr. Lawrence Simpson, Director
Languages Spoken: French, Spanish

Services

TAVERNS: CENTERS OF 18TH CENTURY AMERICAN LIFE
Museums

Ages: 8 to 16
Area Served: All Boroughs, Long Island
Program Hours: Tuesday - Friday: 10:00-11:30 a.m.
Program Capacity: 35/group
Staff/Child Ratio: 1:10, varies
Fees: $40/group, (fee for Taverns program only)
Method of Payment: Individuals: Cash; Group: Check
Medication Administered: No
Transportation Provided: No
Wheelchair Accessible: No
Service Description: This program surveys the importance taverns played in the cultural, social and political lives of early Americans. From places for travelers to drink, eat and sleep, to places to learn local news, discuss business, seek entertainment and celebrate, taverns were an important institution in the fabric of early American life.

FRIENDS OF CROWN HEIGHTS #3

317 Rogers Ave.
Brooklyn, NY 11225

(718) 771-8075 Administrative
(718) 771-5812 FAX

Daryl Davis, Director
Languages Spoken: Spanish

Sites

1. FRIENDS OF CROWN HEIGHTS #3
317 Rogers Ave.
Brooklyn, NY 11225

(718) 771-8075 Administrative
(718) 771-5812 FAX

Daryl Davis, Executive Director

2. FRIENDS OF CROWN HEIGHTS #2
671 Prospect Place
Brooklyn, NY 11216

(718) 638-8686 Administrative

Janis Nichols, Director

Services

Arts and Crafts Instruction
Cooking Classes
Dancing Instruction
Field Trips/Excursions
Music Instruction
Sports, Team/Leagues

Ages: 6 to 10
Area Served: Brooklyn
Program Hours: Monday - Friday: 3-6 p.m.; Full time during the summer months.
Program Capacity: 60
Staff/Child Ratio: 1:8
Medication Administered: No
Transportation Provided: No
Wheelchair Accessible: Yes
Service Description: Provides after school programs that offer a variety of recreational activities for children. Children with special needs are considered on a case-by-case basis.
Sites: 1 2

FRIENDS OF CROWN HEIGHTS DAYCARE

36 Ford St.
Brooklyn, NY 11213

(718) 467-4270 Administrative

E.C. Murrell, Program Director

Services

Arts and Crafts Instruction
Child Care Centers
Computer Classes
Creative Writing
Sports, Individual
Sports, Team/Leagues
Tutoring

Ages: 6 to 11
Area Served: Brooklyn

<continued...>

Program Hours: Monday - Friday: 3-6 p.m., full time during summer months and some school holidays.
Program Capacity: 100
Staff/Child Ratio: 1:10
Fees: Sliding Scale
Medication Administered: No
Transportation Provided: No
Wheelchair Accessible: Yes
Service Description: Provides an after school program which offers a variety of academic and recreational activities. Children with special needs are considered on a case-by-case basis.
Contact: Ms. Velazquez, After School Director

FULTON DAY CARE CENTER

1332 Fulton Ave
Bronx, NY 10456

(718) 378-1330 Administrative

Services

Arts and Crafts Instruction
Child Care Centers
Homework Help Programs
Tutoring

Ages: 6 to 12
Population Served: Learning Disability, Underachiever
Area Served: Bronx
Program Hours: Monday - Friday: 3-5:45 p.m.
Program Capacity: 80
Staff/Child Ratio: 5:40
Fees: Sliding Scale, call for further information.
Medication Administered: No
Transportation Provided: No
Wheelchair Accessible: Yes
Service Description: Child care center providing recreation and education programs.
Contact: Tom Hall, Director of After School Program

FUN TIME VACATION TOURS, INC.

4 Starlight Drive
Commack, NY 11725

(631) 864-5563 Administrative
(631) 864-5563 FAX

Bertram Katz, Director

Services

Travel

Ages: 21 and up
Population Served: Attention Deficit Disorder (ADD/ADHD), Developmental Disability, Learning Disability, Mental Retardation (mild-moderate)
Program Hours: Mid-July. Call for details.
Program Capacity: 40-80

Staff/Child Ratio: 6:1
Fees: Vary according to trip, call for information
Medication Administered: Yes
Transportation Provided: Yes
Wheelchair Accessible: No
Service Description: This travel program serves clients living at home and those residing in group homes. Tours will include hotel trips, and destinations like Lake George. One and two week trips are available, usually in mid-July. We encourage the group to socialize with other clients from other agencies.

FUNWORKS FOR KIDS

201 E. 83rd St.
New York, NY 10028

(212) 759-1937 Administrative

Services

Arts and Crafts Instruction
Dancing Instruction
Music Instruction

Ages: 6 months to 4
Area Served: All Boroughs
Program Hours: Call for information
Fees: Please call for information.
Medication Administered: No
Transportation Provided: No
Service Description: A music, art and movement program willing to include children with mild disabilities on an individual basis. The program develops self-confidence, social awareness and motor skills through creative activities.

GATEWAY NATIONAL RECREATION AREA

Floyd Bennett Field, Bldg. 69
Brooklyn, NY 11234

(718) 318-4300 Breezy Point
(718) 338-4306 Ecology Village
(718) 338-3799 Floyd Bennett Field
(718) 318-4340 Jamaica Bay Wildlife Refuge
(712) 354-4636 Staten Island

Nancy Rivera, Park Ranger

Services

FORT TILDEN GARDEN ASSOCIATION
Nature Centers/Walks
Parks/Recreation Areas

Ages: 9 and up
Area Served: Queens

<continued...>

Program Hours: Seasonal. April to October 31, early morning to early evening (flexible).
Staff/Child Ratio: 1:5
Fees: $25 (fee for Fort Tilden program)
Method of Payment: Cash, Check, Money Order
Medication Administered: No
Transportation Provided: No
Wheelchair Accessible: Yes
Service Description: Gardening program is available from April to October 31. It's an informal program, in which participants can work on the garden from sunrise to sunset. All necessary support and materials are available.

GIRL SCOUTS OF THE USA

420 Fifth Ave.
New York, NY

(212) 852-8000 Administrative

www.girlscouts.org

Helen Orloff, Contact
Languages Spoken: Varies by site

Sites

1. GIRL SCOUTS OF THE USA
420 Fifth Ave.
New York, NY

(212) 852-8000 Administrative

www.girlscouts.org

2. GIRL SCOUT COUNCIL OF GREATER NEW YORK
43 W. 23rd St., 7th Fl.
New York, NY 10010-4283

(212) 645-4000 Administrative
(212) 645-4599 FAX

www.gsc.gsy.org

Aurora Rodriguez, Acting Director

Services

Youth Development

Ages: 5 to 17
Area Served: International
Fees: None
Medication Administered: No
Transportation Provided: No
Service Description: The Girl Scouts of the USA encourage increased skill building and responsibility, and also promote the development of strong leadership and decision making skills. All program activities are age-appropriate and based on the Four Program Goals as well as on the Girl Scout Promise and Law. There are five age levels in Girl Scouting: Daisy Girl Scouts, ages 5-6; Brownie Girl Scouts, ages 6-8; Junior Girl Scouts, ages 8-11; Cadette Girl Scouts, ages 11-14 and Senior Girl

Scouts, ages 14-17. A variety of Girl Scouts programs are held throughout the city, call for information.
Sites: 1 2

GIRLS INC.

120 Wall St.
New York, NY 10005-3902

(800) 374-4475 Toll Free
(212) 509-2000 Administrative
(212) 509-8708 FAX

www.girlsinc.org

Joyce Roche, President/CEO
Languages Spoken: Spanish

Services

Youth Development

Ages: 6 to 18
Area Served: All Boroughs
Program Hours: School year: 3-10 p.m.
Medication Administered: No
Transportation Provided: No
Wheelchair Accessible: Yes
Service Description: A mainstream program that teaches girls how to combat peer pressure while building self-esteem. The goal is to give members the tools necessary to say no to drugs, alcohol and early teenage sex. Call for specific programs in your area.

GOOD SHEPHERD SERVICES

305 Seventh Ave., 9th Fl.
New York, NY 10001

(212) 243-7070 Administrative
(212) 929-3412 FAX

www.goodshepherds.org

Sr. Paulette LoMonaco, Executive Director
Languages Spoken: Spanish

Sites

1. GOOD SHEPHERD SERVICES - FAMILY RECEPTION CENTER
441 Fourth Ave.
Brooklyn, NY 11215

(718) 788-0666 Administrative
(718) 965-0365 FAX

<continued...>

**2. GOOD SHEPHERD SERVICES - RED HOOK
COMMUNITY CENTER**
　　P.S. 15, 71 Sullivan St.
　　Brooklyn, NY 11231

(718) 522-6911 Administrative
(718) 522-4435 FAX

www.goodshepherds.org

**3. GOOD SHEPHERD SERVICES - THE AFTER SCHOOL
CENTER AT PS 12**
　　317 Hoyt Street
　　Brooklyn, NY 11231

(718) 625-5876 Program Director
(718) 625-5748 FAX

www.goodshepherds.org
steve_kennedy@goodshepherds.org

Steve Kennedy, Program Supervisor

**4. GOOD SHEPHERD SERVICES - THE AFTER SCHOOL
CENTER AT MS 293**
　　284 Baltic St.
　　Brooklyn, NY 11201

(646) 739-2392 Administrative
(718) 422-1926 FAX

www.goodshepherds.org
gabriel_dattatreyan@goodshepherds.org

Gabriel Dattatreyan, Coordinator

**5. GOOD SHEPHERD SERVICES - THE AFTER SCHOOL
CENTER AT MS 142**
　　MS 142, 610 Henry St.
　　Brooklyn, NY 11231

(646) 739-2392 Administrative
(718) 422-1926 FAX

www.goodshepherds.org
gabriel_dattatreyan@goodshepherds.org

Gabriel Dattatreyan, Coordinator

**6. GOOD SHEPHERD SERVICES - THE AFTER SCHOOL
CENTER AT PS 27**
　　PS 27, 27 Huntington St.
　　Brooklyn, NY 11231

(718) 722-9561 Administrative
(718) 422-0016 FAX

www.goodshepherds.org
stacey_billups@goodshepherds.org

Stacey Billups, Program Supervisor

<u>Services</u>

Acting Instruction
Arts and Crafts Instruction
Dancing Instruction
Field Trips/Excursions
Homework Help Programs
Music Instruction
Sports, Team/Leagues
Storytelling

Ages: 5 to 10
Area Served: Brooklyn
Program Hours: Monday - Friday: 3-6 p.m.
Program Capacity: 180
Fees: None
Medication Administered: No
Transportation Provided: No
Wheelchair Accessible: No
Service Description: An after school program for 200 elementary school students who attend PS 32 and co-located schools. The Center provides activities that include educational enrichment, sports, arts and crafts, performing arts, homework help, parent workshops, crisis intervention referrals and community service projects.
Sites: 1 3

RED HOOK BEACON
Arts and Crafts Instruction
Computer Classes
Dancing Instruction
Exercise Classes/Groups
Homework Help Programs
Music Instruction
Storytelling
Youth Development

Ages: 6 to 14
Area Served: Brooklyn
Program Hours: Monday - Friday: 3-5 p.m.
Program Capacity: 140
Staff/Child Ratio: 1:10
Fees: None
Medication Administered: No
Transportation Provided: No
Wheelchair Accessible: No
Service Description: The Red Hook Beacon facilitates day, evening, weekend and summer classes, workshops and activities for children and adults, including after-school and summer programs for elementary and middle school students; regular family and parent involvement activities; community-wide special events; the Career Opportunities Resource Center (CORC), Red Hook's only public computer facility; the Women in Motion and Kids in Motion leadership and dance groups; and the "Pathways for Youth Development," three youth development groups for pre-teens and adolescents--the Challengers for 9-to 11-year olds, the Pathfinders for 12-to 15- year olds and Youth on the Move for 16-to 19-year olds.
Sites: 2

<continued...>

Arts and Crafts Instruction
Dancing Instruction
Exercise Classes/Groups
Homework Help Programs
Music Instruction
Sports, Team/Leagues
Youth Development

Ages: 6 to 13
Area Served: Brooklyn
Program Hours: Monday - Friday: 3-6 p.m.
Program Capacity: 235
Staff/Child Ratio: 1:10
Fees: None
Medication Administered: No
Transportation Provided: No
Wheelchair Accessible: No
Service Description: The Center facilitates a wide range of educational, youth development, cultural and artistic, recreational and family support services. Activities include educational enrichment and homework help, team sports, adventure games, youth development and group-building activities and community recognition projects. The program also works with Good Shepherd's other programs at PS 27 and in the Red Hook Community as well as with external service providers and parents.
Sites: 6

THE 21ST CENTURY AFTER SCHOOL PROGRAM AT MS 293
Arts and Crafts Instruction
Dancing Instruction
Exercise Classes/Groups
Homework Help Programs
Music Instruction
Sports, Individual
Tutoring
Youth Development

Ages: 11 to 14
Area Served: Brooklyn
Program Hours: Monday - Thursday: 3-6 p.m.
Program Capacity: 100
Staff/Child Ratio: 1:10
Fees: None
Medication Administered: No
Transportation Provided: No
Wheelchair Accessible: No
Service Description: After school program for 100 middle-school students enrolled in The School for International Studies (formerlly known as MS 293) and The Brooklyn School for Global Studies, providing homework assistance, tutoring, literacy enhancement, community service activities, sports, arts and crafts, and youth leadership activities.
Sites: 4

21ST CENTURY AFTER SCHOOL PROGRAM AT MS 142
Exercise Classes/Groups
Recreational Activities
Sports, Team/Leagues

Ages: 11 to 14

Area Served: Brooklyn
Program Hours: Wednesdays and Fridays
Program Capacity: 100
Staff/Child Ratio: 1:15
Fees: None
Medication Administered: No
Transportation Provided: No
Wheelchair Accessible: No
Service Description: After school program for 100 middle-school students enrolled in MS 142, providing a variety of structured recreational activities in a tournament program that emphasizes the importance of teamwork and fair play.
Sites: 5

GOODWILL INDUSTRIES OF GREATER NEW YORK, INC.

4-21 27th Ave.
Astoria, NY 11102

(718) 728-5400 Administrative
(718) 728-9023 FAX

Sites

1. GOODWILL INDUSTRIES OF GREATER NEW YORK
26-36 4th Ave.
Astoria, NY 11102

(718) 278-9667 Administrative

Tyrone Green

Services

PROJECT SOAR
Computer Classes
Field Trips/Excursions
Homework Help Programs
Tutoring

Ages: 12 to 15
Population Served: Juvenile Offender
Area Served: Queens
Service Description: Program for adolescents on probation, who have been referred by their probation officer. The program develops and individualized plan for each participant, to help meet his or her needs in the way of education, career choices and community support. Included are workshops of interest, cultural field trips, group raps and case management.

Sites: 1

GRACE CHURCH SCHOOL

86 Fourth Ave.
New York, NY 10003

(212) 475-5609 Administrative
(212) 475-5015 FAX
(212) 533-3744 Grace Opportunity Project

www.gcschool.org
gdavison@gcschool.org

George P. Davison, Executive Director

Services

Arts and Crafts Instruction
Computer Classes
Homework Help Programs
Music Instruction
Sports, Individual
Sports, Team/Leagues
Tutoring

Ages: 5 to 14
Population Served: Learning Disability
Area Served: Manhattan
Program Hours: Monday - Friday: 3-5:30 p.m.
Fees: Please call school for information
Medication Administered: No
Wheelchair Accessible: Yes
Service Description: The Grace After School Program (GASP) is designed to provide a natural extension of the school day in a safe, secure and structured environment of the school. Qualified instructors teach several languages, and computer classes; others provide activities in sports, crafts, music and other age-appropriate activities.
Contact: Rich Carroll or Sarah Balkind, After School Program Directors

GRAND STREET SETTLEMENT

80 Pitt St.
New York, NY 10002

(212) 674-1740 Administrative
(212) 358-8784 FAX

www.grandstreet.org

Myrna Simmons, Early Childhood Director
Languages Spoken: Chinese, Spanish

Services

AFTER SCHOOL LATCHKEY PROGRAM
Arts and Crafts Instruction
Homework Help Programs
Tutoring

Ages: 6 to 12
Population Served: Speech/Language Disability
Program Hours: Monday - Friday: 3-6 p.m.
Fees: None
Medication Administered: No

Wheelchair Accessible: Yes
Service Description: Grand Street After School Latchkey Program is a pioneer in providing community-based academic support to low-income children. The creative literacy curriculum embraces an interactive approach to learning and teaching.
Contact: Nora Agrafo, After School Director
212-674-1740 ext. 235

GREENPOINT YMCA

99 Meserole Ave.
Brooklyn, NY 11222

(718) 389-3700 Administrative
(718) 349-2146 FAX

Lori Figuero, Youth and Family Director
Languages Spoken: Polish, Spanish

Services

Acting Instruction
Arts and Crafts Instruction
Creative Writing
Exercise Classes/Groups
Field Trips/Excursions
Homework Help Programs
Recreational Activities
Swimming
Tutoring

Ages: 5 to 12
Area Served: All Boroughs
Program Hours: Monday - Friday: 3-6 p.m.
Program Capacity: 30
Staff/Child Ratio: 1:37
Fees: $280/month
Method of Payment: Cash, Check, Credit Card, Money Order
Medication Administered: No
Transportation Provided: No
Wheelchair Accessible: No
Service Description: Provides after school programs that offer a variety of recreational and educational activities for children. Children with special needs are considered on a case-by-case basis.
Contact: Harvey Grange, Director of After School Program

GREENWICH HOUSE, INC.

27 Barrow St.
New York, NY 10014

(212) 242-4140 Information
(212) 366-4226 FAX
(212) 242-4770 Music School
(212) 691-2900 Counseling Center

www.greenwichhouse.org

<continued...>

gh@greenwichhouse.org
Roy Leavitt, Executive Director
Languages Spoken: Hebrew, Russian, Spanish

Services

Acting Instruction
Arts and Crafts Instruction
Music Instruction

Ages: All Ages
Area Served: All Boroughs
Program Hours: Call for information
Program Capacity: Varies depending on program
Fees: Call for information
Method of Payment: Cash, Check, Credit Card, Money Order, Scholarships are also available
Medication Administered: No
Transportation Provided: No
Wheelchair Accessible: Yes
Service Description: Greenwich House has provided affordable music lessons and musical events for students and audiences of all ages. It has also been a major center for ceramic arts in New York City, offering quality instruction to all ages and providing a series of workshops, lectures, and exhibitions that enrich and inform the community. Children and adults with special needs are considered on a case-by-case basis.

GREENWICH VILLAGE YOUTH COUNCIL, INC. (GUYC)

437 W. 16th St., 2nd Fl.
New York, NY 10014

(646) 935-1943 Administrative

Penelope Williams, Outreach Coordinator

Services

Acting Instruction
Art Therapy
Creative Writing
Tutoring

Ages: 15 to 22
Population Served: AIDS/HIV +, Emotional Disability
Area Served: All Boroughs
Program Hours: Wednesday - Saturday: 5-11 p.m.
Fees: None
Medication Administered: Yes, self administered.
Transportation Provided: Yes. Provide tokens/Metrocard (if needed).
Wheelchair Accessible: Yes
Service Description: The drop-in program for trans, gay and lesbian youth that offers a variety of services, including art therapy, counseling, writing class, drama, peer street outreach, meal program, HIV testing, AIDS education and legal services. There is also a psychiatrist on staff.
Contact: Ladedra Brown, Outreach Coordinator

GROSVENOR NEIGHBORHOOD HOUSE, INC.

176 W. 105th St.
New York, NY 10025

(212) 749-8500 Administrative
(212) 749-4060 FAX

William Rivera, Executive Director
Languages Spoken: Haitian Creole, Spanish

Services

Acting Instruction
Arts and Crafts Instruction
Computer Classes
Music Instruction
Recreational Activities
Tutoring

Ages: 6 to 13
Area Served: All Boroughs
Program Hours: Monday - Friday: 8 a.m.-6 p.m., July 8th - July 30th
Program Capacity: 80
Staff/Child Ratio: 5:10
Fees: $325
Method of Payment: Cash, Check, Credit Card, Money Order
Medication Administered: No
Transportation Provided: No
Wheelchair Accessible: No
Service Description: A summer program that provides educational and recreational activities for all children. Children with special needs are considered on a case-by-case basis.

PROJECT STEPPING STONE
Recreational Activities
Remedial Education
Tutoring

Ages: 6 to 12
Program Hours: Monday - Friday: 3-6 p.m.
Program Capacity: 90
Fees: Nominal annual fee
Method of Payment: Sliding Scale
Medication Administered: No
Transportation Provided: No
Service Description: Provides academic support through theme-based literacy activities including reading, writing and self-expression, as well as tutoring, homework help, recreational and cultural activities to enhance personal development. Children with special needs are considered on a case-by-case basis.

GUGGENHEIM MUSEUM

1071 5th Ave.
New York, NY 10128

(212) 423-3500 Administrative

www.guggenheim.org

Education Program Manager
Languages Spoken: Sign Language

Services

SUMMER STUDIO ART
Arts and Crafts Instruction
Computer Classes
Museums

Ages: 7 to 12
Area Served: All Boroughs
Program Hours: Mondays in July: 1-4 p.m.
Staff/Child Ratio: 1:1
Fees: $60 for 4 sessions, (fee is for Summer Studio Art program)
Method of Payment: Cash, Checks, Money Orders
Medication Administered: No
Transportation Provided: No
Wheelchair Accessible: Yes
Service Description: This new studio-art series for children working in tandem with an adult companion is designed to introduce the Guggenheim Museum Collection through exploration of various media. Led by arts educators, students work with painting, print making and digital media in response to themes and ideas in the collections. Children may enroll in an individual course or complete the series. Children with special needs are considered on a case-by-case basis.

GUIDED TOUR, INC.

7900 Old York Road, Suite 114-B
Elkins Park, PA 19027-2339

(800) 783-5841 Administrative
(215) 635-2637 FAX
(215) 782-1370 Camp Phone

www.guidedtour.com
gtour400@aol.com

Irv Segal, Director

Services

Travel

Ages: 17 and up
Population Served: Learning Disability, Mental Retardation (mild-moderate)
Program Capacity: 170
Fees: Vary by trip length and itinerary
Medication Administered: No
Transportation Provided: Yes
Wheelchair Accessible: Yes (limited)

Service Description: A social agency providing domestic and international travel experiences for persons with developmental and/or learning disabilities on a year-round basis. The Guided Tour has a Seashore Program close to the beach, at Ventnor, Atlantic City, New Jersey, with vacations running from 1 to 12 weeks. There are also two 1-week camps in Lackawaxen, PA., one in June and one in August. People are assisted on flights from all over the U.S. and will be met by Guided Tour staff at the airport, bus or train station. Trips are available for the New Years and Christmas holidays.

GUILD FOR EXCEPTIONAL CHILDREN (GEC)

260 68th St.
Brooklyn, NY 11220

(718) 833-6633 Administrative
(718) 745-2374 FAX

www.gecbklyn.org

Patricia Romano, Ass't Exec. Dir. for Clinical Services
Languages Spoken: Arabic, Chinese, French, Russian, Sign Language, Spanish

Services

Arts and Crafts Instruction
Exercise Classes/Groups
Homework Help Programs
Tutoring

Ages: 3 to 12
Population Served: Developmental Disability
Program Hours: Monday - Friday: 3-6 p.m.
Fees: Call for information
Wheelchair Accessible: Yes
Service Description: Clinical/recreational services for preschool and school age children and their families are offered in afternoon and evening hours.
Contact: Alice Guercio, Assistant Executive Director of Early Childhood Services

HAITIAN AMERICANS UNITED FOR PROGRESS, INC. (HAUP)

221-05 Linden Blvd.
Cambria Heights, NY 11411-0172

(718) 527-3776 Administrative
(212) 276-5481 FAX

haupinc@aol.com

Herold Dasque, Executive Director
Languages Spoken: French, Haitian Creole

< continued...>

Services

Arts and Crafts Instruction
English as a Second Language
Homework Help Programs
Tutoring

Ages: 6 to 21
Population Served: Mental Retardation (mild-moderate), Mental Retardation (severe-profound)
Area Served: Queens
Program Hours: Monday - Wednesday: 3-6 p.m.
Staff/Child Ratio: 1:3
Fees: None
Medication Administered: No
Transportation Provided: Yes
Wheelchair Accessible: Yes
Service Description: Provides after school programs for children with special needs. Focuses primarily on children with Mental Retardation.
Contact: Merline Pierre-Louis, Program Coordinator

HAMILTON-MADISON HOUSE

50 Madison St.
New York, NY 10038

(212) 349-3724 Administrative
(212) 979-8677 FAX

www.hmh100.com
hamiltonmadisonhouse@worldnet.att.net

Frank T. Modica, Executive Director
Languages Spoken: Chinese (Cantonese, Mandarin), Japanese, Korean

Services

Arts and Crafts Instruction
Homework Help Programs
Sports, Team/Leagues
Tutoring

Ages: 2 months to 12 years
Population Served: AIDS/HIV+, Asthma, Attention Deficit Disorder (ADD/ADHD), Cancer, Developmental Delay, Emotional Disability, Gifted, Learning Disability, Physical/Orthopedic Disability, Seizure Disorder, Sickle Cell Anemia, Speech/Language Disability, Underachiever
Area Served: Manhattan
Program Hours: Monday - Friday: 8 a.m.-6 p.m.
Program Capacity: 6 Classrooms
Staff/Child Ratio: 1:10
Fees: Sliding Scale
Method of Payment: Cash, Check
Medication Administered: No
Transportation Provided: No
Wheelchair Accessible: Yes
Service Description: Provides child care services to children with a variety of disabilities within the regular classroom. Special instruction, speech, occupational therapy, physical therapy and counseling services are also available on-site.

HARLEM CENTER FOR EDUCATION, INC.

1 E. 104th St.
New York, NY 10029

(212) 348-9200 Administrative
(212) 831-8202 FAX

www.harlemctred.com

Paula J. Martin, Executive Director
Languages Spoken: Spanish

Services

AFTER SCHOOL PROGRAM
Arts and Crafts Instruction
Computer Classes
Field Trips/Excursions
Homework Help Programs
Tutoring

Ages: 5 to 8
Population Served: Underachiever
Area Served: Manhattan (Upper East Side)
Program Hours: Monday - Thursday: 3-5 p.m.
Program Capacity: 40
Staff/Child Ratio: 2:15
Fees: None
Medication Administered: No
Transportation Provided: No
Wheelchair Accessible: Yes
Service Description: Provides an after school program that offers a variety of activities for neighborhood children.
Contact: Loanda Scheh, Database Specialist

TALENT SEARCH
Computer Classes
Recreational Activities
Test Preparation
Tutoring

Ages: 12 to 19
Population Served: Underachiever
Area Served: All Boroughs
Program Hours: Monday - Friday: 3-5 p.m.
Tutoring: Wednesday and Thursday, 6-8 p.m.
SAT Preparation: Saturday, 10 a.m.-2 p.m.
Program Capacity: 300
Staff/Child Ratio: 40 staff members to 300 students
Fees: None
Medication Administered: No
Transportation Provided: No
Wheelchair Accessible: Yes
Contact: Rita Spinola, Associate Director

HARLEM CHILDREN'S ZONE

2770 Broadway
New York, NY 10025

(212) 866-0700 Administrative
(212) 932-2965 FAX

www.hcz.org
info@harlemchildrenszone.org

Geoffrey Canada, President/CEO
Languages Spoken: Spanish

Sites

1. HARLEM CHILDREN'S ZONE

2770 Broadway
New York, NY 10025

(212) 866-0700 Administrative
(212) 932-2965 FAX

www.hcz.org

2. HARLEM CHILDREN'S ZONE - 147 STREET

147 St. Nicholas Ave., 3rd Fl.
New York, NY 10026

(212) 663-0555 Administrative
(212) 663-0560 FAX

lvural@attmail.com

Laura Vural, Executive Director

Services

YOUTH DEVELOPMENT PROGRAM
Arts and Crafts Instruction
Dancing Instruction
Field Trips/Excursions
Homework Help Programs
Music Instruction
Sports, Individual
Sports, Team/Leagues
Tutoring
Youth Development

Ages: 5 to 10
Population Served: At-Risk, Emotional Disability,
Learning Disability, Substance Abuse
Area Served: Manhattan (Central Harlem, Manhattan
Valley)
Program Hours: Monday - Friday: 12-6 p.m., July -
August
Fees: None
Medication Administered: No
Transportation Provided: No
Wheelchair Accessible: No
Service Description: After school educational and
recreational services for children who have had family
problems, including suspected abuse/neglect, drug use or
truancy. Program offers homework assistance, academic
remediation, recreational sports, music and dance
programs, martial arts and social activities. Summer
program is also offered.

Sites: 1

Arts and Crafts Instruction
Creative Writing
Exercise Classes/Groups
Recreational Activities
Remedial Education
Youth Development

Ages: 12 to 19
Population Served: Emotional Disability,
Learning Disability
Area Served: Manhattan (Central Harlem)
Program Hours: Call for information
Fees: Call for information
Service Description: Comprehensive
youth-development program for adolescents, that
fosters academic growth and career readiness
with an emphasis on the arts and multimedia
technology. Rise and Shine productions is it's
award-winning video and literacy program which
includes "The Real Deal." "Harlem Overheard" is
the only youth-produced newspaper in Harlem
where young writers and entrepreneurs have an
opportunity to develop their communication,
leadership and marketing skills through it's
quarterly publication. The TRUCE nutrition and
fitness center is the first and only
youth-managed fitness center in New York City.
Sites: 2

HARLEM DOWLING WESTSIDE CENTER FOR CHILDREN AND FAMILY SERVICES

2090 Adam Clayton Powell, Jr. Blvd.
New York, NY 10027

(212) 749-3656 Administrative
(212) 864-1908 FAX

Melba Butler, Executive Director

Services

Acting Instruction
Arts and Crafts Instruction
Computer Classes
Homework Help Programs
Mentoring Programs
Respite, Children's Out-of-Home
Tutoring

Ages: 3 to 18
Population Served: Developmental Disability,
Emotional Disability
Area Served: New York
Program Hours: Monday - Friday: 3-6 p.m.
Fees: Call for information
Medication Administered: No
Transportation Provided: No
Service Description: The program provides

< continued . . >

tutorial services, computer skills training, drama and arts and crafts instruction.
Contact: Beverly Brumell, Director of After School Services

HARLEM SCHOOL OF THE ARTS

645 St. Nicholas Ave.
New York, NY 10031

(212) 926-4100 Administrative
(212) 491-6913 FAX

www.harlemlive.org/hsa
info@harlemschoolofthearts.org

Camille Giraud Akeju, President/CEO
Languages Spoken: Russian, Spanish

Services

Acting Instruction
Arts and Crafts Instruction
Dancing Instruction
Homework Help Programs
Music Instruction
Theater Performances

Ages: 4 and up
Area Served: All Boroughs
Program Hours: Monday - Friday: 3-9 p.m.
Program Capacity: 700-800
Fees: Vary depending on class
Medication Administered: No
Transportation Provided: No
Wheelchair Accessible: Yes
Service Description: Provides a variety of educational and recreational activities for all children. Children with special needs are considered on a case-by-case basis.
Contact: Latoya Vethea, Development Assistant

HARLEM YMCA

181 W. 135th St.
New York, NY 10030

(212) 283-8543 Administrative
(212) 283-2809 FAX

A.D. Harris, Program Director

Services

Arts and Crafts Instruction
Homework Help Programs
Recreational Activities
Sports, Team/Leagues
Storytelling
Tutoring

Ages: 2 to 12
Program Hours: Monday - Friday: 3-7 p.m.
Fees: Annual membership fee: $150; Program fee: $40 per month

Method of Payment: Check, Credit Card, Money Order
Medication Administered: No
Transportation Provided: Yes, $75 added fee for transportation.
Wheelchair Accessible: No
Service Description: Provides values development for grade schoolers. Able to accommodate children with disabilities, depending on severity of disability.

HARTLEY HOUSE

413 W. 46th St.
New York, NY 10036

(212) 246-9885 Administrative
(212) 246-9855 FAX

www.hellskitchen.net/resource/hh/index.html

Kathy Faust, Executive Director
Languages Spoken: Spanish

Services

Arts and Crafts Instruction
Dancing Instruction
Exercise Classes/Groups
Homework Help Programs
Tutoring

Ages: 6 to 12
Population Served: Speech/Language Disability, Underachiever
Area Served: Manhattan (from 37th - 57th Streets, between Broadway and 12th Avenue).
Program Hours: Monday - Friday: 3-6 p.m.
Program Capacity: 65 children
Fees: $75 per month
Method of Payment: Check, Credit Card, Money Order
Medication Administered: No
Transportation Provided: No
Wheelchair Accessible: Yes
Service Description: Children who are below grade level in math and reading can receive academic tutoring by volunteer tutors who are supervised by the after school director.

HEARTSHARE HUMAN SERVICES OF NEW YORK

191 Joralemon St.
Brooklyn, NY 11201

(718) 422-4200 Administrative
(718) 422-3324 FAX

www.heartshare.com

William R. Guarinello, Executive Director
Languages Spoken: Spanish

<continued...>

Services

HOLIDAY OVERNIGHT PROGRAM
Respite, Children's Out-of-Home

Ages: 16 and older
Population Served: Developmental Disability
(Mild-Moderate)
Area Served: All Boroughs
Service Description: Provides supervised outings and
activities for teens who have mild to moderate
developmental disabilities.

SCHOOL HOLIDAY PROGRAM
Field Trips/Excursions
Sports, Individual

Ages: 13 to 20
Population Served: Autism, Mental Retardation
(mild-moderate)
Area Served: Brooklyn
Program Hours: Program operates during school
holidays, vacations and during the Summer.
Program Capacity: 23
Staff/Child Ratio: 6:23
Fees: $12 per session, Sliding Scale
Method of Payment: Cash, Check, Money Order
Medication Administered: No
Transportation Provided: Yes, door to door.
Wheelchair Accessible: No

HEBREW EDUCATIONAL SOCIETY

9502 Seaview Ave.
Brooklyn, NY 11236

(718) 241-3000 Administrative
(718) 241-3349 FAX

www.thenewhes.org

Marc Arje, Executive Director
Languages Spoken: Hebrew, Russian

Services

Arts and Crafts Instruction
Computer Classes
Creative Writing
Dancing Instruction
Homework Help Programs
Sports, Team/Leagues
Swimming

Ages: 5 to 12
Population Served: Attention Deficit Disorder
(ADD/ADHD), Developmental Delay, Emotional Disability,
Gifted, Learning Disability
Program Hours: September - June, Monday - Friday:
2:30- 6 p.m. During summer months, staff is available:
12-6 p.m.
Program Capacity: 100
Staff/Child Ratio: 7:10 depending on age

Fees: $320 per month
Method of Payment: 8 payments for 10
months service
Medication Administered: No
Transportation Provided: Yes
Wheelchair Accessible: No
Service Description: The Hebrew Educational
Society's goal is to help children develop a
positive self-image and to be successful at what
they do. Children are provided with a safe,
licensed, non-competitive and nurturing
environment.
Children receive homework help, karate and
gymnastics classes, they also have access to the
large indoor gymnasium and indoor swimming
pool. The program is enriched and individualized.
The children receive a wide range of activities
that support their academic, social and
recreational needs. The Hebrew Educational
Society is a Jewish community center which
respects all faiths and cultures. A learning
disabilities specialist is available at this center.
Contact: Dr. Hanna Bauer, Assistant Executive
Director

HEBREW INSTITUTE OF RIVERDALE

3700 Henry Hudson Parkway
Bronx, NY 10463

(718) 796-4730 Administrative
(718) 884-3206 FAX

Judy Cotrill, Program Administrator

Services

SPECIAL FRIENDS PROGRAM
Recreational Activities

Ages: 14 to 22
Population Served: Cerebral Palsy,
Developmental Disability, Down Syndrome,
Mental Retardation (mild-moderate), Mental
Retardation (severe-profound), Multiple
Disability, Neurological Disability,
Physical/Orthopedic Disability
Area Served: Bronx
Wheelchair Accessible: Yes
Service Description: Offers weekend recreation
for individuals with developmental disabilities.

HENRY STREET SETTLEMENT

265 Henry Street
New York, NY 10002

(212) 766-9200 Administrative
(212) 791-5710 FAX
(212) 254-4700 After School Program

Daniel Kronenfeld, Executive Director

<continued...>

Languages Spoken: Chinese, Spanish

Sites

1. HENRY STREET SETTLEMENT
301 Henry St.
New York, NY 10002

(212) 254-3100 Administrative
(212) 777-1445 FAX

Niwa Pietri, Administrator

Services

Arts and Crafts Instruction
Homework Help Programs
Tutoring

Ages: 5 to 12
Population Served: AIDS/HIV +, Emotional Disability, Health Impairment
Area Served: Manhattan
Program Hours: Monday - Friday: 3-6 p.m.
Fees: Call for information
Medication Administered: No
Transportation Provided: No
Wheelchair Accessible: Yes
Contact: Laura Cole, Director of Educational Services
Sites: 1

HERBERT BERGHOF STUDIO

120 Bank St.
New York, NY 10014

(212) 675-2370 Administrative

Kathryn Eaker, Managing Director

Services

Acting Instruction
Dancing Instruction
Theater Performances

Ages: 9 to 18
Area Served: All Boroughs, Westchester
Program Hours: Varies, (weekends). Classes are usually 1 to 2 hours.
Program Capacity: Varies every term, (10 - 20)
Staff/Child Ratio: Depends on class
Fees: Range from: $200 - $250
Method of Payment: Cash, Check
Medication Administered: No
Transportation Provided: No
Wheelchair Accessible: No
Service Description: A small, not-for-profit studio that offers classes in all aspects of theater, such as acting, voice, speech and musical theater. These classes are high intensity and for children serious about pursuing an acting career. Children with disabilities are considered on case-by-case basis.

HERBERT G. BIRCH SERVICES

275 Seventh Ave., 19th Fl.
New York, NY 10001

(212) 741-6522 Administrative
(212) 741-6739 FAX

www.hgbirch.org

Paul Larsen, CEO
Languages Spoken: Russian, Spanish

Sites

1. HERBERT G. BIRCH SERVICES - EAST 94TH STREET
1321 E. 94th St.
Brooklyn, NY 11236

(718) 257-5500 Administrative
(718) 257-5693 FAX

Sonali Durdan, Residence Manager

2. HERBERT G. BIRCH SERVICES - SPRINGFIELD GARDENS EARLY CHILDHOOD CENTER
145-02 Farmers Blvd.
Springfield Gardens, NY 11434

(718) 527-5220 Administrative
(718) 527-6394 FAX

Lisa Gilday, Disability Service Coordinator

3. HERBERT G. BIRCH SERVICES - WATSON AVENUE EARLY CHILDHOOD CENTER
1880 Watson Ave.
Bronx, NY 10472

(718) 828-3220 Administrative
(718) 409-0816 FAX

Cecil Hodge, Director

4. HERBERT G. BIRCH SERVICES - WASHINGTON HEIGHTS EARLY CHILDHOOD CENTER
554 Fort Washington Ave.
New York, NY 10033

(212) 740-5157 Administrative
(212) 740-8566 FAX

Dr. Karen Hazel, Principal

5. HERBERT G. BIRCH SERVICES - SCHOOL FOR EXCEPTIONAL CHILDREN
71-64 168th St.
Flushing, NY 11365

(718) 591-8100 Administrative
(718) 969-2941 FAX

sec@hgbirch.org

Vincent Russo, Principal

<continued...>

Services

Acting Instruction
Arts and Crafts Instruction
Dancing Instruction
English as a Second Language
Music Instruction
Storytelling

Ages: 2.9 to 6
Population Served: AIDS/HIV +, Asthma, Attention Deficit Disorder (ADD/ADHD), Developmental Delay, Developmental Disability, Emotional Disability, Learning Disability, Mental Retardation (mild-moderate), Multiple Disability, Seizure Disorder, Sickle Cell Anemia, Speech/Language Disability, Spina Bifida, Substance Exposed, Underachiever
Area Served: Bronx, Manhattan
Program Hours: 12-month program, Monday - Friday: 7:30 a.m.-5:45 p.m.
Program Capacity: 190
Staff/Child Ratio: Integrated Class: 1/2:20, 3 yrs: 1/2:17, 4 yrs: 1/2:20, 5 yrs: 1/2:22
Fees: Sliding Scale
Method of Payment: Cash, Money Orders
Medication Administered: No
Transportation Provided: Yes, special needs students are picked-up and droped-off at home.
Wheelchair Accessible: Yes
Service Description: Funded through the New York City Administration for Children's Services/Agency for Child Development (ACS/ACD). The mission is to create a nurturing environment that is rich in educational content, as well as supportive of each child's emotional and social growth. A multidisciplinary team identifies each child's developmental needs and objectives, sets attainable goals and then works toward meeting those goals.
Sites: 3

Arts and Crafts Instruction
Computer Classes
Exercise Classes/Groups
Homework Help Programs
Swimming

Ages: 3 to 20
Population Served: Autism, Developmental Delay, Developmental Disability, Learning Disability, Mental Retardation (mild-moderate), Speech/Language Disability
Area Served: Queens
Program Hours: Tuesdays, Wednesdays, Thursdays: 3-6 p.m.
Program Capacity: 37
Fees: $7.50 per day, includes transportation service home; $6 per day without transportation
Method of Payment: Cash, Check, Money Order
Medication Administered: No
Transportation Provided: Yes
Wheelchair Accessible: No
Service Description: Age-appropriate, supervised recreational and educational programming for participants in a safe school setting. If space is available, matron-monitored, one-way dismissal transportation

services will be provided for participants in one of three privately contracted mini-vans. Ninety, 3-hour sessions are provided throughout the school year from October to May to eligible participants from Queens.
Contact: Nannette Kirkland, Program Coordinator
Sites: 5

Arts and Crafts Instruction
Computer Classes
English as a Second Language
Exercise Classes/Groups
Homework Help Programs

Ages: 3 to 5
Population Served: Attention Deficit Disorder (ADD/ADHD), Developmental Delay, Developmental Disability, Down Syndrome, Learning Disability, Mental Retardation (mild-moderate), Speech/Language Disability
Area Served: Bronx, Manhattan
Program Hours: Year round, weekdays: 2- 6 p.m.
Program Capacity: 40
Staff/Child Ratio: 2:12
Fees: State funded, income eligibility required
Medication Administered: No
Transportation Provided: No
Wheelchair Accessible: No
Service Description: The program provides pre-school learning experiences in all domains of learning, with particular emphasis on social/emotional development, language development and nutrition. Referrals are made for children suspected of having developmental delays. Families are provided with support during and after the evaluation process. Families experiencing difficulties with housing, nutrition and mental health issues are provided with assistance, resources and support.
Contact: Diana Vasquez-Spiegler, Head Start Program Supervisor
Sites: 4

English as a Second Language
Storytelling

Ages: 3 to 5
Population Served: Asthma, Autism, Developmental Delay, Emotional Disability, Speech/Language Disability
Area Served: Brooklyn, Queens
Program Hours: Monday - Friday: 1:15-5:45 p.m.
Program Capacity: 36
Staff/Child Ratio: 1/2:18
Fees: Call center for information.
Transportation Provided: No
Wheelchair Accessible: No
Service Description: The ACS Head Start program is a collaborative program that provides

< continued... >

special needs children attending our program an extended day opportunity and typically developing community-based children an afternoon program option. All children and families receive comprehensive Head Start services ranging from nutrition and mental health services to on-going well health care monitoring.
Contact: Marjory Antoine, Education Director
Sites: 2

Exercise Classes/Groups
Homework Help Programs
Sports, Individual
Swimming

Ages: 9 to 35
Population Served: Autism, Developmental Disability, Mental Retardation (mild-moderate), Mental Retardation (severe-profound), Seizure Disorder, Speech/Language Disability
Area Served: Brooklyn, Queens
Program Hours: Evenings during the week. Day hours on weekend.
Program Capacity: 20
Staff/Child Ratio: 1:1
Fees: Rates are established by the Office of Mental Retardation and Developmental Disabilities
Method of Payment: Medicaid
Medication Administered: No
Transportation Provided: Yes
Wheelchair Accessible: No
Service Description: In-home services for people with developmental disabilities. Services include training in activities of daily living; travel training, shopping skills and community inclusion.
Contact: Chartayne Dunning, Waiver Coordinator
Sites: 1

HERO, INC.

123 Main St.
White Plains, NY 10601-3104

(914) 428-3451 Administrative

Brenda Spyer, Ed.D., Creative Director

Services

Dance Therapy
Recreational Activities

Ages: 3 to Seniors
Population Served: All Disabilities
Area Served: All Boroughs, Nassau, Putnam, Westchester
Staff/Child Ratio: 2:12/15 (instructor plus volunteers, depending on disability)
Wheelchair Accessible: Yes
Service Description: HERO's mission is to reach out to as many physically challenged, developmentally delayed, emotionally disabled and at-risk children, teens and adults as possible, and provide them with the same

recreational chances as are available to those without disabilities. HERO runs adaptive tennis, Tai Chi, dance and pet therapy activities.

HETRICK-MARTIN INSTITUTE

2 Astor Pl.
New York, NY 10003-6998

(212) 674-2400 Administrative
(212) 674-8650 FAX
(212) 674-8695 TDD

www.hmi.org
info@hmi.org

David Mensah, Executive Director
Languages Spoken: Spanish

Services

DROP-IN CENTER
Arts and Crafts Instruction
Film Making Instruction
Film Presentations
Music Instruction

Ages: 13 and up
Program Hours: Monday - Friday: 3-6:30 p.m.
Fees: None
Medication Administered: No
Transportation Provided: No
Wheelchair Accessible: No
Service Description: Offers education and support for gay and lesbian teenagers. A safe and fun space in which youth can learn about themselves, their peers and the larger world. The Drop-In Center offers a wide variety of youth programming which includes: photography, fine arts, music and video production workshops.

HIGHBRIDGE ADVISORY COUNCIL

880 River Ave.
Bronx, NY 10452

(718) 992-1321 Administrative
(718) 992-8539 FAX

Patricia Bellamy, Director
Languages Spoken: Spanish

<continued...>

Sites

1. HIGHBRIDGE ADVISORY COUNCIL - NELSON AVE. CENTER

1181 Nelson Ave.
Bronx, NY 10452

(212) 681-5215 Administrative

2. HIGHBRIDGE ADVISORY COUNCIL - DORIS E. STONE CENTER

1165 University Ave.
Bronx, NY 10452

(718) 588-1513 Administrative
(718) 681-5888 FAX

Demetrice Hawkins, Director

Services

Arts and Crafts Instruction
Dancing Instruction
Field Trips/Excursions
Music Instruction
Storytelling

Ages: 3 to 5
Population Served: AIDS/HIV +, Attention Deficit Disorder (ADD/ADHD), Developmental Delay, Learning Disability, Speech/Language Disability, Underachiever
Program Hours: Saturdays: 8 a.m.-6 p.m.
Program Capacity: 20 children
Staff/Child Ratio: 3:20
Fees: ACD determines fees
Method of Payment: Cash, Money Order, Voucher
Medication Administered: No
Transportation Provided: No
Wheelchair Accessible: No
Service Description: Children receive a snack in the morning, lunch and supper. They make arts and crafts projects, play games, take field trips, participate in movement and storytelling hours.
Sites: 1 2

DAY CARE CENTER
Arts and Crafts Instruction
Child Care Centers
Computer Classes
Creative Writing
Homework Help Programs
Sports, Team/Leagues
Tutoring

Ages: 5 to 12
Population Served: AIDS/HIV +, Asthma, Attention Deficit Disorder (ADD/ADHD), Developmental Delay, Gifted, Learning Disability, Underachiever
Program Hours: Monday - Friday: 3-7:30 p.m., Saturday: 8:30 a.m.-4 p.m.
Program Capacity: 40 children
Staff/Child Ratio: 4:40
Fees: ACD determines fees
Method of Payment: Cash, Money Order, Voucher

Medication Administered: No
Transportation Provided: No
Wheelchair Accessible: Yes
Service Description: Children receive a snack, lunch and supper. Services provided are as follows: homework help, one-on-one tutoring, arts and crafts, creative writing, educational games, field trips, various sports and computer training.
Sites: 1

HIGHBRIDGE COMMUNITY LIFE CENTER

979 Ogden St.
Bronx, NY 10452

(718) 681-2222 Administrative

Sister Ellen Rita, Contact
Languages Spoken: Spanish

Sites

1. HIGHBRIDGE COMMUNITY LIFE CENTER - YOUTH SERVICES CENTER

1248 Nelson Ave.
New York, NY 10452

(718) 293-6103 Administrative

Kyrstel Wright, Director

Services

Homework Help Programs
Mentoring Programs
Recreational Activities
Social Skills Training
Tutoring

Ages: 6 to 16
Program Hours: Monday - Friday: 3-6 p.m., Saturday: 12-3 p.m.
Program Capacity: 75 children
Fees: None
Medication Administered: No
Transportation Provided: No
Wheelchair Accessible: No
Service Description: A mainstream recreational and educational after school program. Children with special needs are accepted on a case-by-case basis.
Contact: Mary Ann Flanagan, Youth Development
Sites: 1

HUDSON GUILD, INC.

441 W. 26th St.
New York, NY 10001

(212) 760-9800 Administrative
(212) 760-9822 Counseling Services
(212) 268-9983 FAX

hguild@hudsonguild.org

Janice McGuire, Executive Director
Languages Spoken: Spanish

Sites

1. HUDSON GUILD, INC. - CHILDREN'S CENTER

459 W. 26th St.
New York, NY 10001

(212) 760-9831 Administrative
(212) 268-9983 FAX

Luz Cabezas, Director, Children's Center

Services

CHILDREN'S CENTER
Child Care Centers
Dancing Instruction
Field Trips/Excursions
Music Instruction

Ages: 2 months to 12 years of age
Population Served: All Disabilities
Program Hours: Monday - Friday: 8 a.m.-6 p.m.
Program Capacity: Preschool: 150, Family Day Care: 49, School Age: 35
Fees: $1 - $90/week (Sliding Scale)
Method of Payment: Cash, Check, Postal Money Order
Medication Administered: Yes, with doctor's documentation, ACD/ACS approval and parent's/guardian's written authorization.
Transportation Provided: No
Wheelchair Accessible: Yes
Service Description: The Children's Center provides child care services to children between the ages of 2 months to 12 years of age, all year round. Hot meals are provided on-site all children in our center-based programs. All children participate in music, dance, gymnastics and trips. Individualized age-appropriate curriculum with emphasis on language arts, math, science, celebration of diversity and parent involvement. All programs are licensed by the New York City Department of Health.
Sites: 1

HUDSON RIVER MUSEUM

511 Warburton Ave.
Yonkers, NY 10701-1899

(914) 963-4550 [212] Administrative
(914) 963-4550 [243] Education Department
(914) 963-8558 FAX

www.hrm.org

Zoe Lindsey, Public Information

Services

Museums

Ages: All Ages
Area Served: All Boroughs
Program Hours: May - September: Wednesday - Sunday, Noon-5 p.m., Friday , Noon-9 p.m.; October - April: Wednesday - Sunday, Noon-5 p.m.
Fees: $4 per adult, $3 per child (members free)
Medication Administered: No
Transportation Provided: No
Wheelchair Accessible: Yes

HUDSON VALLEY CHILDREN'S MUSEUM

Nyack Seaport
21c Burd St.
Nyack, NY 10960

(845) 358-2191 Administrative
(845) 358-2642 FAX

Services

Museums

HUNTER COLLEGE

695 Park Ave. North Bldg. Rm. 100
New York, NY 10021

(212) 650-3850 Administrative
(212) 650-3336 FAX

Languages Spoken: Spanish

Services

Acting Instruction
Arts and Crafts Instruction
Creative Writing
Dancing Instruction
Exercise Classes/Groups
Music Instruction
Recreational Activities
Remedial Education

<continued...>

Theater Performances

Ages: 2 to 12
Area Served: All Boroughs
Program Hours: Hours vary; Call for information
Program Capacity: Varies from program to program.
Fees: Fees vary depending on program. Call for information
Method of Payment: Check, Credit Card (American Express, Discover, MasterCard or Visa), Money Order
Medication Administered: No
Transportation Provided: No
Wheelchair Accessible: Yes
Service Description: Hunter College provides a variety of weekend programs for children. Please contact the school for a complete listing.

HUNTINGTON LEARNING CENTER

1556 Third Ave., Suite 209
New York, NY 10128

(212) 534-3200 Administrative
(212) 534-8638 FAX

Deborah Briggs, Director

Services

Remedial Education
Test Preparation
Tutoring

Ages: 5 to 17
Population Served: Attention Deficit Disorder (ADD/ADHD), Developmental Disability, Gifted, Learning Disability, Neurological Disability, Underachiever
Area Served: All Boroughs
Staff/Child Ratio: 1:1 if needed (as per initial conference), all individual programs, no group instruction
Fees: $49.50 - $75 per session
Method of Payment: Cash, Check, Credit Card, Money Order
Medication Administered: No
Wheelchair Accessible: Yes
Service Description: Provides supplemental instruction in reading, writing, mathematics, study skills, phonics, and related areas.

IMMIGRANT SOCIAL SERVICE, INC.

137 Henry St.
New York, NY 10002

(212) 571-1840 Administrative
(212) 571-1848 FAX

Victor Papa
Languages Spoken: Chinese, Haitian Creole, Russian, Sign Language, Spanish

Services

Arts and Crafts Instruction
Homework Help Programs
Recreational Activities
Tutoring

Ages: 5 to 14
Program Hours: Monday - Friday: 3-6 p.m.
Staff/Child Ratio: 1:1
Fees: Call for information
Medication Administered: No
Transportation Provided: No
Wheelchair Accessible: No
Service Description: A mainstream after school program offering tutoring services in subjects such as reading and math. Children with disabilities are considered on a case-by-case basis.

INSPIRICA

850 Seventh Ave.
New York, NY 10019

(212) 245-3888 Administrative

Anita Brownstern

Services

Homework Help Programs
Remedial Education
Test Preparation
Tutoring

Ages: All Ages
Population Served: All Disabilities
Program Hours: Schedule is flexible, depending on needs of client.
Staff/Child Ratio: 1:1
Fees: $200 - $400 per hour
Medication Administered: No
Transportation Provided: No
Wheelchair Accessible: Yes
Service Description: Tutoring sessions are custom designed to fit the needs of all children and sessions are on an individual basis. Educational plan is designed for each child individually.

INSTITUTE FOR THEATRE-LEARNING, INC.

56-15A Utopia Parkway
Fresh Meadows, NY 11365

(718) 357-4532 Administrative

www.theatrelearning.org
TLStages@aol.com

Maxine Fields, MS, Program Director

< continued... >

Services

Drama Therapy
Social Skills Training
Theater Performances

Ages: 9 to 14
Population Served: At-Risk, Attention Deficit Disorder (ADD/ADHD), Emotional Disability, Learning Disability, Pervasive Developmental Disorder (PDD/NOS), Speech/Language Disability
Area Served: Queens
Service Description: A mainstream and special needs theatre program. The STAGES program is specifically for at-risk children who are learning disabled, socially inhibited, withdrawn or have Attention Deficit Disorder. Theatre games and improvisional role playing help increase self-esteem and social competency. A second program for children who have cognitive delays, and auditory processing difficulties provides a social hour for children in order to improve their interaction skills.

INSTITUTES OF APPLIED HUMAN DYNAMICS - CENTERS FOR THE MULTIPLY HANDICAPPED (IAHD)

3625 Bainbridge Ave.
Bronx, NY 10467

(718) 920-0800 Administrative
(718) 920-0896 FAX

Dr. Elias S. Gootzeit, Executive Director
Languages Spoken: Spanish, Tagalog

Services

Arts and Crafts Instruction
Recreational Activities
Respite, Children's Out-of-Home
Sports, Individual
Sports, Team/Leagues
Swimming

Ages: 4 to 20
Population Served: Cerebral Palsy, Developmental Delay, Developmental Disability, Mental Retardation (mild-moderate), Mental Retardation (severe-profound)
Area Served: All Boroughs
Program Hours: Sunday: 10 a.m.-3 p.m.
Fees: None
Transportation Provided: No
Wheelchair Accessible: Yes
Service Description: A weekend recreational program for children and teens.

INTERFAITH NEIGHBORS, INC.

210 E. 86th St., Suite 401
New York, NY 10028

(212) 717-1119 Administrative
(212) 717-1522 FAX

www.ifneighbors.org
info@ifneighbors.org

Eileen Lyons, CSW, Executive Director
Languages Spoken: Spanish

Sites

1. INTERFAITH NEIGHBORS, INC.
210 E. 86th St., Suite 401
New York, NY 10028

(212) 717-1119 Administrative

www.ifneighbors.org

Eileen Lyons, CSW, Executive Director

2. TEEN LEARNING CENTER
247 E. 82nd St.
New York, NY 10028

(212) 472-3567 Administrative
(212) 472-5317 FAX

www.ifneighbors.org

Theresa Phenjad, Director

3. INTERFAITH NEIGHBORS, INC. - NEW BEGINNINGS AT P.S. 38
P.S. 38, 232 E. 103rd St.
New York, NY 10029

(212) 860-5882 Administrative
(212) 860-6093 FAX

4. GIRLSPACE - A CENTER FOR GIRLS IN EAST HARLEM
14 E. 109th St., 2nd Fl.
New York, NY 10029

(212) 427-0457 Administrative
(212) 410-9384 FAX

Mary Bitel, CSW, Director

Services

EDUCATION PLUS
Acting Instruction
Arts and Crafts Instruction
Creative Writing
Exercise Classes/Groups
Homework Help Programs
Music Instruction
Tutoring

Ages: 12 to 16
Population Served: Asthma, Attention Deficit Disorder (ADD/ADHD), Gifted, Learning Disability
Program Hours: Monday - Friday: 3-7 p.m.

<continued...>

Program Capacity: 100
Staff/Child Ratio: 1:15
Fees: Call center for information
Medication Administered: No
Transportation Provided: No
Wheelchair Accessible: Yes
Service Description: The Teen Learning and Leadership Center provides after school programs in areas of academics (homework help, tutoring, reading lab) and social programs (rap groups, issue-based workshops).
Sites: 2

NEW BEGINNINGS AT P.S. 38
Acting Instruction
Arts and Crafts Instruction
Creative Writing
Dancing Instruction
Exercise Classes/Groups
Homework Help Programs
Sports, Individual
Sports, Team/Leagues
Tutoring

Ages: 5 to 11
Population Served: Asthma, At-Risk, Learning Disability
Area Served: New York
Program Hours: Monday - Friday: 3-6 p.m.
Fees: None
Medication Administered: No
Transportation Provided: No
Wheelchair Accessible: Yes
Service Description: The primary goal of New Beginnings is encouraging children to enjoy using their minds, whether they're getting tutorial help or intellectually exploring in the library, reading rooms, writing corner, or computer lab. Activities such as arts and crafts, science discussion groups, dance, acting, video-making, double-dutch, basketball and martial arts stretch their worlds beyond the fences of poverty. Every aspect of New Beginnings is to instill individual worth and promote mutual respect and cooperation.
Sites: 3

GIRLS' LOUNGE
Acting Instruction
Arts and Crafts Instruction
Dancing Instruction
Recreational Activities

Ages: 10 to 15
Population Served: At Risk, Developmental Delay, Developmental Disability, Emotional Disability, Learning Disability, Speech/Language Disability, Underachiever
Area Served: All Boroughs
Program Hours: Saturday. Call for information
Fees: None
Medication Administered: No
Transportation Provided: No
Service Description: Girls' Lounge is the newest GirlSpace program, it offers girls an opportunity to relax and have fun. A variety of activities and programs are offered.
Sites: 4

PANTRY SISTERS
Acting Instruction
Arts and Crafts Instruction
Creative Writing
Dancing Instruction
Exercise Classes/Groups
Field Trips/Excursions
Homework Help Programs
Mentoring Programs
Sports, Team/Leagues
Storytelling
Swimming
Tutoring

Ages: 10 to 15
Population Served: Asthma, Attention Deficit Disorder (ADD/ADHD), Developmental Delay, Emotional Disability, Gifted, Learning Disability, Substance Exposed, Underachiever
Program Hours: September 15 - June: Monday - Friday, 3-7 p.m.; November 1 - April 30: Saturday, 12-3 p.m.; Summer Camp: July - August, Monday - Friday, 8:30 a.m.-3 p.m.
Program Capacity: 150
Fees: None
Medication Administered: No
Transportation Provided: No
Wheelchair Accessible: No
Service Description: Girlspace provides girls with a variety of learning and enrichment programs, including: Youth-4-Youth, a leadership and job internship program; tutoring; homework help; Young Women's Voices, a creative writing program and math lab. Girlspace also offers art, drama, dance, sports, writing, cooking, cultural exploration, rap groups, newsletter and book clubs.
Sites: 4

READING LAB
Creative Writing
Storytelling
Tutoring

Ages: 12 to 16
Population Served: At Risk, Developmental Delay, Developmental Disability, Emotional Disability, Learning Disability, Speech/Language Disability, Underachiever
Area Served: New York
Program Hours: Twice per week. Monday and Thursday: 3:30-7 p.m.
Staff/Child Ratio: 1:1
Fees: None
Transportation Provided: No
Wheelchair Accessible: Yes
Service Description: In twice-weekly sessions with a trained tutor, students master phonics skills, read aloud a book of their choice and discuss it through journal entries - a blend of activities that sharpen word-study reading and writing skills. Lesson plans are hand-tailored to each child's learning curve by the labs' expert staff.

< continued... >

Sites: 1 2

JACOB RIIS NEIGHBORHOOD SETTLEMENT HOUSE

10-25 41st Ave.
Long Island City, NY 11101

(718) 784-7447 Administrative
(718) 729-2063 FAX

www.riissettlement.org

Dennis Brown, Acting Director

Services

OUR KIDS AFTER SCHOOL PROGRAM
Arts and Crafts Instruction
Homework Help Programs

Ages: 5 to 12
Area Served: Queens
Program Hours: Monday - Friday: 3-6 p.m.
Fees: Call for information
Medication Administered: No
Transportation Provided: No
Wheelchair Accessible: Yes
Service Description: Provides after school programs. Children with special needs are considered on a case-by-case basis.
Contact: Vanessa Quiñones, Program Coordinator

JAMAICA CENTER FOR ARTS AND LEARNING

161-04 Jamaica Ave.
Jamaica, NY 11432

(718) 658-7400 Administrative
(718) 658-7922 FAX

Efeyinna Acosta, Educational

Services

Acting Instruction
Arts and Crafts Instruction
Computer Classes
Creative Writing
Dancing Instruction
Exercise Classes/Groups
Music Instruction
Theater Performances

Ages: 4 and up
Area Served: All Boroughs
Program Hours: Call for information
Fees: Please call for information.
Medication Administered: No
Transportation Provided: No
Service Description: An arts center offering dance instruction, arts instruction, drama classes, writing courses, computer classes, exercise programs and theater productions. Children with special needs are considered on a case-by-case basis.

JAMES WELDON JOHNSON COMMUNITY CENTER

2201 First Ave.
New York, NY 10029

(212) 860-7250 Administrative
(212) 860-0053 FAX

Barbara Ramage, Executive Director

Services

Arts and Crafts Instruction
Homework Help Programs
Tutoring

Ages: 2.5 to 13
Population Served: Attention Deficit Disorder (ADD/ADHD), Autism, Cancer, Cardiac Disorder, Cerebral Palsy, Cystic Fibrosis, Developmental Disability, Diabetes, Down Syndrome, Emotional Disability, Health Impairment, Learning Disability, Mental Retardation (mild-moderate), Mental Retardation (severe-profound), Multiple Disability, Neurological Disability, Pervasive Developmental Disorder (PDD/NOS), Physical/Orthopedic Disability, Seizure Disorder, Sickle Cell Anemia, Speech/Language Disability, Substance Abuse, Tourette Syndrome, Underachiever, Visual Disability/Blind
Program Hours: Monday - Thursday: 3-6:30 p.m., Friday: 3-5:45 p.m.
Fees: $15 per month
Method of Payment: Cash, Check, Credit Card, Money Order
Medication Administered: No
Transportation Provided: No
Wheelchair Accessible: Yes
Service Description: ACD-funded early childhood, educational, Head Start, recreational and after school programs with licensed teachers, providing services to both mainstream and special needs children.

JESPY TOURS, INC.

2518 Spruce St.
Union, NJ 07083

(908) 688-1704 Administrative
(908) 688-1770 FAX

Myra Trinkler, Director

<continued...>

Services

Travel

Ages: 21 and up
Population Served: Attention Deficit Disorder (ADD/ADHD), Autism, Developmental Disability, Diabetes, Learning Disability, Mental Retardation (mild-moderate), Neurological Disability, Physical/Orthopedic Disability, Seizure Disorder, Speech/Language Disability
Staff/Child Ratio: 1:6
Fees: Call for information
Method of Payment: Payment Plan
Medication Administered: No
Transportation Provided: Yes
Wheelchair Accessible: No
Service Description: Offers six travel and recreational opportunities each year. The trips are well planned, innovative, supervised and fun. All trips are carefully researched to accommodate the travelers' special needs.

JEWISH BOARD OF FAMILY AND CHILDREN'S SERVICES (JBFCS)

120 W. 57th St.
New York, NY 10019

(212) 582-9100 Administrative
(212) 245-2096 FAX

www.jbfcs.org
admin@jbfcs.org

Alan B. Siskind, Ph.D., Executive Director
Languages Spoken: Spanish

Sites

1. JEWISH BOARD OF FAMILY AND CHILDREN'S SERVICES - STATEN ISLAND OFFICE / MADELEINE BORG COMMUNITY SERVICES

2795 Richmond Ave.
Staten Island, NY 10314

(718) 698-5307 Warm Line
(718) 370-1142 Warm Line FAX
(718) 982-6982 Case Management

Eileen Duva, RN, Parent Advocate, Parent Resource Center

2. JEWISH BOARD OF FAMILY AND CHILDREN'S SERVICES - BORO PARK OFFICE / MADELEINE BORG COMMUNITY SERVICES

1273 53rd St.
Brooklyn, NY 11219

(718) 435-5700 Administrative
(718) 854-5495 FAX

Services

BIG BROTHER/BIG SISTER
Mentoring Programs

Ages: 7 to 16
Area Served: Brooklyn
Program Capacity: No limit
Fees: None
Medication Administered: No
Transportation Provided: No
Wheelchair Accessible: No
Service Description: The Big Brother-Big Sister program provides a socializing experience for a child through participation in regularly scheduled activities, while building a relationship based upon trust, support and consistancy. The Big Brothers-Big Sisters are regularly supervised by the child's therapist on an ongoing basis to maximize the growth and development of a mutually positive and rewarding relationship. Children with special needs are considered on a case-by-case basis.
Contact: Miriam Turk, CSW
Sites: 2

STATEN ISLAND TEEN LOUNGE CENTER
Recreational Activities
Social Skills Training

Ages: 13 to 19
Population Served: Developmental Disability, Learning Disability, Mental Retardation (mild-moderate)
Area Served: Staten Island
Wheelchair Accessible: Yes
Service Description: A drop-in center where teens with special needs gather and receive special attention from social workers. Outreach to potential teen clients is provided.
Contact: Susan Brenner, CSW, Coordinator
Sites: 1

JEWISH CHILD CARE ASSOCIATION (JCCA)

120 Wall St., 12th Fl.
New York, NY 10005

(212) 425-3333 Administrative
(212) 425-9397 FAX

www.jewishchildcareny.org

Paul Gitelson, DSW, Executive Vice President
Languages Spoken: Russian, Spanish

< continued...>

Sites

1. JEWISH CHILD CARE ASSOCIATION (JCCA)
120 Wall St., 12th Fl.
New York, NY 10005

(212) 425-3333 Administrative
(212) 425-9397 FAX

www.jewishchildcareny.org

2. JEWISH CHILD CARE ASSOCIATION - BROOKLYN PROGRAM OFFICE - SWYFT
3003 Ave. H
Brooklyn, NY 11210

(718) 859-4500 Administrative
(718) 859-5708 FAX

Charyn Wilson, Director

3. JEWISH CHILD CARE ASSOCIATION - QUEENS OFFICE
97-45 Queens Blvd.
Rego Park, NY 11374

(718) 793-7890 Administrative
(718) 275-0143 FAX

Rebecca Koffler, Director, Early Childhood Programs

Services

Social Skills Training

Ages: Birth to 21
Population Served: Emotional Disability
Area Served: NYC Metro Area
Program Hours: Call for information
Transportation Provided: No
Wheelchair Accessible: Yes
Service Description: Provides socialization training for children and young adults.
Sites: 2

TWO TOGETHER / SCHOLARSHIP PROGRAM
Tutoring

Ages: 9 to 17
Population Served: Learning Disability
Area Served: All Boroughs
Program Hours: Tuesday, Wednesday, Thursday: 5-8 p.m.
Program Capacity: 100
Staff/Child Ratio: 1:1
Fees: Call for information
Medication Administered: No
Transportation Provided: Reimbursement for token.
Wheelchair Accessible: Yes
Service Description: Program provides free individual remedial math and reading instruction to school age children. Trained volunteers tutor children under the supervision of learning specialists. Workshops for parents, cultural experiences and educational projects reinforce program goals. Staff also work with parents toward educational goals. Referrals are from schools,

parents and the community. The Two Together Rego Park program primarily serves immigrants from the former Soviet Union.
Sites: 1 3

JEWISH COMMUNITY HOUSE OF BENSONHURST

7802 Bay Parkway
Brooklyn, NY 11214

(718) 331-6800 [28] Administrative
(718) 232-8461 FAX

Faye Levine, Director of Social Services
Languages Spoken: Russian

Services

Arts and Crafts Instruction
Child Care Centers
Dancing Instruction
Homework Help Programs
Sports, Team/Leagues
Tutoring

Ages: 5 to 12
Population Served: Attention Deficit Disorder (ADD/ADHD), Learning Disability
Area Served: Brooklyn (Southwest section)
Program Hours: Monday - Friday: 3-6:30 p.m.
Program Capacity: 15-20
Staff/Child Ratio: 1:4
Fees: $260 per month
Method of Payment: Cash, Check, Credit Card, Income based scholarship
Transportation Provided: Yes, from district 20 and 21.
Wheelchair Accessible: No
Service Description: Provides after school activities for children with special needs. Activities include homework assistance, 1:1 tutoring, and gymnastics. Children in special needs program are integrated with mainstream children for participation in sports, arts and crafts, and dance. Snacks are provided.
Contact: Gelena Blishteyn, 718-331-6800 x25

JEWISH MUSEUM (THE)

1109 Fifth Ave. at 92nd St.
New York, NY 10128

(212) 423-3200 Administrative
(212) 423-3225 Scheduling Coordinator
(212) 423-3232 FAX

www.thejewishmuseum.org

Siri Steinberg, Administrative Associaate
Languages Spoken: Sign Language

<continued...>

Services

Museums

Ages: K-12
Program Capacity: 28 Students per group maximum.
Staff/Child Ratio: Varies
Fees: $55 per school group, $75 per group on Sundays.
Method of Payment: Cash, Check, Credit Card.
Wheelchair Accessible: Yes

JOSEPH DEMARCO CHILD CARE CENTER

36-49 11th St.
Long Island City, NY 11106

(718) 786-1166 Administrative

Waleska Martinez, Educational Director
Languages Spoken: Spanish

Services

Arts and Crafts Instruction
Child Care Centers
Homework Help Programs

Ages: 2.9 to 9
Population Served: Attention Deficit Disorder
(ADD/ADHD), Cerebral Palsy, Developmental Disability,
Emotional Disability, Learning Disability, Multiple
Disability, Speech/Language Disability
Area Served: All Boroughs
Fees: Call for information
Wheelchair Accessible: Yes
Service Description: Child care center offering head
start, preschool and after school programs. Call for more
information.

JOSEPH P. ADDABBO FAMILY HEALTH CENTER

67-10 Rockaway Beach Blvd.
Arverne, NY 11692

(718) 945-7150 Administrative
(718) 474-5076 PRYSE
(718) 945-2596 FAX

Fern Zagor, Director, Mental Health Services
Languages Spoken: Spanish

Services

Recreational Activities

Ages: 5 to 18
Population Served: AIDS/HIV +, Attention Deficit
Disorder (ADD/ADHD), Emotional Disability
Area Served: Queens (Rockaway peninsula)
Program Hours: Call for information
Fees: Call for information

Transportation Provided: No
Wheelchair Accessible: Yes
Service Description: Offers an evening
therapeutic program and parent support group.

KAPLAN, INC.

888 7th Ave.
New York, NY 10106

(212) 492-5800 Administrative

www.kaplan.com

Services

Test Preparation

Ages: All Ages
Area Served: All Boroughs
Program Hours: Call for information
Staff/Child Ratio: Dependant upon program
Fees: Vary depending on program
Method of Payment: Cash, Check, Credit Card,
Money Order
Medication Administered: No
Transportation Provided: No
Wheelchair Accessible: Yes
Service Description: Kaplan gives students and
professionals the best in test preparation
combined with unbeaten convenience and
flexibility. Kaplan offers preparation for 35
standardized tests, including entrance exams for
secondary school, college, and graduate school
as well as English language and professional
licensing exams. Kaplan also provides tutoring.

KIDS WITH A PROMISE

132 Madison Ave.
New York, NY 10016

(212) 684-1016 Administrative

*Heide Goode, Director, After School and Day
Camp*
Languages Spoken: Spanish

Sites

**1. KIDS WITH A PROMISE - CHURCH OF THE
REVELATION**
1154 White Plains Rd.
Bronx, NY 10472

< continued... >

2. KIDS WITH A PROMISE - EVANGELICAL CHRISTIAN CHURCH

692 Union Ave.
Bronx, NY 10455

3. KIDS WITH A PROMISE - FORDHAM MANOR REFORMED CHURCH

2705 Reservoir Ave.
Bronx, NY 10468

4. KIDS WITH A PROMISE - FORT WASHINGTON COLLEGIATE CHURCH

729 W. 181st. St.
New York, NY 10033

5. KIDS WITH A PROMISE - LIVING WATERS FELLOWSHIP

265 Stanhope St.
Brooklyn, NY 11237

Services

Arts and Crafts Instruction
Homework Help Programs
Religious Activities
Tutoring

Ages: 6 to 12
Area Served: Bronx, Brooklyn, Manhattan
Wheelchair Accessible: Yes (some sites)
Service Description: After school programs provide group instruction in reading, writing, math and other activities. Willing to accept children with disabilities on a case-by-case basis. Fort Washington and Living Waters are wheelchair accessible. Call main office for information on programs at all sites.
Sites: 1 2 3 4 5

KINGS BAY LITTLE LEAGUE CHALLENGER

2670 Coyle St.
Brooklyn, NY

(718) 934-6345 Administrative
(Call between: 7:30 & 9:30 p.m.)

Services

CHALLENGER DIVISION
Sports, Team/Leagues

Ages: 5 to 18
Population Served: All Disabilities
Area Served: All Boroughs
Program Hours: Wednesday: 6-8 p.m.; Saturday: 9 a.m.-12 p.m.; Sunday: 9 a.m.-12 p.m.
Program Capacity: Unlimited
Staff/Child Ratio: 1:10

Wheelchair Accessible: Yes
Service Description: Provides after school Little League baseball program for children with special needs.
Contact: Mike Silver Bush, Vice President

KINGS BAY YM-YWHA

3495 Nostrand Ave.
Brooklyn, NY 11229

(718) 648-7703 Administrative
(718) 648-0758 FAX

www.kingsbayy.org

Edna Wildman, Director
Languages Spoken: Russian

Services

Acting Instruction
Arts and Crafts Instruction
Exercise Classes/Groups
Field Trips/Excursions
Homework Help Programs
Mentoring Programs
Recreational Activities
Sports, Individual
Sports, Team/Leagues
Swimming

Ages: 5 to 12
Population Served: Asperger Syndrome, Attention Deficit Disorder (ADD/ADHD), Developmental Disability, Emotional Disability, Learning Disability, Multiple Disability
Area Served: Brooklyn
Program Hours: Monday - Friday: 3-6 p.m.
Program Capacity: 25
Staff/Child Ratio: 1:4
Fees: $12 per day plus Kings Bay YM-YWHA membership.
Method of Payment: Cash, Check, Credit Card
Medication Administered: Yes
Wheelchair Accessible: Yes
Service Description: Trained professional staff provides children with developmental and learning disabilities with homework assistance, snacks, and activities.
Contact: Neil S. Grossman, Children's Services Supervisor

KINGSBRIDGE HEIGHTS COMMUNITY CENTER, INC.

3101 Kingsbridge Terrace
Bronx, NY 10463

(718) 884-0700 Administrative
(718) 884-0858 FAX

Charles Shayne, Executive Director
Languages Spoken: Spanish

Services

Arts and Crafts Instruction
Music Instruction
Sports, Team/Leagues
Storytelling

Ages: 5 to 17
Population Served: Autism, Diabetes, Health Impairment, Mental Retardation (mild-moderate), Mental Retardation (severe-profound), Neurological Disability, Seizure Disorder, Speech/Language Disability
Area Served: Bronx
Program Hours: Monday - Friday: 8 a.m.-6 p.m.; two weeks in August.
Program Capacity: 25
Staff/Child Ratio: 1:5
Fees: None
Medication Administered: Yes
Wheelchair Accessible: Yes
Service Description: Provides working parents with full day respite after school ends. The program offers children an opportunity to participate in socialization, athletic sports, arts and crafts, music, storytelling, and outdoor activities.

KINGSLAND HOMESTEAD - QUEENS HISTORICAL SOCIETY

143-35 37th Ave.
Flushing, NY 11354

(718) 939-0647 Administrative
(718) 539-9885 FAX

www.preserve.org/queens
qhs@juno.com

Mitchell Grubler, Executive Director

Services

Museums

Program Hours: Tuesday, Saturday and Sunday: 2:30-4:30 p.m.

LAGUARDIA COMMUNITY COLLEGE

31-10 Thomson Ave.
Long Island City, NY 11101

(718) 482-5250 Office of Students with Disabilities
(718) 482-5324 Program for Deaf Adults
(718) 482-5279 The Learning Project
(718) 482-5293 Registration for College
(718) 482-5311 TDD

www.lagcc.cuny.edu

Alexis Frazie

Services

COLLEGE FOR CHILDREN
Arts and Crafts Instruction
Dancing Instruction
Music Instruction
Recreational Activities
Remedial Education

Ages: 5 to 18
Program Hours: Call for information
Fees: Call for information
Service Description: Programs offer tutorial classes in math, reading, and college preparation for students. Also provides workshops in art, cartooning, puppet making and creative writing. Children with special needs are accepted on a case-by-case basis.

LANGSTON HUGHES COMMUNITY LIBRARY AND CULTURAL CENTER

100-01 Northern Blvd.
Corona, NY 11368

(718) 672-2710 Administrative

Dr. Ruby Sprott, Homework Program
Languages Spoken: Spanish

Services

Homework Help Programs
Remedial Education

Ages: 6 to 13
Population Served: Emotional Disability
Area Served: Queens
Program Hours: Monday - Friday: 3-6 p.m.
Program Capacity: 100
Staff/Child Ratio: 1:8
Fees: None
Medication Administered: No
Transportation Provided: No
Wheelchair Accessible: Yes
Service Description: Offers after school homework help programs for all children. Children with special needs are considered on a case-by-case basis.

LAURELTON THEATRE OF PERFORMING & VISUAL ARTS

228-05 Merrick Blvd.
Laurelton, NY 11413

(718) 481-8840 Administrative

Claretta F. King, Executive Director

Services

Acting Instruction
Dancing Instruction
Music Instruction

Ages: 6 to 18
Population Served: Health Impairment, Physical/Orthopedic Disability
Area Served: All Boroughs
Fees: Vary
Method of Payment: Payment Plan
Wheelchair Accessible: Yes
Service Description: Cultural program available after school and on Saturdays for children. Children with health impairments and limited physical disabilities are mainstreamed on the basis of an interview. Includes workshops in visual arts, dance, drama, piano, voice, scene studies and stage performances.

LEARNING FOR LIFE

1601 York Ave., #3B
New York, NY 10028

(212) 414-5100 Administrative

slo@hewittsch.com

Sue Lux

Services

Test Preparation
Tutoring

Ages: 3 to 16
Population Served: Attention Deficit Disorder (ADD/ADHD), Learning Disability
Area Served: Manhattan
Program Hours: Call for information
Fees: Call for information
Medication Administered: No
Transportation Provided: No
Service Description: Specializes in multisensory tutoring in phonics, reading, writing, math, study skills, organization and ERB test preparation.

LEARNING TREE

125 E. 23rd St., Suite 203
New York, NY 10010

(212) 465-3294 Administrative
(212) 533-5844 FAX

Lourdes Blanco, CSW, Director
Languages Spoken: Chinese, French, Spanish

Services

Remedial Education
Study Skills Assistance
Test Preparation
Tutoring

Ages: 4 and up
Population Served: Attention Deficit Disorder (ADD/ADHD
Area Served: All Boroughs
Fees: Call for information
Service Description: Provides individual instruction and support in all subject areas: study skills assistance, organization workshops, test preparation, remedial and enrichment services.

LEHMAN COLLEGE

250 Bedford Park Blvd. W.
Bronx, NY 10468-1589

(718) 960-8441 Office of Special Student Services
(877) 534-6261 Toll Free

www.lehman.cuny.edu

Jose Magdaleno, Vice President of Student Affairs

Services

LEARNING DISABILITIES CLINIC
Remedial Education

Ages: 6 and up
Population Served: Learning Disability
Area Served: All Boroughs
Fees: None.
Service Description: Learning Disabilities Clinic offers tutoring and remedial services for children ages 6 and older. Call for more information.

LEISURE TRAX

460 W. 34th St., 11th Fl.
New York, NY 10001

(212) 273-6254 Administrative
(212) 273-6161 FAX

www.YAI.org

Iran Buckler, Coordinator
Languages Spoken: Spanish

Services

Travel

Ages: 21 and up
Population Served: Mental Retardation (mild-moderate)
Area Served: NYC Metro Area
Fees: Free membership; trip prices vary accordingly
Transportation Provided: Yes
Service Description: Trips supervised by YAI-experienced chaperones. Offers vacation and travel opportunities, including weekend and extended vacations with domestic and international destinations. Group rates and custom-designed trips available.

LENOX HILL NEIGHBORHOOD HOUSE

331 E. 70th St.
New York, NY 10021

(212) 744-5022 Administrative
(212) 288-0722 FAX

www.lenoxhill.org

Nancy Wackstein, Executive Director

Services

Acting Instruction
Arts and Crafts Instruction
Computer Classes
Creative Writing
Dancing Instruction
Homework Help Programs
Mentoring Programs
Music Instruction
Storytelling
Swimming
Tutoring

Ages: 5 to 12
Program Hours: Monday - Friday: 3-6 p.m. Full day for Board of Education closings.
Program Capacity: 140
Staff/Child Ratio: 2:15
Fees: $260 per month
Medication Administered: No
Transportation Provided: No
Wheelchair Accessible: No
Service Description: Program provides recreational, educational, and cultural activities for children. Program operates September to June, following the public school

calendar year. Dinner is served daily. Medical clearance and results of the HGB blood test and TB test are required for all participants. 1:1 tutoring is offered.
Contact: Meeta Sharma-Holt, Director of Youth Services

LENOX HILL TEAM PROGRAM
Acting Instruction
Arts and Crafts Instruction
Computer Classes
Homework Help Programs
Mentoring Programs
Music Instruction
Sports, Individual
Swimming
Tutoring

Ages: 12 to 18
Population Served: Attention Deficit Disorder (ADD/ADHD), Asthma, Deaf-Blind, Developmental Disability, Emotional Disability, Gifted, Juvenile Offender, Learning Disability, Underachiever, Visual Disability/Blind
Area Served: Bronx, Brooklyn, Manhattan, Queens
Program Hours: Ocober - August: Tuesday - Friday: 6-9 p.m., Wednesday, 6-8 p.m.
Program Capacity: 150
Staff/Child Ratio: 1:15
Fees: $40
Method of Payment: Payment plans, financial aid.
Service Description: Academic, physical and social development of teens are promoted through sports, arts, clubs, computer training, tutoring, college preparation and SAT help. Dinner served nightly at no additional cost. 1:1 tutoring available.
Contact: Tabitha Gamonski, Teen Coordinator

Child Care Centers

Ages: 3 to 5
Population Served: Emotional Disability, Gifted, Health Impairment, Speech/Language Disability.
Program Hours: Mon-Fri, 8a.m.-6p.m.
Program Capacity: 148
Staff/Child Ratio: 1:8, 1:10
Fees: Headstart income guidelines (80 participants), ACD funded (68 participants)
Method of Payment: ACD fee agreement/ Voucher accepted.
Medication Administered: No
Transportation Provided: No
Wheelchair Accessible: No
Service Description: Comprehensive pre-school program. Curriculum includes literacy activities, pre-math skills, art, music, movement, field trips, outdoor play, and swimming.
Contact: Deborah Carroll, Director of Family Services

LIBERTY SCIENCE CENTER

Liberty State Park
Jersey City, NJ 07305

(201) 451-0006 Administrative
(201) 200-1000 Reservation Line
(201) 451-0006 [317] School Coordinator
(201) 451-0006 [417] School Coordinator

www.lsc.org

Deb Wanko, Groups and Tours

Services

Museums

Service Description: A hands-on experiential science education center. Will try to accommodate groups with special needs if they call ahead.

LIFESPIRE/ACRMD

345 Hudson St., 3rd Fl.
New York, NY 10014

(212) 741-0100 Administrative

www.lifespire.org

Art Rosa, Executive Director

Sites

1. LIFESPIRE - RECREATION PROGRAM
Jib Lanes, 67-19 Parsons Boulevard
Flushing, NY 11365

(718) 539-8091 Information

Gary Lewis, Recreation Coordinator

Services

SUNDAY EARLY BOWLING
Recreational Activities

Ages: 16 to 22
Population Served: Developmental Disability
Area Served: Queens
Program Hours: Sunday mornings
Program Capacity: 120
Fees: $1.00 per week dues
Service Description: Sunday Morning Bowling League provides socialization, recreation and exercise for the developmentally disabled in the borough of Queens.
Contact: Larry Hirsch
Sites: 1

LINCOLN CENTER FOR THE PERFORMING ARTS, INC.

70 Lincoln Center Plaza
New York, NY 10023

(212) 875-5375 Administrative
(212) 875-5414 FAX

Bobbi Wailes, Director, PSPD

Services

PROGRAMS AND SERVICES FOR PEOPLE WITH DISABILITIES
Music Performances
Theater Performances

Ages: 6 to 12
Area Served: All Boroughs
Fees: Call for information
Wheelchair Accessible: Yes
Service Description: Family weekend program provides an opportunity for children with disabilities, their parents and siblings to experience performances at Lincoln Center on Saturdays. The school program provides opportunities for children with disabilities to come to Lincoln Center during the school day to partake in direct contact and interaction with professional artists.
Contact: Bobbi Wailes, Director, PSPD

LINCOLN ROAD PLAYGROUND

c/o Prospect Park
95 Prospect Park West
Brooklyn, NY 11215

(718) 965-8999 Main Info Line
(718) 965-8951 Recording

www.prospectpark.org
info@prospectpark.org

Services

Parks/Recreation Areas

Population Served: All Disabilities
Area Served: All Boroughs
Wheelchair Accessible: Yes
Service Description: A playground that welcomes children with or without disabilities. Also has a reading playground equipped with a performing stage, dragon fountain, animal cutout figures, a children's village, and bronze sculptures.

LINDAMOOD-BELL LEARNING CENTER

153 Waverly Pl., 9th Fl.
New York, NY 10014

(212) 627-8576 Administrative
(212) 627-8561 FAX

www.lblp.com
lblpny@lblp.com

Liz Craynon, Ali Prigg, Clinic Directors

Services

Remedial Education

Ages: 5 to Adult
Population Served: Asperger Syndrome, Asthma, Attention Deficit Disorder (ADD/ADHD), Autism, Developmental Delay, Developmental Disability, Gifted, Learning Disability, Neurological Disability, Pervasive Developmental Disorder (PDD/NOS), Speech/Language Disability, Underachiever
Area Served: All Boroughs
Program Hours: Monday - Friday: 8:30 a.m.-5:30 p.m.
Program Capacity: 20
Staff/Child Ratio: 1:1
Fees: $89 per hour
Method of Payment: Credit Card, Check
Medication Administered: Yes, with permission.
Wheelchair Accessible: Yes
Service Description: A one on one learning center that fosters sensory cognitive processing. Students include those who are diagnosed with dyslexia, hyperlexia and comprehension issues.

LITERACY ASSISTANCE CENTER, INC.

84 William St., 14th Fl.
New York, NY 10038

(212) 803-3333 Referral Line
(212) 803-3300 Administrative
(212) 785-3685 FAX

www.lacnyc.org
lacinfo@lacnyc.org

Michael Hirschhorn, Executive Director
Languages Spoken: Chinese, Haitian Creole, Spanish

Services

English as a Second Language

Ages: All ages
Area Served: All Boroughs
Service Description: Provides training and technical assistance and support to literacy programs in New York City. The Referral Hotline provides over-the-phone information about basic education, English to speakers of other languages and GED preparation classes to adults and out-of-school youth.

LONG ISLAND CITY YMCA

32-23 Queens Blvd.
Long Island City, NY 11101

(718) 392-7932 Administrative
(718) 392-0544 FAX

www.ymcanyc.org
licymca@ymcanyc.org

Paul Mohabir, Executive Director

Services

Arts and Crafts Instruction
Field Trips/Excursions
Homework Help Programs
Sports, Individual
Sports, Team/Leagues
Swimming

Ages: 5 to 12
Area Served: Queens
Program Hours: Monday - Friday: 3-6 p.m.
Program Capacity: 60
Staff/Child Ratio: 1:10, varies based on age of child.
Fees: Full-time enrollment (4-5 days), $210 per month; Part-time enrollment (1-3 days), $150 per month.
Medication Administered: No
Transportation Provided: Yes, additional fee.
Wheelchair Accessible: Yes
Service Description: Offers various recreational and educational after school activities for school age children. Snack provided. Accepts children with disabilities on a case-by-case basis.
Contact: Renee Nikita, Site Coordinator

LONG ISLAND MUSEUM OF AMERICAN ART, HISTORY AND CARRIAGES

1200 Route 25A
Stony Brook, NY 11790

(631) 751-0066 [212] Administrative

www.longislandmuseum.org
educators@longislandmuseum.org

Services

Museums

Ages: 5 to 18
Area Served: All Boroughs
Program Hours: 1 to 1.5 hours
Fees: $4.50 per student. Fee may increase depending on specific program.
Wheelchair Accessible: Yes
Service Description: Children will learn about art through exploring the works of different

<continued...>

painters, and also through tours of the museum.

LUCILLE MURRAY CHILD DEVELOPMENT CENTER

296 E. 140th St.
Bronx, NY 10454

(718) 665-0780 Administrative
(718) 665-1188 FAX

Arlene Kelly, Executive Director
Languages Spoken: African, Albanian, Spanish

Services

Arts and Crafts Instruction
Homework Help Programs

Ages: 3 to 6
Population Served: Developmental Delay,
Developmental Disability, Down Syndrome, Learning
Disability, Speech/Language Disability
Area Served: All Boroughs
Program Hours: Call for information
Program Capacity: 20
Staff/Child Ratio: 3:20
Fees: ACD determines fees
Medication Administered: No
Wheelchair Accessible: Yes
Service Description: Early childhood center offering arts
and crafts and homework assistance.

LUCY MOSES SCHOOL FOR MUSIC AND DANCE

129 W. 67th St.
New York, NY 10023

(212) 501-3303 Administrative
(212) 874-7865 FAX

www.ekcc.org

Services

Acting Instruction
Arts and Crafts Instruction
Dancing Instruction
Music Instruction

Ages: 3 and up
Area Served: All Boroughs
Program Hours: Call for information
Program Capacity: Varies
Fees: $305 per half semester, $555-$625 per full year.
Service Description: Offers classes in visual and
performing arts. Children explore, ballet, jazz,
instrumental study, etc. Children with disabilities are
accepted on a case-by-case basis.

MAIMONIDES MEDICAL CENTER

4802 Tenth Ave. (48th St.)
Brooklyn, NY 11219

(718) 283-6000 Information
(718) 283-7500 Pediatrics

www.maimonidesmed.org

Steven Shelov, MD, Chairman of Pediatrics
Languages Spoken: Interpreters available

Services

Arts and Crafts Instruction
Homework Help Programs
Tutoring

Ages: 7 to 15
Population Served: All Disabilities
Area Served: Brooklyn
Program Hours: Call for information
Fees: Call for information
Wheelchair Accessible: Yes
Service Description: Offers an after school
program for clients of the hospital's Child and
Adolescent Outpatient Services and their
parents. Summer and weekend programs are
also offered. Call for further information.
Contact: Dr. Alan Hilfer, Program Director

MANHATTAN CENTER FOR LEARNING

590 West End Ave.
New York, NY 10024

(212) 787-5712 Administrative

Dr. Judith Baumrin, Executive Director

Services

Remedial Education

Ages: 5 to Adult
Population Served: Learning Disability
Area Served: All Boroughs
Fees: $500 - $1200 diagnostic; $75 per hour
Service Description: Provides
Neuropsychological testing and individual
remediation. Call for more information.

MANHATTAN VALLEY YOUTH PROGRAM

1047 Amsterdam Ave.
New York, NY 10025

(212) 222-2110 Administrative
(212) 220-4671 FAX

John Bess, Executive Director

< continued... >

Languages Spoken: Spanish

Services

Computer Classes
Tutoring
Youth Development

Ages: 7 to 18
Service Description: Manhattan Valley Youth Program provides GED Programs and Computer Classes. Tutoring is provided for children from Elementary through High School. A leadership program is also available. Children with disabilities are accepted on a case-by-case basis.

MARTIAL ARTS FOR THE DEAF

c/o Fukasa-Kai
PO Box 20619
New York, NY 10021-0072

(212) 737-2097 Voice/TDD

soke@fukasakai.com

Cary Nemeroff-Soke, President

Services

Sports, Individual

Ages: All Ages
Population Served: Deaf/Hard of Hearing
Area Served: All Boroughs
Wheelchair Accessible: Yes
Service Description: Offers the deaf and hard of hearing community martial arts seminars and class instruction in both sign language and voice. Presently held at three locations; the Sol Goldman Y at 344 E. 14th St.; the Jewish Community Center on Amsterdam/76th St., and LaGuardia Community College in Long Island City. If you would like to communicate through TDD, e-mail first so that arrangements can be made.

MARY MCDOWELL CENTER FOR LEARNING

20 Bergen St.
Brooklyn, NY 11201

(718) 625-3939 Administrative
(718) 625-1456 FAX

info@mmcl.net

Debbie Zlotowitz, Head of School

Services

Social Skills Training

Ages: 5 to 12
Population Served: Learning Disability
Area Served: All Boroughs
Program Hours: Tuesday and Thursday, call for hours

Fees: Call for information
Wheelchair Accessible: Yes
Service Description: The Center's approach is grounded in the Quaker values of respect for individuals, personal, and social responsibility, peaceful resolution of conflict, the importance of diversity and the value of service. Challenging and building on the strengths of each child, the Center cherishes the uniqueness of every student.

MCBURNEY YMCA

122 W. 17th St.
New York, Ny 10011

(212) 741-8725 Administrative
(212) 741-9702 FAX

www.ymca.org

Stan Holland, Executive Director
Languages Spoken: Spanish

Services

Arts and Crafts Instruction
Homework Help Programs
Recreational Activities
Sports, Team/Leagues

Ages: 5 to 12
Population Served: Learning Disability
Area Served: All Boroughs
Program Hours: Monday - Friday: 3-6 p.m. during school year
Program Capacity: 35
Staff/Child Ratio: 2:12
Fees: Member: $220 for 11 1/2 week session, 2 days per week
Non-Member: $240 for 11 1/2 week session, 2 days per week
Service Description: After school program provides a fun, safe and supervised environment. Children receive homework assistance and snacks and may participate in arts and crafts, games, sports, and so much more.
Contact: Angela Ford, Child Care Director

MENTORING PARTNERSHIP OF NEW YORK

Chanin Building
122 E. 42nd St., Suite 1520
New York, NY 10128

(800) 839-6884 Toll Free
(212) 953-0945 Administrative

www.mentoring.org

Kathryn Straub, Program Director

<continued...>

Services

Mentoring Programs

Service Description: Provides referrals to member organizations providing mentoring programs for youth.

MENTORING USA

113 E. 13th St.
New York, NY 10003

(212) 253-1194 Administrative
(212) 253-1267 FAX

www.mentoringusa.org
musa@mentoringusa.org

Deborah E. Lans, Executive Director

Services

Mentoring Programs

Ages: 5 to 14
Area Served: All Boroughs
Service Description: Links children in grades K through 8 with mentors; provides academic tutoring and mentoring to prevent school drop-out.

METROPOLITAN MUSEUM OF ART (THE)

1000 Fifth Ave.
New York, NY 10028

(212) 879-5500 [3561] Access Programs
(212) 650-2304 Discoveries Program
(212) 570-3782 FAX
(212) 570-3828 TDD

Languages Spoken: Sign Language

Services

Arts and Crafts Instruction
Museums

Ages: All Ages
Population Served: Deaf/Hard of Hearing, Developmental Disability, Physical/Orthopedic Disability, Visual Disability/Blind
Area Served: All Boroughs
Program Hours: Call for information
Program Capacity: Varies depending on program.
Fees: Vary depending on program.
Method of Payment: Cash, Check, Credit Card
Medication Administered: No
Transportation Provided: No
Wheelchair Accessible: Yes
Service Description: The Metropolitan Museum of Art offers a variety of programs and activities for children with special needs. Call the museum for a complete listing of programs, dates, hours and fees.

MIDWOOD DEVELOPMENT CORPORATION

1416 Ave. M
Brooklyn, NY 11210

(718) 376-0999 Administrative
(718) 382-6453 FAX

Linda Goodman, Executive Director
Languages Spoken: Sign Language, Spanish

Services

Arts and Crafts Instruction
Homework Help Programs
Recreational Activities
Sports, Team/Leagues

Ages: 8 to 22
Population Served: Developmental Delay, Developmental Disability, Down Syndrome, Learning Disability, Mental Retardation (mild-moderate)
Program Capacity: 100
Fees: $45/per month for transportation
Transportation Provided: Yes
Wheelchair Accessible: Yes
Service Description: Two after school programs for special education students: (1) homework, crafts, activities and evening recreation for young adults 16 and older, and (2) an after-school, evening and weekend program of recreation and socialization for children with developmental disabilities and deafness. Includes aerobic dancing, weight training, arts and crafts, team sports, homework assistance, vocational counseling, theme parties and games.
Contact: Liz Cazo, Youth Director

MORNINGSIDE CHILDREN'S CENTER

311 W. 120 St.
New York, NY 10027

(212) 864-0400 Administrative
(212) 665-2645 FAX

Rorry Scott, Director

Services

Homework Help Programs
Tutoring

Ages: 6 to 10
Area Served: All Boroughs
Fees: Call for information
Medication Administered: No
Wheelchair Accessible: Yes
Service Description: Provides an after school program including special activities, field trips, and homework help programs. Children with special needs are accepted on a case-by-case

< continued... >

basis. Call for more information.

MORRIS-JUMEL MANSION

65 Jumel Terrace
New York, NY 10032

(212) 923-8008 Administrative

Gregory Bynum, Director of Education

Services

Museums

MOUNT VERNON HOTEL MUSEUM AND GARDEN

421 E. 61st St.
New York, NY 10021

(212) 838-6878 Administrative
(212) 838-7390 FAX

mvhmedu@aol.com

Robin Sue Marcato, Public Relations Coordinator
Languages Spoken: French, Russian

Services

Museums

MUSEUM OF AMERICAN FINANCIAL HISTORY

28 Broadway
New York, NY 10004

(877) 983-4626 Toll Free
(212) 908-4519 Administrative
(212) 908-4601 FAX

www.financialhistory.org
mventrudo@financialhistory.org

Brian Thompson, Director

Services

Museums

Ages: 4 and up
Area Served: All Boroughs
Program Hours: Monday - Friday: 10 a.m.-4 p.m.
Program Capacity: 30 per group.
Fees: $50 per group.
Service Description: Narrated school group tours. School programs take approximately 45 minutes.

MUSEUM OF AMERICAN FOLK ART

Columbus Ave. and 66th St.
New York, NY

(212) 977-7298 Administrative

Susan Flamm

Services

Museums

MUSEUM OF JEWISH HERITAGE (THE)

18 First Place
Battery Park City
New York, NY 10004

(212) 509-6130 Information
(212) 945-0039 Tickets

www.mjhnyc.org

Services

Museums

MUSEUM OF MODERN ART

33rd Street @ Queens Blvd.
Long Island City, NY 11101

(212) 708-9864 Accessibility Programs
(212) 708-9400 Administrative
(212) 333-1118 FAX
(212) 247-1230 TTY

www.moma.org
specialneeds@moma.org

Leah Schroder, Accessibility Programs
Languages Spoken: Sign Language

Services

Museums

Area Served: All Boroughs
Wheelchair Accessible: Yes
Service Description: After-School Hours focuses on topics that introduce high school students to MoMA and other arts institutions. Each thematic program consists of three sessions led by a Museum educator. Recent programs included visits to the Studio Museum of Harlem, The Metropolitan Museum of Art, the Dia Center for the Arts, and Chelsea galleries.
Contact: Department of Education, 212-708-9805

MUSEUM OF TELEVISION & RADIO

25 W. 52nd St.
New York, NY 10019

(212) 621-6600 Administrative

www.mtr.org

Rebekah Fisk, Manager, School and Family Programs

Services

Museums

Ages: 5 to 12
Area Served: All Boroughs
Program Hours: Monday - Friday: 10 a.m.-12 Noon
Program Capacity: 35 per class.
Fees: $50 per group of 35 or less
Method of Payment: Cash or Check
Wheelchair Accessible: Yes
Service Description: Programs for school groups are conducted on a wide range of subjects relating to school curriculum and are accessible to children with special needs. Teachers should call in advance for class listings and to make reservations. Weekend programs for families are also accessible. There are daily screenings and exhibits, a radio listening room, and a wheelchair-accessible library where visitors may select programs to watch at a private viewing console.

MUSEUM OF THE CITY OF NEW YORK

1220 5th Ave. at 103rd St.
New York, NY 10029

(212) 534-1672 Administrative

www.mcny.org

DeJamea White, Education

Services

Museums

Ages: K-12
Area Served: All Boroughs
Fees: $2 per child; $3 per adult
Service Description: Groups visit three galleries with experienced docents, who focus on visual literacy strategies and New York City history. Tours are available in Spanish upon requests, and "please touch" activities may be arranged for the visually impaired.

MUSEUM OF THE MOVING IMAGE

3601 35 Ave.
Astoria, NY 11106

(718) 784-4520 Administrative
(718) 784-4681 FAX

www.ammi.org
info@ammi.org

Dawn Williams, Memberships/Visitor Services Coordinator

Services

Museums

MUSIC FOR LIVING CENTER FOR MUSIC THERAPY

175 Wolf Hill Road
Melville, NY 11747

(516) 850-8917 Administrative

John Carpente, MA, CMT, NRMT, Executive Director

Services

Music Therapy

Ages: 3 to 18
Population Served: Autism, Developmental Delay, Developmental Disability, Learning Disability, Mental Retardation (mild-moderate), Mental Retardation (severe-profound), Speech/Language Disability
Area Served: Long Island, Manhattan, Queens
Program Hours: Monday, Wednesday, Thursday: 12-7 p.m. Saturday: 9 a.m.-5 p.m.
Program Capacity: 15
Fees: Individual Sessions: $40 per session; Group Sessions: $25 per child per session
Method of Payment: Cash, Check, Credit Card, Money Order
Medication Administered: No
Transportation Provided: No
Wheelchair Accessible: Yes
Service Description: Participants are involved in musical activities selected to address specific clinical goals and appropriate to the maturity level of the group. Each musical composition or improvisation is designed to stimulate pleasurable and satisfying involvement; each individual is encouraged to participate to their fullest extent. Personal and social integration are among the goals of group therapy. Individual therapy sessions are also available.

MY FRIEND'S HOUSE OF DOUGLASTON, NEW YORK INC.

41-14 240th St.
Douglaston, NY 11363

(718) 631-8874 Administrative

Cecilia LaRock, Director

Services

Recreational Activities

Ages: 4.9 to 21
Population Served: Cerebral Palsy, Developmental Delay, Developmental Disability, Down Syndrome, Health Impairment, Learning Disability, Mental Retardation (mild-moderate), Mental Retardation (severe-profound), Multiple Disability, Neurological Disability, Physical/Orthopedic Disability, Seizure Disorder, Speech/Language Disability, Spina Bifida, Technology Supported
Fees: $350/10 sessions, $650/20 sessions
Wheelchair Accessible: Yes
Service Description: An inclusionary after school and weekend recreation program serving children with mental retardation and/or physical disabilities and their siblings. Sessions may include music, dance, arts, crafts, cooking, games, trips.

NATIONAL JEWISH COUNCIL FOR THE DISABLED

11 Broadway, 13th Fl.
New York, NY 10004

(212) 613-8229 Administrative
(212) 613-0796 FAX

www.ou.org
njcd@ou.org

Dr. Jeffrey Lichtman, Executive Director
Languages Spoken: Hebrew, Sign Language, Yiddish

Services

GOOD SPORTS ATHLETIC PROGRAM
Sports, Individual
Sports, Team/Leagues

Ages: 5 and up
Population Served: Autism, Deaf/Hard of Hearing, Mental Retardation (mild-severe), Neurological Disability, Seizure Disorders
Program Hours: Once a month, Sundays 10:00 a.m.- 1:00 p.m.
Fees: Call for information
Service Description: Athletic program for deaf children, under the guidance of a coach and interpreter. Separate gyms for boys and girls. Held at Edward Murrow High School, 1600 Ave. L, Brooklyn NY. Must be of Jewish religion. Call for more information.

Contact: Information, 212-613-8234

YACHAD FOR THE DEVELOPMENTALLY DISABLED
Recreational Activities

Ages: 5 and up
Population Served: All Disabilities, Attention Deficit Disorder (ADD/ADHD), Asperger Syndrome, Autism, Cerebral Palsy, Deaf/Hard of Hearing, Developmental Disability, Down Syndrome, Emotional Disability, Learning Disability, Mental Retardation (Mild-Moderate), Neurological Disability, Pervasive Developmental Disorder, Seizure Disorder, Tourette Syndrome, Traumatic Brain Injury.
Area Served: All Boroughs
Program Hours: Call for information
Fees: Call for information
Medication Administered: Yes
Transportation Provided: Yes
Wheelchair Accessible: Yes
Service Description: Provides social, educational and recreational "mainstreamed" programs for the developmentally disabled and deaf. Call for more information.

NATIONAL MUSEUM OF THE AMERICAN INDIAN

One Bowling Green
New York, NY 10004

(212) 514-3700 Information
(212) 514-3705 Group Reservation

www.nmai.si.edu

Russ Tall Chief, Public Affairs
Languages Spoken: Spanish

Services

Museums

Ages: K-12
Area Served: All Boroughs
Wheelchair Accessible: Yes
Service Description: Provides activity based educational programs that interpret the museum's exhibition. Native American staff members guide and direct teachers and chaperones as they lead students through hands-on learning experiences. All reservations must be made in advance. Museum will make accomodations for children with special needs. Please call ahead.

NATIONAL THEATER WORKSHOP OF THE HANDICAPPED

354 Broome St., Suite 5F
New York, NY 10013

(212) 941-9511 Administrative

www.ntwh.org
ntwh@aol.com

Services

Acting Instruction
Dancing Instruction
Music Instruction
Theater Performances

Ages: 5 to 13
Population Served: Asthma, Cardiac Disorder, Cerebral Palsy, Deaf-Blind, Deaf/Hard of Hearing, Diabetes, Physical/Orthopedic Disability, Seizure Disorder, Speech/Language Disability, Spina Bifida, Traumatic Brain Injury, Visual Disability/Blind
Area Served: All Boroughs
Program Hours: Call for times.
Program Capacity: 24
Staff/Child Ratio: 1:4 or 1:5
Fees: $100 but generous scholarships available
Wheelchair Accessible: Yes
Service Description: Theater program for young children with physical disabilities . This workshop is designed to provide children with a supportive atmosphere in which they are free to discover theatre, music and movement. Through monologues, songs, relaxation and movement exercises, children will have the opportunity to become comfortable in front of an audience and have an outlet to explore their creativity.
Contact: Laura Cline, Director of Children's Programs, New York

NATIONAL THEATRE OF THE DEAF

55 Van Dyke Ave., Suite 312
Hartford, CT 06106

(800) 300-5179 Toll Free
(860) 724-5179 Administrative
(860) 550-7974 FAX
(860) 724-5179 TDD

www.ntd.org
info@ntd.org

Jerry Goehring, Executive Director
Languages Spoken: American Sign Language

Services

Theater Performances

NEIGHBORHOOD CARE TEAM

111-54 Merrick Blvd.
St. Albans, NY 11433

(718) 739-3000 Administrative
(718) 739-3054 FAX

ncareteam@aol.com

Carrie Johnson, Executive Director
Languages Spoken: French, German, Spanish

Services

Computer Classes
Homework Help Programs
Respite, Children's Out-of-Home

Ages: 5 to 14
Population Served: At-Risk, Attention Deficit Disorder (ADD/ADHD), Emotional Disability, Learning Disability, Pervasive Developmental Disorder (PDD/NOS), Speech/Language Disability
Area Served: Queens
Program Hours: Monday - Friday: 3:30-6:30 p.m.
Program Capacity: 20
Staff/Child Ratio: 1:10
Fees: None
Medication Administered: Yes
Transportation Provided: No
Wheelchair Accessible: No
Service Description: Provides an after school program with various recreational and educational activities.

NEIGHBORHOOD SERVICE AND DEVELOPMENT AGENCY

2913 Glenwood Road
Brooklyn, NY 11210

(718) 421-0650 Administrative

Dr. Emil D. De Loache, Director
Languages Spoken: French/Creole, Spanish

Services

Arts and Crafts Instruction
Music Instruction

Ages: 5 to 12
Area Served: Brooklyn
Program Capacity: 35
Fees: $83 per week
Method of Payment: Payment Plan
Medication Administered: Yes
Service Description: A summer camp and year-round after school program that will include

<continued...>

children with special needs. The children enjoy music, art and sports.

NETWORKING PROJECT FOR YOUNG ADULTS WITH DISABILITIES

610 Lexington Ave.
New York, NY 10022

(212) 735-9766 Administrative
(212) 223-6438 FAX
(212) 735-9767 TDD

Suzy Blumenthal, Executive Director

Services

Mentoring Programs

Ages: 13 to 21
Population Served: Cerebral Palsy, Deaf/Hard of Hearing, Developmental Disability, Learning Disability, Neurological Disability, Physical/Orthopedic Disability, Speech/Language Disability, Spina Bifida, Visual Disability/Blind
Area Served: All Boroughs
Program Hours: Sundays: 12-2 p.m.
Fees: None
Transportation Provided: Yes
Wheelchair Accessible: Yes
Service Description: The Networking Project is a mentoring and empowerment program for young adults with physical and/or sensory disabilities. The program provides advocacy training, other pre-employment activities including transportation skills for teenagers with physical and sensory disabilities including cerebral palsy, spina bifida and neurological impairments. Eligibility determined through an interview.

NEVINS DAY CARE CENTER, INC.

460 Atlantic Ave.
Brooklyn, NY 11217

(718) 855-2621 Administrative
(718) 855-2560 FAX

Gloria Armstrong, Director

Services

Arts and Crafts Instruction
Child Care Centers
Field Trips/Excursions
Film Presentations
Homework Help Programs

Ages: 6 to 12
Area Served: All Boroughs
Program Hours: Monday - Friday: 3-6 p.m.; full day during the summer and holidays.
Program Capacity: 50

Staff/Child Ratio: 2:25
Fees: Sliding Scale
Medication Administered: No
Transportation Provided: No
Wheelchair Accessible: Yes
Service Description: Provides after school, summer and holiday programs for children. Children with special needs are considered on a case-by-case basis.

NEW ALTERNATIVES FOR CHILDREN

37 W. 26th St., 6th Fl.
New York, NY 10010

(212) 696-1550 Administrative
(212) 696-1602 FAX
(212) 696-1550 TDD

NACAG@aol.com

Dr. Arlene Goldsmith, Executive Director
Languages Spoken: Arabic, Italian, Japanese, Sign Language, Spanish

Services

FOSTER CARE AND ADOPTION
Creative Writing
Equestrian Therapy
Homework Help Programs
Mentoring Programs
Photography Exhibits
Respite, Children's Out-of-Home
Sports, Individual
Sports, Team/Leagues
Swimming

Ages: Birth to 21
Program Hours: Monday-Thursday: 8:45 a.m.-8 p.m.; Friday: 8:45 a.m.-5:30 p.m.; Saturday: 9 a.m.-5 p.m.
Program Capacity: 140 Children
Fees: None
Transportation Provided: Yes
Contact: Mary Moe, Director , Foster Care and Adoption

NEW DIRECTIONS

5276 Hollister Ave., #207
Santa Barbara, CA 93111

(888) 967-2841 Toll Free
(805) 964-7344 FAX

www.newdirectionstravel.com
newdirec@silcom.com

Dee Duncan, Director

< continued... >

Services

Travel

Ages: 7 and up
Population Served: Autism, Cerebral Palsy, Down Syndrome, Emotional Disability, Mental Retardation (mild-moderate), Mental Retardation (severe-profound), Visual Disability/Blind
Program Capacity: 500
Staff/Child Ratio: 1:4; 1:1 available for special assistance as needed
Fees: According to tour
Transportation Provided: Yes
Wheelchair Accessible: Yes
Service Description: Takes people with physical, emotional and developmental disabilities on tour all over the world all year round. Holiday tours available. Bike tours, tours to cities and resorts throughout the United States and abroad. Twenty-four hour supervision is given. Special attention, such as feeding, oxygen, or dialysis available. New Directions runs an international educational exchange for people with disabilities and has participated with people in Mexico, Italy and Israel.

NEW MUSEUM OF CONTEMPORARY ARTS

583 Broadway
New York, NY 10012

(212) 219-1222 Administrative
(212) 431-5328 FAX

www.newmuseum.org
newmu@newmuseum.org

Ann Barlow, Director of Education

Services

Museums

NEW VICTORY THEATRE

229 W. 42nd St., 10th Fl.
New York, NY 10036

(646) 223-3020 Administrative
(646) 223-3090 Education
(212) 882-8550 Hands On
(646) 562-0175 FAX

Edie Demas, Director of Education

Services

Theater Performances

Service Description: A perfroming arts institution devoted to programming for youth and families. Offers public performances as well as School Time matinees for school groups. Hands On provides select sign

interpreted performances of each production. Assistive listening devices are also available. Wheelchair accessible seating must be ordered in advance, and is subject to availability.

NEW YORK AQUARIUM

Boardwalk and W. 8th St.
Brooklyn, NY 11224

(718) 265-3448 Education
(718) 265-3474 Administrative
(718) 265-3451 FAX

www.nyaquarium.com

Louis Garibaldi, Director

Services

Arts and Crafts Instruction
Storytelling
Zoos/Wildlife Parks

Ages: All Ages
Population Served: All Disabilities
Area Served: All Boroughs
Program Hours: Dates and hours vary depending on program.
Fees: Fees vary depending on programs.
Method of Payment: Cash, Check, Credit Card, Money Order
Medication Administered: No
Transportation Provided: No
Wheelchair Accessible: Yes
Service Description: The New York Aquarium provides a variety of programs and activities for children of all ages and their parents. Children with special needs can be accommodated.

NEW YORK BOTANICAL GARDEN

Southern Blvd. and 200th St.
Bronx, NY 10458

(718) 817-8700 Administrative

www.nybg.org

Services

Parks/Recreation Areas

Ages: 5 to 12
Area Served: All Boroughs
Program Hours: Tuesday - Sunday: 1 p.m.-5 p.m.
Fees: Free on Wednesday, call for regular fees.
Service Description: Semester-long after school program located in the Hunts Point section of the South Bronx. This culminates in weekend "field experiences" for the participating children and their families. Most events are on a drop-in basis.

< continued... >

Will accept children with disabilities.
Contact: Ellen McArthy

NEW YORK CITY ADMINISTRATION FOR CHILDREN'S SERVICES - AGENCY FOR CHILD DEVELOPMENT

150 William St., 18th Fl.
New York, NY 10038

(800) 342-3720 Child Abuse Report
(212) 676-9421 Parents' and Children's Rights
(212) 676-7055 Administrative
(212) 676-9034 FAX

www.kidsnyc.org

William C. Bell, Commissioner
Languages Spoken: Spanish

Sites

1. AGENCY FOR CHILD DEVELOPMENT
66 John St., 8th Fl
New York, NY 10038

(212) 361-6200 Child Care Helpline
(718) 367-5437 Administrative

www.kidsnyc.org

Penny Schneier, Acting Director, Bureau of Program Dev.

2. AGENCY FOR CHILD DEVELOPMENT - BRONX
400 E. 145th St., 2nd Fl.
Bronx, NY 10452

(718) 367-5437 Child Care Helpline
(718) 401-2036 Administrative
(718) 401-2035 Administrative
(718) 401-2034 Administrative

Rosemary Kennedy, Resource Area Director

3. AGENCY FOR CHILD DEVELOPMENT - BROOKLYN/STATEN
151 Lawrence St., 3rd Fl.
Brooklyn, NY 11201

(718) 367-5437 Child Care Helpline
(718) 488-5280 Administrative
(718) 488-5279 Administrative
(718) 488-5278 Administrative

Anita Folkerth, Resource Area Director

4. AGENCY FOR CHILD DEVELOPMENT - MANHATTAN
109 E. 16th St., 5th Fl.
New York, NY 10003

(718) 367-5437 Child Care Helpline
(212) 835-7718 Administrative
(212) 835-7715 Administrative

Elise Moses, Resource Area Director

5. AGENCY FOR CHILD DEVELOPMENT - QUEENS
90-75 Sutphin Blvd., 5th Fl.
Jamaica, NY 11435

(718) 367-5437 Child Care Helpline
(718) 523-6872 Administrative
(718) 523-6826 Administrative
(718) 523-6799 FAX

Virginia Heyward, Resource Area Director

Services

Child Care Resource and Referral
Area Served: All Boroughs
Service Description: Provides information and referral for parents and caregivers seeking child care for children with or without special needs in New York City.
Sites: 1 2 3 4 5

NEW YORK CITY DEPARTMENT OF HEALTH

125 Worth St.
New York, NY 10013

(800) 825-5448 Central Information and Referral

www.nycdoh.org

Thomas Frieden, M.D., M.P.H, Commissioner
Languages Spoken: Spanish

Services

BUREAU OF DAY CARE
Child Care Resource and Referral

Service Description: The Bureau of Day Care is the licensing and monitoring unit for child care; information on registered family day care providers; licensed infant, toddler and preschool group family day care; licensed child day care centers; nursery school and school-aged child care.

NEW YORK CITY DEPARTMENT OF YOUTH AND COMMUNITY DEVELOPMENT

156 William St., 3rd Fl
New York, NY 10038

(800) 246-4646 YOUTHLINE
(212) 788-5677 Administrative
(212) 227-7007 FAX
(800) 246-4699 TDD

www.nycyouthline.com

< continued... >

Jeanne B. Mullgrav, Commissioner

<u>Sites</u>

1. NEW YORK CITY DEPARTMENT OF YOUTH AND COMMUNITY DEVELOPMENT - BEACON PROGRAMS
156 William St., 4th Fl.
New York, NY 10038-2609

(212) 676-8255 Administrative

Christopher Darwin, Beacon Coordinator

<u>Services</u>

BEACON PROGRAMS
Homework Help Programs
Recreational Activities

Service Description: Offers youth the opportunity to develop a sense of social connection through participation in positive group activities ranging from sports and drama groups to entrepreneurial training and community service. A variety of after school and summer programs are offered. The Department funds many community based organizations to provide after school programs.

BRONX BEACONS

C.E.S. 11
MOSAIC
1257 Ogden Avenue
Bronx, NY 10452
718-590-0101

C.I.S. 117
ACPD Choices and Community Beacon
1865 Morris Avenue
Bronx, NY 10453
718-466-1806

C.I.S. 148
Beacon Center 148
3630 Third Avenue, Rm. 227
Bronx, NY 10456
718-293-5454

I.S. 200 (CS 214)
Beacon Program, Rm. 146
1970 West Farms Road
Bronx, NY 10460
718-991-6338

M.S. 201
Beacon Extended Hours
Weekend Program
730 Bryant Avenue
Bronx, NY 10474
718-542-6850

I.S. 116
SISDA Beacon
977 Fox Street

Bronx, NY 10459
718-589-6509

I.S. 139 (MOTT HAVEN)
Project B.E.A.M.
345 Brook Avenue, Rm. 109
Bronx, NY 10454
718-585-3353

I.S. 192
650 Hollywood Avenue
Bronx, NY 10456
718-239-4080

M.S. 45
Community Beacon M.S. 45
2502 Lorillard Place
Bronx, NY 10458
718-367-9577

M.S. 80
149 East Mosholu Parkway
Bronx, NY 10467
718-882-5929

M.S. 113
Beacons III
3710 Barnes Avenue
Bronx, NY 10467
718-654-5881

P.S. 86 (Kingsbridge)
2756 Reservoir Avenue
Bronx, NY 10468
718-563-7410

BROOKLYN BEACONS

GRAND STREET CAMPUS H.S.
850 Grand Street
Brooklyn, NY 11211
718-387-2800, ext. 313

I.S. 35
Extended Day, Family Center & Enrichment
272 Macdonough Street
Brooklyn, NY 11233
718-453-7004

I.S. 68
956 East 82nd Street
Brooklyn, NY 11236
718-241-2555

I.S. 96
Seth Low J.H.S.
99 Avenue P
Brooklyn, NY 11204
718-232-2266

I.S. 111 Beacon (I.S. 347-349)
35 Starr Street

< continued... >

Brooklyn, NY 11221
718-366-7821

I.S. 218
370 Fountain Avenue
Brooklyn, NY 11208
718-277-1928

I.S. 220
Pershing Beacon
4812 9th Avenue, Rm. 252
Brooklyn, NY 11220
718-436-5270

I.S. 232
Winthrop Beacon Community Center
905 Winthrop Street
Brooklyn, NY 11203
718-221-8880

I.S. 259
McKinley
7301 Ft. Hamilton Parkway
Brooklyn, NY 11228
718-836-3620

I.S. 271
1137 Herkimer Street
Brooklyn, NY 11233
718-345-5904

I.S. 285
5909 Beverly Road, Rm. 107
Brooklyn, NY 11203
718-629-9188

I.S. 291
231 Palmetto Street
Brooklyn, NY 11221
718-574 3288

I.S. 296
Ridgewood Bushwick Beacon
125 Covert Street, Rm. 149B
Brooklyn, NY 11207
718-919-4453

I.S. 302
Cypress Hills East New York Beacon
350 Linwood Street
Brooklyn, NY 11208
718-277-3522

J.H.S. 50
El Puente Community Center
183 South Third Street
Brooklyn, NY 11211
718-486-3936/48

J.H.S. 126
424 Leonard Street, Rm.105
Brooklyn, NY 11222

718-388-5546

J.H.S. 166
School Based Community
Restoration Center
800 Van Sicklen Avenue
Brooklyn, NY 11207
718-257-7003

I.S. 263
Educators for Children, Youth & Families
210 Chester Street
Brooklyn, NY 11212
718-498-7030

J.H.S. 265
101 Park Avenue
Brooklyn, NY 11205
718-694-0601

J.H.S. 275
PAL Brownsville Beacon
School Based Community
985 Rockaway Avenue, Room 111
Brooklyn, NY 11212
718-485-2719

M.S. 2 (FLATBUSH)
Beacon II at I.S. 2
655 Parkside Avenue
Brooklyn, NY 11226
718-826-2889

M.S. 136
Dewey M.S. 136 Beacon
4004 4th Ave
Brooklyn, NY 11232
718-788-4972

P.S. 15
Red Hook Community Center
71 Sullivan Street
Brooklyn, NY 11231
718-422-1900, ext. 32

P.S. 138
801 Park Pl.
Brooklyn, NY 11217
718-735-9380

P.S. 269
Beacon Center
1957 Nostrand Avenue
Brooklyn, NY 11210
718-462-2597

P.S. 288
Surfside Beacon School
2959 West 25th Street
Brooklyn, NY 11224
718-714-0103

< continued... >

P.S. 314
Center for Family Life
330 59th Street
Brooklyn, NY 11220
718-439-5986

MANHATTAN BEACONS

I.S. 70
333 West 17th Street
New York, NY 10011
212-243-7574

I.S. 88
Beacon at Wadleigh
215 West 114th Street
New York, NY 10026
212-932-7895

I.S. 118
154 West 93rd Street
New York, NY 10025
212-866-0009

I.S. 131
Beacon Center
100 Hester Street
New York, NY 10002
212-219-8393

I.S. 195
Beacon School
625 West 133rd Street
New York, NY 10027
212-368-1827, 1622

I.S. 217
645 Main Street
Roosevelt Island, NY 10044
212-527-2505

J.H.S. 22
Highroad
111 Columbia Street
New York, NY 10002
212-505-6338

J.H.S. 45
EHCCI/El Faro Beacon
2351 First Avenue, Rm. 154
New York, NY 10035
212-410-4227, ext. 226

J.H.S. 60
University Settlement Beacon
420 East 12th Street
New York, NY 10009
212-598-4533

J.H.S. 99
La Isla De Barrio Beacon

410 East 100th Street
New York, NY 10029
212-987-8743

J.H.S. 143
La Plaza Community Center
515 West 182nd Street
New York, NY 10030
212-928-4992

M.S. 54
Booker T. Washington Community Center
103 West 107th Street
New York, NY 10025
212-866-5579

P.S. 194
Countee Cullen Community Center
242 West 144th Street
New York, NY 10030
212-234-4500

P.S. 198
1700 Third Avenue
New York, NY 10028
212-628-6342

J.H.S. 164
401 West 164th Street
New York, NY 10032
212-927-7251

MARTA VALLE H.S.
145 Stanton St.
New York, NY 10002
212-505-5660

QUEENS BEACONS

I.S. 5
50-40 Jacobus Street
Flushing, NY 11373
718-429-8752

I.S. 10
45-11 31st Avenue
Astoria, NY 11103
718-777-9202

I.S. 43
160 Beach 29th Street
Far Rockaway, NY 11691
718-471-7875

I.S. 72
133-25 Guy R. Brewer Blvd.
Jamaica, NY 11434
718-276-7728

I.S. 93
Greater Ridgewood Youth Council
66-56 Forest Avenue

< continued... >

Ridgewood, NY 11385
718-628-8702, ext.23

I.S. 168
158-40 76th Road
Flushing, NY 11366
718-820-0760

J.H.S. 8
New Preparatory School for Technology
108-35 167th Street
Jamaica, NY 11433
718-523-7338

J.H.S. 141
37-11 21st Avenue
Astoria, NY 11105
718-777-9200

J.H.S. 189
Flushing Y Beacon Center
144-80 Barclay Avenue
Flushing, NY 11355
718-961-6014

J.H.S. 190
Forest Hills Community House
68-17 Austin Street
Flushing, NY 11375
718-830-5233

J.H.S. 194
Beacon Center
154-60 17th Avenue
Whitestone, NY 11355
718-747-3644

J.H.S. 198
Rev. Thomas Mason
Community Center
365 Beach 56th Street
Arverne, NY 11692
718-945-7845

J.H.S. 204
Street Outreach /
Youth Enhancement
36-41 28th Street
LIC, NY 11106
718-433-1989

I.S. 210
93-11 101st Avenue
Ozone Park, NY 11416
718-659-7710

J.H.S. 216
64-20 175th Street
Fresh Meadows, NY 11365
718-445-6983

J.H.S. 226

Beacons School III
121-10 Rockaway Blvd.
South Ozone Park, NY 11420
718-848-2890

J.H.S. 231
Beacon III
145-00 Springfield Blvd.
Springfield Gardens, NY 11413
718-528-1743

M.S. 158
Beacon Program
46-35 Oceania Street
Bayside, NY 11364
718-423-2266

M.S. 172
81-14 257th Street
Floral Park, NY 11004
718-347-3279

P.S. 176
120-45 235th St.
Cambria Heights, NY 11411
718-902-7813

P.S. 19 (CORONA)
Coalition for Culture
4032 99th Street
Corona, NY 11368
718-651-4656

P.S. 149
93-11 34th Avenue
Jackson Heights, NY 11372
718-426-0888

STATEN ISLAND BEACONS

I.S. 2
33 Midland Avenue
Staten Island, NY 10306
718-668-9176

I.S. 49
101 Warren Street, B-33
Staten Island, NY 10304
718-556-1565

P.S. 18
School Based Multi-Services
Community Center
221 Broadway
Staten Island, NY 10310
718-448-4834

TOTTENVILLE H.S.
100 Luten Avenue
Staten Island, NY 10312
718-984-9225

< continued... >

Sites: 1

NEW YORK CITY FIRE DEPARTMENT MUSEUM

278 Spring St.
New York, NY 10013

(212) 691-1303 Administrative
(212) 924-0430 FAX

www.nycfiremuseum.org

Steve Arkin, Director

Services

Museums

Ages: 5 and up
Area Served: All Boroughs
Program Hours: Tuesday - Friday: 10 a.m.-12 p.m.
Program Capacity: 35
Fees: $3 per child.
Wheelchair Accessible: Yes
Service Description: Museum provides organized tours for groups consisting of a minimum of 10 individuals and a recommended maximum of 35. One adult leader is admitted free of charge for every 10 children. Programs are on fire safety and burn prevention. Will accomodate children with special needs.

NEW YORK CITY MISSION SOCIETY

105 E. 22nd St.
New York, NY 10010

(212) 674-3500 Administrative
(212) 979-5764 FAX

Maria Orengo, Associate Executive Director, Planning
Languages Spoken: Spanish

Sites

1. NEW YORK CITY MISSION SOCIETY
105 E. 22nd St.
New York, NY 10010

(212) 674-3500 Administrative
(212) 979-5764 FAX

Maria Orengo, Associate Executive Director, Planning

2. NEW YORK CITY MISSION SOCIETY - MINISINK TOWNHOUSE
646 Malcolm X Blvd.
New York, NY 10037

(212) 368-8400 Administrative
(212) 926-4431 FAX

Kimberley Hayes, Director

Services

Homework Help Programs
Recreational Activities
Tutoring

Ages: 11 to 14; 14 to 18
Area Served: All Boroughs
Program Hours: Monday - Friday 3-7 p.m.
Program Capacity: 11 to 14 years old, 70; 14 to 18 years old, 100
Staff/Child Ratio: 1:9 to 1:17
Fees: None
Service Description: Offers college preparation, SAT preparation, tutoring, homework help and recreational games. Some extended and weekend hours. Children with special needs are accepted on a case-by-case basis.
Contact: Tracey Gardner
Sites: 2

TEAM ROC
Sports, Team/Leagues
Youth Development

Ages: 5 and up
Population Served: At-Risk
Area Served: All Boroughs
Wheelchair Accessible: Yes
Service Description: Organized basketball teams are used as a platform from which at-risk youth are taught effective life and leadership skills.
Sites: 1 2

NEW YORK FAMILIES FOR AUTISTIC CHILDREN, INC.

95-16 Pitkin Ave.
Ozone Park, NY 11417

(718) 641-3441 Administrative
(718) 641-4452 FAX

www.nyfac.org

Andrew Baumann, President
Languages Spoken: Spanish

Services

Arts and Crafts Instruction
Dancing Instruction
Equestrian Therapy
Recreational Activities
Sports, Individual
Sports, Team/Leagues
Swimming

Population Served: Autism, Developmental Disability
Area Served: Queens
Program Hours: Weekends. Call for information

<continued...>

Fees: Call for information
Medication Administered: No
Transportation Provided: No
Service Description: All recreational programming except swimming are fully integrated community based programs. Children are paired or play with their typically developing peers. Activities are supervised by parents and guided by professionals in that recreational area. Programs are not designed to be respite. All programs require family participation.

NEW YORK HALL OF SCIENCE

47-01 111th St.
Flushing Meadows, NY 11368

(718) 699-0005 Administrative
(718) 699-0005 [349] Education Department
(718) 699-1341 FAX

www.nyhallsci.org

Jan Rosensky, Manager, Visitor Services & Volunteers
Languages Spoken: American Sign Language, Arabic, German, Hebrew, Hindi, Italian, Russian, Spanish

Services

Museums

Ages: All ages
Population Served: All Disabilities
Area Served: All Boroughs
Wheelchair Accessible: Yes
Service Description: Educational programs available to groups on weekdays. Workshops are available for the general public on weekends. Programs can be modified to meet special needs. Please call in advance for details and reservations.
Contact: Sylvia Perez, Manager of Public Programs

NEW YORK SERVICES FOR THE HANDICAPPED

853 Broadway, Suite 605
New York, NY 10003

(212) 533-4020 Administrative
(212) 533-4023 FAX

nysh@aol.com

Marvin A. Raps, Executive Director
Languages Spoken: Spanish

Services

Respite, Children's Out-of-Home

Ages: 8 to Adult
Population Served: Cerebral Palsy, Developmental Disability, Neurological Disability, Physical/Orthopedic Disability, Spina Bifida, Traumatic Brain Injury (TBI)

Area Served: All Boroughs
Wheelchair Accessible: Yes
Service Description: An out-of-home respite program for children who are physically disabled, mentally alert and living with their parents or caregivers. The program is held at Camp Oakhurst in Monmouth Co., N.J. in winterized facilities. The children have an active recreational program indoors and out, depending on the time of year. Independence involving self-care and decision-making are stressed. The sessions are planned around school holidays.

NEW YORK STATE OFFICE OF PARKS, RECREATION AND HISTORIC PRESERVATION - NEW YORK CITY REGIONAL OFFICE

c/o Riverbank State Park
675 Riverside Dr.
New York, NY 10031

(212) 694-3722 Administrative
(212) 694-3741 FAX

www.nysparks.com

James Moogan, Assistant Deputy Commissioner
Languages Spoken: Spanish

Sites

1. NEW YORK STATE OFFICE OF PARKS, RECREATION AND HISTORIC PRESERVATION - NEW YORK CITY REGIONAL OFFICE

c/o Riverbank State Park
675 Riverside Dr.
New York, NY 10031

(212) 694-3722 Administrative

www.nysparks.com

Jim Moogan, Assistant Deputy Commissioner

2. NEW YORK STATE OFFICE OF PARKS, RECREATION AND HISTORIC PRESERVATION - BAYWATER POINT STATE PARK

1479 Point Breeze Pl.
Far Rockaway, NY 11691

(212) 694-3722 Administrative

3. NEW YORK STATE OFFICE OF PARKS, RECREATION AND HISTORIC PRESERVATION - CLAY PIT PONDS PRESERVE

83 Nielsen Ave.
Staten Island, NY 10309

(718) 967-1976 Administrative

<continued...>

4. NEW YORK STATE OFFICE OF PARKS, RECREATION AND HISTORIC PRESERVATION - EMPIRE-FULTON FERRY STATE PARK

26 New Dock St.
Brooklyn, NY 11201

(718) 858-4708 Administrative

5. NEW YORK STATE OFFICE OF PARKS, RECREATION AND HISTORIC PRESERVATION - RIVERBANK STATE PARK

679 Riverside Dr.
New York, NY 10031

(212) 694-3607 Administrative

6. NEW YORK STATE OFFICE OF PARKS, RECREATION AND HISTORIC PRESERVATION - ROBERTO CLEMENTE STATE PARK

W. Tremont and Mattewson Rd.
Bronx, NY 10453

(718) 299-8750 Administrative

7. NEW YORK STATE OFFICE OF PARKS, RECREATION AND HISTORIC PRESERVATION - GANTRY PLAZA STATE PARK

49th Ave. and E. River
Long Island City, NY 11101

(212) 694-3724 Administrative
(718) 786-6385 Administrative

<u>Services</u>

Parks/Recreation Areas
Sports, Individual
Sports, Team/Leagues

Area Served: All Boroughs
Service Description: Sponsors the Empire State Summer and Winter Games (amateur athletic competition) and the Empire State Games for the Physically Challenged (athletic programs for youth with disabilities). Holds concerts, arts program, fairs and festivals, sports and athletics for people of all ages and abilities in the state parks located in New York City.
Sites: 1 2 3 4 5 6 7

NEW YORK STATE PARKS GAMES FOR THE PHYSICALLY CHALLENGED

Belmont Lake State Park, PO Box 247
Babylon, NY 11720

(631) 669-1000 [295] Administrative

Pam Maryjanowski, Games Coordinator

<u>Services</u>

Sports, Individual
Sports, Team/Leagues

Ages: 5 to 21
Population Served: Cerebral Palsy, Deaf/Hard of Hearing, Physical/Orthopedic Disability, Visual Disability/Blind
Area Served: New York State
Wheelchair Accessible: Yes
Service Description: Offers a free program of competition in track, field, slalom, swimming, archery and table tennis events. Workshops, with instruction by Adapted Physical Education coaches and physically challenged athletes are available. No experience is necessary to enter competition.

NICHOLAS CARDELL DAY CARE CENTER

84 Vermilyea Ave.
New York, NY 10034

(212) 942-6757 Administrative
(212) 942-6792 FAX

Norma So, Executive Director

<u>Services</u>

Child Care Centers

Ages: 2.5 to 5
Population Served: Speech/Language Disability
Area Served: Manhattan
Program Hours: Monday - Friday: 8 a.m.-6 p.m.
Program Capacity: 20
Staff/Child Ratio: 4:20
Fees: None
Medication Administered: No
Transportation Provided: No
Wheelchair Accessible: No
Service Description: A day care program where emphasis is placed on the refinement of motor skills.

NORDOFF-ROBBINS CENTER FOR MUSIC THERAPY

82 Washington Square E., 4th Fl.
New York, NY 10003

(212) 998-5151 Administrative

Kenneth Aigen, Alan Turry, Co-Directors

< continued... >

Services

Music Therapy

Ages: All Ages
Population Served: All Disabilities
Area Served: All Boroughs
Wheelchair Accessible: Yes
Service Description: Offers a music therapy program for children, teenagers and adults with special needs. Live music with client involvement at all levels is available to children with any disability. Improvisational approach brings flexibility of music to the service of the individual. Thorough documentation and close parent contact is essential to the program. Call for more information.

NORTH BRONX FAMILY SERVICE CENTER

2190 University Ave.
Bronx, NY 10453

(718) 365-1400 Administrative
(718) 365-1411 FAX

Diana Torres, Program Director, Youth & Family Support
Languages Spoken: Spanish

Services

Arts and Crafts Instruction
Computer Classes
English as a Second Language
Homework Help Programs
Tutoring

Ages: 6 to 12
Population Served: Asthma, Attention Deficit Disorder (ADD/ADHD), Autism, Cerebral Palsy, Developmental Delay, Developmental Disability, Diabetes, Learning Disability, Multiple Disability, Sickle Cell Anemia, Spina Bifida
Area Served: All Boroughs
Program Hours: Monday - Friday: 3-6 p.m.
Program Capacity: 150
Staff/Child Ratio: 1:6
Fees: $70 per week, tutoring $10 per week.
Wheelchair Accessible: Yes
Service Description: Provides after school recreational and educational activities for children.
Contact: Mr. Irving, Child Program Director, 718-365-7755

NORTH BROOKLYN YMCA

570 Jamaica Ave.
Brooklyn, NY 11208

(718) 277-1600 Administrative
(718) 277-2081 FAX

Cid Rivera Jr., Executive Director

Services

Arts and Crafts Instruction
Creative Writing
Dancing Instruction
Homework Help Programs
Recreational Activities
Sports, Team/Leagues
Swimming
Tutoring

Ages: 5 to 12
Population Served: Deaf/Hard of Hearing, Gifted, Learning Disability,
Area Served: Brooklyn, Queens
Program Capacity: 40
Staff/Child Ratio: 1:6
Fees: $70 per week, $10 per person
Transportation Provided: Yes
Service Description: Offers various after school educational and recreational actitivies including 1:1 tutoring.

NORTHSIDE CENTER FOR CHILD DEVELOPMENT

35 E. 110th St.
New York, NY 10029

(212) 426-3400 Administrative
(212) 410-7561 FAX - Clinic
(212) 426-8976 FAX - TECC

Thelma Dye, Ph.D., Executive Director
Languages Spoken: Spanish

Services

SATURDAY RECREATION PROGRAM
Child Care Centers
Computer Classes
Field Trips/Excursions
Homework Help Programs
Mentoring Programs
Sports, Team/Leagues
Tutoring

Ages: 6 to 17
Population Served: Attention Deficit Disorder (ADD/ADHD), Autism (mild), Learning Disability, Physical/Orthopedic Disability, Speech/Language Disability
Area Served: Bronx, Manhattan
Program Hours: Saturdays. Call for information
Program Capacity: 32

<continued...>

Staff/Child Ratio: 1:3
Medication Administered: Yes
Service Description: A 10-week Saturday recreational program open to children who are patients at the facility or children whose parents are patients. Tutoring offered on a 1:1 basis.
Contact: Leslie Blankfein, 212-426-3400

NORTHSIDE COMMUNITY DEVELOPMENT COUNCIL, INC.

551 Driggs Ave.
Brooklyn, NY 11211

(718) 384-0380 Administrative
(718) 384-6599 FAX

Annette LaMatto, Executive Director
Languages Spoken: Polish, Spanish

Services

Arts and Crafts Instruction
Sports, Team/Leagues

Ages: 5 to 21
Population Served: Gifted, Learning Disability, Underachiever
Area Served: Brooklyn, (Williamsburg)
Program Hours: Monday - Thursday: 3-5 p.m.
Program Capacity: 75-80
Staff/Child Ratio: 1:10
Wheelchair Accessible: Yes
Service Description: After school program primarily serving children attending PS 17.

ON YOUR MARK

645 Forest Ave., Suite 2A
Staten Island, NY 10310

(718) 720-9233 Administrative
(718) 720-9331 FAX

www.onyourmark.org
info@onyourmark.org

Lucy Birbiglia, Director of Service Coordination
Languages Spoken: Sign Language

Services

Dancing Instruction
Recreational Activities
Sports, Team/Leagues
Swimming

Ages: 5 to 18
Population Served: Autism, Cerebral Palsy, Developmental Delay, Developmental Disability, Down Syndrome, Learning Disability, Mental Retardation (mild-moderate), Neurological Disability, Seizure Disorder
Area Served: Staten Island

Program Hours: Call for information
Service Description: Offers, therapeutic recreation, after school programs, and a Saturday program. Activities include, bowling, yoga, aerobics, drama, social development and cooking.
Contact: Jim Allocco

ORGANIZED STUDENT (THE)

220 W. 93rd St.
New York, NY 10025

(212) 769-0026 Administrative

www.organizedstudent.com

Donna Goldberg, Director

Services

Study Skills Assistance

Ages: 10 to 25
Population Served: Attention Deficit Disorder (ADD/ADHD), Developmental Disability, Learning Disability, Neurological Disability
Area Served: All Boroughs
Service Description: Helps students develop organizational skills. Sessions are held in the home to teach students the value of good organizational skills that will eliminate stress and build a foundation for academic success. Works with students to develop personalized systems for time management, paper management, space design, and clutter control.

OTSAR FAMILY SERVICES, INC.

2334 W. 13th St.
Brooklyn, NY 11223

(718) 946-7301 Administrative
(718) 946-7966 FAX

otsarinc@aol.com

Betty Pollack, Executive Director
Languages Spoken: Hebrew, Yiddish

Services

Arts and Crafts Instruction
Dancing Instruction
Exercise Classes/Groups

Ages: 5 to 21
Population Served: Developmental Disabilities
Area Served: Brooklyn, Manhattan, Queens
Program Hours: Sundays and holidays, 10 a.m.-3 p.m.
Fees: None
Medication Administered: Yes
Transportation Provided: Yes

<continued...>

Wheelchair Accessible: Yes
Service Description: Provides a variety of recreational activities for children with developmental disabilities.
Contact: Chenie Friedler, Assistant Program Director

OUTWARD BOUND USA

100 Mystery Point Road
Garrison, NY 10524-9757

(845) 424-4000 Administrative
(888) 882-6863 Toll Free

www.outwardbound.com

Sites

1. OUTWARD BOUND USA

100 Mystery Point Road
Garrison, NY 10524-9757

(800) 243-8520 Administrative

www.outwardbound.com

2. NEW YORK CITY OUTWARD BOUND CENTER

29-46 Northern Blvd.
Long Island City, NY 11101

(718) 706-9900 Administrative
(718) 433-0500 FAX

www.nycoutwardbound.org

Richard Stopol, Executive Director

Services

Wilderness Training

Fees: $120/por day
Transportation Provided: Yes
Sites: 1 2

PADRES PARA PADRES

2301 Amsterdam Ave.
New York, NY 10033

(212) 781-5500 Administrative

Jose Josega, Director
Languages Spoken: Spanish

Services

Recreational Activities
Sports, Individual
Sports, Team/Leagues

Ages: 5 to 21
Population Served: Attention Deficit Disorder (ADD/ADHD), Autism, Cerebral Palsy, Developmental Delay, Developmental Disability, Down Syndrome, Health Impairment, Learning Disability, Mental Retardation (mild-moderate), Mental Retardation (severe-profound), Multiple Disability, Neurological Disability, Physical/Orthopedic Disability, Seizure Disorder, Speech/Language Disability, Spina Bifida, Technology Supported
Area Served: Manhattan (Inwood, Washington Heights)
Program Hours: Saturday: 10 a.m.-4 p.m.
Service Description: Offers games, reading, music, art, trips, sports and outdoor activities for children with special needs.

PAL-O-MINE EQUESTRIAN, INC.

33 Lloyd Harbor Road
Huntington, NY 11743

(631) 427-6105 Administrative
(631) 427-2596 FAX

www.pal-o-mine.org
info@pal-o-mine.org

Lisa Gatti, Executive Director
Languages Spoken: Sign Language

Services

Equestrian Therapy

Ages: 3 and up
Population Served: Attention Deficit Disorder (ADD/ADHD), Autism, Cerebral Palsy, Developmental Delay, Developmental Disability, Down Syndrome, Emotional Disability, Health Impairment, Learning Disability, Mental Retardation (mild-moderate), Mental Retardation (severe-profound), Multiple Disability, Neurological Disability, Physical/Orthopedic Disability, Rare Disorder, Seizure Disorder, Sickle Cell Anemia, Speech/Language Disability, Spina Bifida, Substance Abuse, Technology Supported, Underachiever, Visual Disability/Blind
Area Served: New York Metro Area
Program Capacity: 200 students
Staff/Child Ratio: Dependant on severity of disability, 1:1 or 3:1
Fees: $60 initial evaluation, $40 private lesson
Method of Payment: Scholarships available. Cash/check required before lesson.
Service Description: A therapeutic horseback riding program.

PARK SLOPE TUTORIAL SERVICES

487 12th St.
Brooklyn, NY 11215

(718) 499-3899 Administrative

Judith Ferrenbach, Contact

Services

Tutoring

Ages: 10 to 18
Population Served: Mild Learning Disability
Area Served: Brooklyn (Park Slope)
Fees: $60 per session
Service Description: General academic tutoring and test preparation for children with mild learning disability only.

PEDRO ALBIZU CAMPOS COMMUNITY CENTER

611 E. 13th St.
New York, NY 10009

(212) 677-1801 Administrative
(212) 533-0244 FAX

William Nieves, Executive Director

Services

Arts and Crafts Instruction
Homework Help Programs
Music Instruction
Recreational Activities
Sports, Individual
Tutoring

Ages: 6 to 12
Population Served: All Disabilities
Area Served: Manhattan (Lower East Side)
Program Hours: Monday - Friday: 2:30-6 p.m., September - June
Program Capacity: 50
Staff/Child Ratio: 1:10
Fees: $25/season
Method of Payment: Money Orders only
Medication Administered: No
Transportation Provided: No
Wheelchair Accessible: Yes
Service Description: An after school program that includes homework help, arts and crafts and recreational activities. Children with special needs are accepted on a case-by-case basis.

PESACH TIKVAH

18 Middleton St.
Brooklyn, NY 11206

(718) 875-6900 Administrative
(718) 875-6999 FAX

ptikvah@aol.com

Neal C. Goldberg, Ph.D., Executive Director
Languages Spoken: Spanish

Services

Arts and Crafts Instruction
Homework Help Programs
Respite, Children's Out-of-Home

Ages: 6 to 17
Area Served: Brooklyn
Fees: None
Transportation Provided: Yes
Wheelchair Accessible: Yes
Service Description: An after school program 4 days a week and Sundays for children and teens. Children with all disabilities are eligible after evaluation. Parent and sibling groups formed according to the child's disability are also available.

PIERPONT MORGAN LIBRARY

29 E. 36th St.
New York, NY 10016

(212) 685-0008 Administrative

Karen Brosins Powell

Services

Museums

PLAYGROUND FOR ALL CHILDREN (THE) - MANHATTAN

NYC Dept. of Parks and Recreation
Asher Levy Center, 23rd St. at FDR Dr.
New York, NY 10010

(212) 447-2027 Administrative

Lisa Henry, Director

Services

Parks/Recreation Areas

PLAYGROUND FOR ALL CHILDREN (THE) - QUEENS

111-01 Corona Ave.
Corona, NY 11368

(718) 699-8283 Administrative

www.nycparks.org

Mark Edwards, Director
Languages Spoken: Spanish

Services

Parks/Recreation Areas

PLAYGROUND FOR ALL CHILDREN (THE) - STATEN ISLAND

1150 Clove Road
Staten Island, NY 10301

(718) 477-5471 Program Director

Marie M.LaCurtis, Program Director

Services

Parks/Recreation Areas

Ages: All Ages
Population Served: All Disabilities
Area Served: Staten Island
Wheelchair Accessible: Yes
Service Description: An adaptive playgroup and outreach recreation center providing therapeutic recreation programs all year round. The focus is on visits by special-needs classes, workshops, day habilitation and day treatments. Fun, socialization and goal/skills enhancement are stressed. Classes for mainstream children are also offered. Classes for children and teens on sensitivity toward people with disabilities are offered. Teachers and group leaders should call to schedule a visit.

PLAYING 2 WIN (P2W)

1330 Fifth Ave.
New York, NY 10026

(212) 369-4077 Administrative
(212) 369-7046 FAX

www.playing2win.org
info@playing2win.org

Rahsaan Harris, Executive Director

Services

Arts and Crafts Instruction
Field Trips/Excursions
Homework Help Programs
Music Instruction

Ages: 7 and up
Population Served: Asthma, Autism, Cancer, Developmental Disability, Diabetes, Emotional Disability, Gifted, Health Impairment, Sickle Cell Anemia, Substance Abuse, Substance Exposed
Area Served: All Boroughs
Program Hours: Tuesday - Friday: 3:30-5:30 p.m.
Program Capacity: 10-15 per class.
Staff/Child Ratio: 1:10
Fees: $75 per year
Method of Payment: Cash, Check, Credit Card, Money Order
Medication Administered: Yes
Wheelchair Accessible: Yes
Service Description: Children receive homework help, tutoring and participate in special projects.
Contact: Debbie Bailey, Recruitment Coordinator/Manager

POLICE ATHLETIC LEAGUE, INC. (PAL)

34 1/2 12th St.
New York, NY 10003

(212) 477-9450 Administrative

www.palnyc.org

Dr. John Ryan
Languages Spoken: Arabic, French, German, Spanish

Sites

1. POLICE ATHLETIC LEAGUE, INC. (PAL)
34 1/2 12th St.
New York, NY 10003

(212) 477-9450 Administrative

www.palnyc.org

Joe Loughran, Director

2. POLICE ATHLETIC LEAGUE, INC. (PAL) - PART-TIME YOUTH CENTER
City Island Center
190 Fordham Rd.
Bronx, NY 10454

Joe Loughran, Director

<continued...>

3. POLICE ATHLETIC LEAGUE, INC. (PAL) - HOWARD HOUSES CENTER

90 Watkins St.
Brooklyn, NY 11212

(718) 495-4089 Administrative
(718) 495-4096 FAX

Liodia Rendon, Director

4. POLICE ATHLETIC LEAGUE, INC. (PAL) - FOSTER LAURIE

199-10 112th Ave.
Hollis, NY 11412

(718) 468-1888 Administrative
(718) 468-4824 FAX

Chris Douglas, Director

5. POLICE ATHLETIC LEAGUE, INC. (PAL) - CAPTAIN SWEENEY

31 Snyder Ave.
Brooklyn, NY 11226

(718) 856-1113 Administrative

Robert Lopez, Director

6. POLICE ATHLETIC LEAGUE, INC. (PAL) - BELMONT COMMUNITY CENTER

2410 Arthur Ave.
Bronx, NY 10458

(718) 364-9118

7. POLICE ATHLETIC LEAGUE, INC. (PAL) - ARNOLD AND MARIE SCHWARTZ COMMUNITY CENTER

127 Pennsylvania Ave.
Brooklyn, NY 11207

(718) 342-4098 Administrative
(718) 485-2970 FAX

Diane Harris, Acting Director

8. POLICE ATHLETIC LEAGUE, INC. (PAL) - WESTERN QUEENS NURSERY SCHOOL

10-26 41st Ave.
Long Island City, NY 11101

(718) 784-2080 Administrative
(718) 786-2142 FAX

Carmencita Fiesta, Director

9. POLICE ATHLETIC LEAGUE, INC. (PAL) - NEW HARLEM CENTER

441 Manhattan Ave.
New York, NY 10026

(212) 665-8699 Administrative
(212) 665-2164 FAX

Barbara Samuels, Director

10. POLICE ATHLETIC LEAGUE, INC. (PAL) - CAREY GARDENS DAY CARE CENTER

2964 W. 23rd St.
Brooklyn, NY 11224

(718) 372-4044 Administrative
(718) 372-1288 FAX

Mona Essman, Director

11. POLICE ATHLETIC LEAGUE, INC. (PAL) - NEW SOUTH BRONX CENTER

991 Longwood Ave.
Bronx, NY 10459

(718) 991-2447 Administrative

Rodney Johnson, Program Director

Services

Child Care Centers
Recreational Activities

Ages: 2.9 to 21
Area Served: All Boroughs
Staff/Child Ratio: 1:9
Fees: $5 per year
Wheelchair Accessible: At most locations.
Service Description: Offers educational and recreational programs to underserved youth living in neighborhoods throughout the five boroughs.
Sites: 1 2 3 4 5 6 7 8 9 10

POLICE ATHLETIC LEAGUE ON HORSEBACK (P.A.L.O.H.)
Equestrian Therapy

Service Description: A therapeutic horseback riding program incorporating many of the principles of adaptive physical education and therapy.
Sites: 1 11

Remedial Education

Ages: 6 to 12
Sites: 9

POLISH AND SLAVIC CENTER, INC.

177 Kent St.
Brooklyn, NY 11222

(718) 383-5290 Administrative
(718) 383-5159 FAX

www.pscenter.org
psc@pscenter.org

Kaja Sawczuk, Executive Director
Languages Spoken: Polish, Russian

<continued...>

Sites

1. POLISH AND SLAVIC CENTER, INC.
176 Java St.
Brooklyn, NY 11222

(718) 389-5366 Administrative
(718) 349-1143 Immigration Program
(718) 349-7937 FAX

Services

Arts and Crafts Instruction
Homework Help Programs
Music Instruction
Recreational Activities

Ages: 5 to 12
Population Served: All Disabilities
Area Served: Brooklyn, (Greenpoint)
Program Hours: Monday - Friday: 2-6 p.m.
Fees: Sliding scale fee on weekly basis.
Transportation Provided: Yes, pick up service from school.
Service Description: Provides after school program for children of new Polish immigrants, in the Greenpoint section of Brooklyn. Services include, pick up service from three local schools, hot meals, homework help, arts and craft, music and recreational activities. Also has educational workshops for parents.
Sites: 1

PRATT INSTITUTE

200 Willoughby Ave.
South Hall, 2nd Fl.
Brooklyn, NY 11205

(718) 636-3637 Administrative

Susan Martin

Services

SATURDAY ARTS SCHOOL
Arts and Crafts Instruction

Ages: 4 to 17
Population Served: AIDS/HIV +, Asthma, Cancer, Gifted, Learning Disability, Mental Retardation (mild-moderate), Underachiever
Area Served: All Boroughs
Program Hours: Saturday: 10 a.m.-12 p.m.
Program Capacity: 300
Staff/Child Ratio: 1:10
Fees: $120 per semester and $30 for materials.
Method of Payment: Offers scholarship through schools.
Service Description: Hands-on arts and crafts project and classes.
Contact: Veronica Doby, 718-636-3505

PRESBYTERIAN INFANT AND CHILD CARE CENTER

61 Haven Ave.
New York, NY 10032

(212) 927-2723 Administrative
(212) 740-7376 FAX

Elaine Rexdale, Director

Services

Child Care Centers

Ages: 2 months to 5 years
Population Served: All Disabilities
Area Served: Manhattan
Program Hours: Monday - Friday: 6:15 a.m.-6 p.m.
Program Capacity: 66
Staff/Child Ratio: 23 staff members
Fees: Varies, $240 - $275/week
Method of Payment: Cash, Check, Credit Card, Money Order
Medication Administered: No
Transportation Provided: No
Wheelchair Accessible: No
Service Description: A child care center that provides services to staff members of the Presbyterian medical center. Children with special needs are considered on a case-by-case basis.

PRINCETON REVIEW (THE)

2315 Broadway
New York, NY 10024

(212) 874-8282 Administrative
(212) 874-0775 FAX

Services

Test Preparation

Ages: All Ages
Area Served: All Boroughs
Program Hours: Call for information
Staff/Child Ratio: 1:8/12
Fees: Vary depending on program
Method of Payment: Cash, Check, Credit Card, Money Order
Medication Administered: No
Transportation Provided: No
Wheelchair Accessible: Yes
Service Description: Personalized attention is a top priority for The Princeton Review. Small classes mean that teachers can provide their students with the attention they need for the best results. Classes are also grouped by ability level, so the class will progress at a pace that is appropriate for that particular group.

PROFESSIONAL SERVICE CENTERS FOR THE HANDICAPPED (PSCH)

22-44 119th St.
College Point, NY 11356

(718) 445-4700 Administrative
(718) 358-7502 FAX

Cathy Varano, Director
Languages Spoken: Spanish

Services

Arts and Crafts Instruction
Recreational Activities

Ages: 16 to 21
Population Served: Asperger Syndrome, Autism, Cerebral Palsy, Developmental Disability, Down Syndrome, Mental Retardation(mild/moderate), Mental Retardation(severe/profound), Mulitple Disability, Neurological Disability, Pervasive Developmental Disorder, Seizure Disorder, Traumatic Brain Injury
Area Served: Queens
Program Hours: Tuesday-Saturday. Call for times.
Program Capacity: Up to 30
Staff/Child Ratio: 1:2 or 3
Fees: Only nominal admission fees as needed per recreation outing.
Transportation Provided: Yes
Wheelchair Accessible: Yes
Service Description: Community-based recreation program for small groups of developmentally disabled children and adults, with transportation provided.
Contact: June Solomon, Family Support Coordinator

Field Trips/Excursions

Ages: 5 to adult
Population Served: Developmental Delay, Developmental Disability
Area Served: Queens
Program Hours: Monday - Friday and one day on the weekend. Call for times.
Program Capacity: 45
Fees: Call for information
Medication Administered: No
Transportation Provided: Yes
Service Description: Participants are grouped by appropriate age and activity. Trips to parks, recreational areas, museums, bowling alleys and other places of interest.
Contact: Jannie Smalls

PROJECT BRIDGE

144 Bleecker St.
Brooklyn, NY 11221

(718) 455-4649 Administrative
(718) 455-9311 FAX

Stacey C. Lawrence, Project Director
Languages Spoken: Spanish

Services

PROJECT BRIDGE LIFE SKILLS/YOUTH COUNCIL NETWORK
Homework Help Programs
Recreational Activities
Remedial Education

Ages: 6 to 21
Population Served: Gifted, Underachiever
Area Served: Brooklyn (Bushwick, East New York, Williamsburgh)
Wheelchair Accessible: Yes
Service Description: Caters to at-risk youth in danger of school drop out, drug abuse and teenage pregnancy. Offers homework assistance, dropout prevention programs, and recreation.

PROJECT HAPPY

425 E. 25th St.
New York, NY 10010

(212) 772-4613 Administrative

Penny Shaw, Executive Director

Services

Dancing Instruction
Recreational Activities
Sports, Individual
Sports, Team/Leagues

Ages: 6 to 26
Population Served: Mental Retardation (mild/moderate), Physical/Orthopedic Disability.
Area Served: All Boroughs
Program Hours: Saturday: 10 a.m.-4 p.m., September to December and February to May
Program Capacity: 80-100
Staff/Child Ratio: 1:2
Transportation Provided: Yes, for children with Orthopedic Disabilities (very limited).
Wheelchair Accessible: Yes
Service Description: All sports Saturday program for young people with orthopedic disabilities. Open to all who are referred by health professionals. Activities include aquatics, dance, bowling, floor hockey, fitness and wheelchair sports.

PROJECT TEEN AID

51 St. Edwards St.
Brooklyn, NY 11205

(718) 834-8553 Administrative
(718) 403-9432 FAX

ptafsi@netzero.net

Lynn Henderson, Executive Director

Services

Arts and Crafts Instruction
Computer Classes
Homework Help Programs

Ages: 9 to 14
Area Served: All Boroughs
Program Hours: Monday - Friday: 3:15 - 5:15p.m.
Program Capacity: 35
Fees: None
Wheelchair Accessible: No
Service Description: Provides after school activities such as information technology workshops, arts and crafts, homework help and life skills preparation. Snacks provided. Children with special needs are accepted on a case-by-case basis.
Contact: Janiki Dickson

PROSPECT PARK

95 Prospect Park West
Brooklyn, NY 11215

(718) 965-8951 Administrative

Tupper Thomas, Administrator
Languages Spoken:

Sites

1. PROSPECT PARK
95 Prospect Park West
Brooklyn, NY 11215

(718) 965-8951 Administrative

Tupper Thomas, Administrator

2. PROSPECT PARK WILDLIFE CENTER
450 Flatbush Ave.
Brooklyn, NY 11225

(718) 399-7339 Administrative

Services

Parks/Recreation Areas
Storytelling

Ages: Vary depending on program.
Population Served: Gifted, Physical/Orthopedic Disability
Area Served: All Boroughs
Program Hours: Weekends: 1- 5 p.m. School and

private programs by appointment.
Program Capacity: Varies depending on program.
Fees: Vary depending on program.
Method of Payment: Cash, Checks, Credit Cards
Medication Administered: No
Transportation Provided: No
Wheelchair Accessible: Yes
Service Description: Prospect Park offers a variety of programs for children of all ages. The Children's Historic House Museum located in Prospect Park offers interactive educational programs such as: Early American Tools and Toys - A year round, all ages program with sessions lasting 1 hour and 15 minutes, where children study the day to day lives of African American, Native American and Dutch American children at Lefferts; Who Lived Here? - Research teams choose a person to learn about from the exhibit provided; Grandmother's Stories, Discovery: Play Sessions and Quilts are other programs offered by Prospect Park.
Sites: 1

Zoos/Wildlife Parks
Sites: 2

PROSPECT PARK YMCA

357 9th St.
Brooklyn, NY 11215

(718) 768-7100 Administrative

Maria Herman, Executive Director
Languages Spoken: Haitian Creole, Spanish

Services

Arts and Crafts Instruction
Child Care Centers
Tutoring

Ages: 2.5 to 18
Population Served: Gifted, Underachiever
Area Served: All Boroughs
Program Hours: Monday - Friday: 3-6 p.m.
Program Capacity: After school, 70; Virtual Y, 130.
Staff/Child Ratio: 1:10
Fees: After school, $165 per month; Virtual Y, Free, must be in school.
Transportation Provided: Yes, only for pick-up at P.S. 39 and drop off at P.S. 321 where the virtual Y and after school programs are held.
Wheelchair Accessible: Yes
Service Description: Virtual Y provides free literacy program with homework help and other activities. After school program offers arts and crafts and tutoring.

PROTECTORS OF PINE OAK WOODS

80 Mann Ave.
Staten Island, NY 10314

(718) 761-7496 Administrative

Dick Buegler, President

Services

Nature Centers/Walks

PUBLIC SCHOOL 274 AFTER SCHOOL PROGRAM

800 Bushwick Ave.
Brooklyn, NY 11221

(718) 443-5551 Administrative

Languages Spoken: Spanish

Services

Arts and Crafts Instruction
Creative Writing
English as a Second Language
Field Trips/Excursions
Homework Help Programs
Mentoring Programs
Remedial Education
Tutoring

Ages: 4 to 17
Population Served: Asthma, Attention Deficit Disorder (ADD/ADHD), Gifted, Learning Disability, Underachiever
Area Served: Brooklyn, (Bedford Stuyvesant)
Program Hours: October - June, Tuesday - Thursday: 3-5 p.m.
Program Capacity: 27
Staff/Child Ratio: 1:27, along with teacher aide.
Fees: Free
Medication Administered: Yes, with consent form
Wheelchair Accessible: No
Service Description: After school program offering instructional classes, tutoring, homework help and guest speakers. Learning Disability specialist available. Tutoring offered both on a 1:1 basis and group level.

PUBLIC SCHOOL 81 AFTER SCHOOL PROGRAM

990 Dekalb Ave.
Brooklyn, NY 11221

(718) 443-5551 Administrative

Rev. Molly Golden, Executive Director
Languages Spoken: Spanish

Services

Arts and Crafts Instruction
English as a Second Language
Field Trips/Excursions
Homework Help Programs
Mentoring Programs
Remedial Education
Tutoring

Ages: 4 to 17
Population Served: Asthma, Attention Deficit Disorder (ADD/ADHD), Gifted, Learning Disability, Underachiever
Area Served: Brooklyn, particularly Bedford Stuyvesant
Program Hours: Tuesday - Thursday: 3-5 p.m., October - June
Program Capacity: 27
Staff/Child Ratio: 1:27, teacher aide available
Fees: None
Medication Administered: Yes, with consent form
Service Description: After school program offering instructional classes, tutoring, homework help and guest speakers. Learning Disability specialist available. Tutoring offered both on a 1:1 basis and group level.

PUERTO RICAN COUNCIL DAY CARE

180 Suffolk St.
New York, NY 10002

(212) 674-6731 Administrative
(212) 253-7110 FAX

Beatriz Ladiana, Executive Director
Languages Spoken: Spanish

Services

Acting Instruction
Arts and Crafts Instruction
Child Care Centers
Computer Classes
English as a Second Language
Field Trips/Excursions
Homework Help Programs
Music Instruction
Sports, Team/Leagues
Storytelling
Tutoring

Ages: 6 to 9
Population Served: Asthma, Emotional Disability, Gifted, Health Impairment, Learning Disability, Speech/Language Disability, Underachiever
Area Served: All Boroughs
Program Hours: Summer and holidays, 8 a.m.-6 p.m., After school 3-6 p.m.
Program Capacity: 70

<continued...>

Staff/Child Ratio: 1:22 or 24
Fees: Fee scaled according to income.
Wheelchair Accessible: Yes
Service Description: Provides tutoring in all subjects, homework help programs and other recreational activities in an academic environment. Holiday, summer, and after school programs provided in school setting. Tutoring is on a 1:1 basis or group level. Also available are mentoring programs focusing on child awareness and violence control.

PURPLE CIRCLE DAY CARE CENTER

251 W. 100th St.
New York, NY 10025

(212) 866-9193 Administrative

Mary Jane Lewis, Executive Director

Services

Child Care Centers

Ages: 2 to 6
Area Served: Manhattan
Program Hours: Monday - Friday: 2-6 p.m.
Program Capacity: 55
Staff/Child Ratio: 1:5.5
Fees: $9500 per year
Wheelchair Accessible: No
Service Description: Offers a late day program for children. Activities include arts and crafts, reading, storytelling, and outdoor play. Children with special needs are accepted on a case-by-case basis.
Contact: Elaine Karas, Director

QUALITY SERVICES FOR THE AUTISM COMMUNITY (QSAC)

30-10 38th St., 3rd Fl.
Astoria, NY 11103

(718) 728-8476 Administrative
(718) 204-7570 FAX

www.qsac.com
info@qsac.com

Gary Maffei, Executive Director
Languages Spoken: Spanish

1. QUALITY SERVICES FOR THE AUTISM COMMUNITY (QSAC) - PRESCHOOL

12-10 150th St.
Whitestone, NY 11357

(718) 747-6674 Administrative

Debra Gruber, Director

Services

Respite, Children's Out-of-Home

Ages: 5 to 15
Population Served: Autism
Program Hours: Saturdays (approximately 40 sessions per year) 11 a.m.-3 p.m.
Program Capacity: 10
Staff/Child Ratio: 2:1
Fees: None
Transportation Provided: Yes, transportation to and from the program
Service Description: Offered at the Whitestone location, this program provides structured recreation, including group activities on site and community trips to local parks and museums.
Contact: Farzana Karim, Director of Service Coordination
Sites: 1

QUEENS BOTANICAL GARDEN

43-50 Main St.
Flushing, NY 11355

(718) 886-3800 Administrative

Fred Gerber

Services

Nature Centers/Walks
Parks/Recreation Areas

Ages: Pre-K to 8th Grade
Population Served: All Disabilities
Area Served: All Boroughs
Program Hours: Monday - Friday: 9:30 a.m.-4 p.m.
Program Capacity: 32 per class (mainstream); 20 per class (special needs)
Staff/Child Ratio: 1 instructor per class with or without an assistant
Fees: Workshops and tours $65 per class plus materials fee (variable). $5 per child for "Just for Kids" drop-in workshop program.
Method of Payment: Advance payment by check required for classes.
Wheelchair Accessible: Yes
Service Description: Program offers a wide variety of hands-on workshop experiences for students pre-K through 8th grade. All programs

<continued...>

have been adapted to special needs audiences.
There are also drop-in "Just for Kids" week-end programs.
Contact: Betty Scott, Education Coordinator

QUEENS CHILD GUIDANCE CENTER

60-02 Queens Blvd., Lower Level
Woodside, NY 11377

(718) 651-7770 Administrative
(718) 651-5029 FAX

www.qcgc.org
info@qcgc.org

Languages Spoken: Bengali, Chinese (Cantonese, Mandarin), French, Gujarti, Hindi, Kannada, Korean, Marathi, Oriya, Punjabi, Russian, Tagalog, Urdu, Spanish

Sites

1. QUEENS CHILD GUIDANCE CENTER - ASIAN OUTREACH

87-08 Justice Ave., Suite C7
Elmhurst, NY 11373

(718) 899-9810 Administrative
(718) 899-9699 FAX

2. QUEENS CHILD GUIDANCE CENTER - SOUTH JAMAICA CLINIC

115-15 Sutphin Blvd.
Jamaica, NY 11434

(718) 659-4000 Administrative
(718) 659-1405 FAX

Linda Ford

3. QUEENS CHILD GUIDANCE CENTER - WOODSIDE CLINIC

67-14 41st Ave.
Woodside, NY 11377

(718) 458-4243 Administrative
(718) 458-4481 FAX

Services

READING ASSISTANCE PROGRAM (RAP)
Tutoring

Ages: Birth to 18
Population Served: Emotional Disability
Area Served: Queens
Fees: Sliding Scale. Some school-based services are provided at no cost.
Method of Payment: Medicaid, Child Health Plus, Private Insurance
Wheelchair Accessible: Yes
Service Description: Provides after school reading improvement and tutoring program, as well as, academic/recreational programs.
Sites: 1 2 3

QUEENS COUNTY FARM MUSEUM

73-50 Little Neck Parkway
Floral Park, NY 11004

(718) 347-3276 Administrative
(718) 347-3243 FAX

www.queensfarm.org
info@queensfarm.org

Amy Fischetti, Executive Director
Languages Spoken: Spanish

Services

Recreational Activities
Zoos/Wildlife Parks

Ages: 4 to 12
Population Served: AIDS/HIV+, Asthma, Attention Deficit Disorder (ADD/ADHD), Autism, Cancer, Cardiac Disorder, Cerebral Palsy, Cystic Fibrosis, Deaf-Blind, Deaf/Hard of Hearing, Developmental Delay, Developmental Disability, Diabetes, Down Syndrome, Emotional Disability, Gifted, Health Impairment, Juvenile Offender, Learning Disability, Mental Retardation (mild-moderate), Mental Retardation (severe-profound), Multiple Disability, Neurological Disability, Physical/Orthopedic Disability, Sickle Cell Anemia, Speech/Language Disability, Substance Exposed, Technology Supported, Tourette Syndrome, Underachiever, Visual Disability/Blind
Area Served: All Boroughs
Program Hours: Monday - Friday: 10-11:30 a.m., or 12:30-2 p.m.
Program Capacity: 20 to 50 children
Staff/Child Ratio: Varied, depending on needs of children.
Fees: $6 per child
Wheelchair Accessible: Yes
Service Description: Program emphasizes general farm life. The tour highlights animals, planting fields and farmers. Animal feeding and hayride are included. A small craft project can be substituted for hayride.
Contact: Dianne Miller, Education Coordinator

QUEENS MUSEUM

Flushing Meadows - Corona Park
Flushing, NY 11368

(718) 592-9700 Administrative
(718) 592-5778 FAX
(718) 592-2847 TDD

www.queensmuse.org

Kit Shapiro, Special Needs Coordinator
Languages Spoken: Spanish

<continued...>

Services

Museums

Population Served: Deaf/Hard of Hearing, Emotional Disability, Learning Disability, Mental Retardation (mild-moderate), Physical/Orthopedic Disability, Visual Disability/Blind
Area Served: All boroughs
Program Hours: Tuesday - Friday: 10 a.m.-4 p.m.
Fees: $5 per student
Service Description: The Art Access program features a guided tour, a hands-on art workshop and multisensory experiences for students with special needs. Programs are designed for students with learning, emotional and physical disabilities, mental retardation and sensory impairments.

QUEENS PARENT RESOURCE CENTER

88-50 165th St., 2nd Fl., Suite B
Jamaica, NY 11433

(718) 523-6953 Administrative
(718) 523-7261 FAX

Ana Magalee, Executive Director
Languages Spoken: Haitian Creole, Spanish

Services

AFTER SCHOOL RESPITE PROGRAM
Arts and Crafts Instruction
Computer Classes
Creative Writing
Homework Help Programs
Tutoring

Ages: 5 to 12
Population Served: Developmental Disability, Emotional Disability, Mental Retardation (mild-moderate)
Area Served: Queens
Program Hours: Monday - Friday: 3:30-6:30 p.m.
Fees: None
Transportation Provided: Yes
Service Description: Program takes place at the Beacon 43, 160 Beach 29th St., Far Rockaway. Children take part in arts and crafts, computer lab, creative writing workshops, homework help, recreational activities, tutoring and a Friday book club. They can also participate in martial arts and a community movie night. Children with special needs are integrated with mainstream students.
Contact: Carol Harris

FUN WITH FRIENDS
Homework Help Programs
Recreational Activities
Sports, Team/Leagues

Ages: 5 to 12
Population Served: Developmental Disability, Emotional Disability, Mental Retardation (mild-moderate)

Area Served: Queens
Program Hours: Call for information
Fees: Call for information
Transportation Provided: Yes
Service Description: Offers experiences for children who have had limited opportunities to socialize and enjoy recreational activities. Events include activities such as sporting events, bowling, concerts, exercise, arts and crafts, homework help, recreation, gym activities, game room and movies.
Contact: Marcia Walker

QUEENS WILDLIFE CENTER

53-51 111th St.
Flushing Meadows, NY 11368

(718) 271-7761 Administrative

Services

Zoos/Wildlife Parks

QUEENSBRIDGE DAY CARE CENTER

38-11 27th St.
Long Island City, NY 11101

(718) 937-7640 Administrative
(718) 392-7928 FAX

Languages Spoken: Southeast Asian, Spanish

Services

Arts and Crafts Instruction
Child Care Centers
Computer Classes
Dancing Instruction
Storytelling

Ages: 2.9 to 6
Population Served: Developmental Delay, Developmental Disability, Speech Delay
Area Served: Queens
Program Hours: Monday - Friday: 8 a.m.-6 p.m.
Program Capacity: 135
Staff/Child Ratio: 1:7
Fees: Sliding scale fee
Method of Payment: Cash or Money Order
Wheelchair Accessible: Yes
Contact: Rodolfo Aquino, Educational Director

R.E.A.C.H. (RECREATION, EDUCATION, ATHLETICS AND CREATIVE ARTS FOR THE HANDICAPPED) - BROOKLYN

1555 Linden Blvd.
Brooklyn, NY 11212

(718) 485-4633 [22] Administrative

Carol Black

Services

Recreational Activities

Ages: 18 and up
Population Served: Developmental Disability
Area Served: Brooklyn (Brownsville)
Wheelchair Accessible: No
Service Description: Provides recreational activities for individuals with developmental challenges to help develop motor and social skills.

R.E.A.C.H. (RECREATION, EDUCATION, ATHLETICS AND CREATIVE ARTS FOR THE HANDICAPPED) - STATEN ISLAND

1150 Clove Road
Staten Island, NY 10301

(718) 816-5558 Administrative
(718) 390-8080 FAX

William LeCurtis, Executive Director
Languages Spoken: Sign Language

Services

Arts and Crafts Instruction
Field Trips/Excursions
Recreational Activities

Ages: 6 and up
Population Served: AIDS/HIV +, Attention Deficit Disorder (ADD/ADHD), Autism, Deaf/Hard of Hearing, Developmental Disability, Emotional Disability, Health Impairment, Learning Disability, Mental Retardation (mild-moderate), Mental Retardation (severe-profound), Neurological Disability, Physical/Orthopedic Disability, Seizure Disorder, Speech/Language Disability, Technology Supported, Visual Disability/Blind
Program Hours: Call for information.
Program Capacity: 45
Staff/Child Ratio: 1:5
Fees: The Parents Association fees are on a sliding scale, based on session and need.
Method of Payment: Payment Plan
Service Description: Provides diverse and exciting recreational and educational activities during the year, which is divided into a fall/winter, spring and summer seasons. These activities include: client-interactive dinners; arts and crafts; modified physical games; gardening; photography; bingo; team sports; drama and

music therapy; adaptive aquatics, tennis, golf; a special bowling league; overnight respite; monitored personal management/prevocational community-orientation programs; a huge variety of holiday and themed parties, dances, dinners and socials; and an ongoing training camp for Special Olympics, etc. Participants also go on a full gamut of off-site field trips, such as the movies, museums, shows, zoos, sports matches, city-wide parks and recreation centers, etc. Limited openings for camps and schools to visit the center weekly during morning hours for special trips.

READING REFORM FOUNDATION

1680 York Ave., 4F
New York, NY 10128

(212) 396-1947 Administrative

Bonnie Lee, Reading Consultant

Services

Tutoring

Ages: 5 to 9
Population Served: Developmental Disability, Gifted, Underachiever
Program Hours: Monday - Friday (after school) and/or Saturday
Staff/Child Ratio: 1:1 or small group
Fees: $75/hour, sliding scale if necessary.
Method of Payment: Check or cash
Transportation Provided: No
Service Description: Through informal diagnostic testing, individual academic plans are developed to increase the child's motivation, self-esteem and reading level. Tutoring services focus on reading, writing and spelling. Bonnie Lee and staff are Harvard-trained reading specialists.

RESOURCES FOR CHILDREN WITH SPECIAL NEEDS, INC.

116 E. 16th St., 5th Fl.
New York, NY 10003

(212) 677-4650 Administrative
(212) 254-4070 FAX

www.resourcesnyc.org
info@resourcesnyc.org

Karen Thoreson Schlesinger, Executive Director
Languages Spoken: Spanish

<continued...>

Services

Child Care Resource and Referral
Recreational Activities
Tutoring

Ages: All Ages
Population Served: All Disabilities
Area Served: All Boroughs
Wheelchair Accessible: Yes
Service Description: Provides information and referral services to parents seeking childcare, tutoring, recreation and and a wide range of other after school services for children with special needs.

RESPITE FOUNDATION, INC.

113-04 219th St.
Queens Village, NY 11429

(718) 217-4461 Voice/FAX

Yvonne Secreto, RN, Director
Languages Spoken: Spanish

Services

Respite, Children's Out-of-Home

Ages: 6 to 12
Population Served: Autism, Cerebral Palsy, Mental Retardation (mild to profound), Neurological Disability, Seizure Disorder
Area Served: Brooklyn
Program Hours: Saturday. Call for information
Wheelchair Accessible: Yes
Service Description: Offers Saturday respite program for children with special needs.

RIDGEWOOD BUSHWICK SENIOR CITIZENS COUNCIL, INC.

217 Wyckoff Ave.
Brooklyn, NY 11237

(718) 497-1808 Administrative
(718) 381-9680 FAX

Elena Zullo, Assistant Executive Director
Languages Spoken: Spanish

Sites

1. RIDGEWOOD BUSHWICK SENIOR CITIZENS COUNCIL, INC. - BEACON PROGRAM AT I.S. 296
125 Convert Street
Brooklyn, NY 11207

(718) 919-4453 Administrative
(718) 919-4517 FAX

Judy Valerio, Director

Services

RIDGEWOOD BUSHWICK BEACON PROGRAM
AT IS 296
Arts and Crafts Instruction
Homework Help Programs
Music Instruction

Ages: 6 to 21
Population Served: Juvenile Offender, Substance Abuse
Area Served: Brooklyn (Bushwick), Queens (Ridgewood)
Wheelchair Accessible: Yes
Service Description: An educational and recreational community center offering an after school program, arts and crafts, computers, games, homework assistance, parties, sports and trips. Call for more information.
Contact: Janine Dilorenzo
Sites: 1

RIVERDALE COMMUNITY CENTER

660 W. 237th St.
Bronx, NY 10463

(718) 796-4724 Administrative

Ferne LaDue, Executive Director

Services

Tutoring

Ages: 10 to 16
Area Served: Bronx
Program Hours: October 1 - May 31, Tuesday, Wednesday, Thursday: 3-5 p.m.
November 1 - May 2, Friday: 7-10 p.m.
Wheelchair Accessible: Yes
Service Description: A drop-in after school program offering reading and math tutorial services, library center, teen theater, and a Friday evening Teen Center. Tutoring is offered in group format.

RIVERDALE EQUESTRIAN CENTER

254th St. and Broadway
Bronx, NY 10471

(718) 548-4848 Administrative

www.dcriders.org
info@dcriders.com

Denise Colón, CSW, Director

< continued... >

Services

Sports, Individual

Ages: 5 to 18
Population Served: Asperger Syndrome, Autism, Cerebral Palsy, Developmental Disability, Down Syndrome
Area Served: All Boroughs
Program Hours: Monday and Friday afternoons and Saturday mornings.
Program Capacity: Limited space, 3 outdoor seasonal series.
Staff/Child Ratio: 2/3:1
Fees: $200/8 lessons
Method of Payment: Partially funded
Service Description: Provide outdoor and indoor riding lessons for adults and children of all ages and levels of experience. Pony rides are available on Saturdays for children under the age of 6. By appointment only. Call for more information.

RIVERDALE NEIGHBORHOOD HOUSE

5521 Mosholu Ave.
Bronx, NY 10471

(718) 549-8100 Administrative
(718) 884-1645 FAX

Esther Levy Bar-Shai, CSW, Director of Family Center
Languages Spoken: Spanish

Services

Arts and Crafts Instruction
Homework Help Programs
Sports, Individual
Sports, Team/Leagues
Tutoring

Ages: 6 to 12
Population Served: All Disabilities
Area Served: All Boroughs
Program Hours: Monday - Friday: 3-6 p.m.
Program Capacity: 72
Staff/Child Ratio: 1:12
Fees: $85/5 days; $80/4 days; $75/3 days; $67/2 days
Method of Payment: Scholarships available
Medication Administered: No
Transportation Provided: No
Wheelchair Accessible: Yes (limited)
Service Description: Provides an after school program which offers a variety of academic and recreational activities. Children with special needs are considered on a case-by-case basis.
Contact: Cathy Duffy, Administrative Director of School Age Programs

RIVERDALE YM-YWHA

5625 Arlington Ave.
Bronx, NY 10471

(718) 548-8200 Administrative
(718) 796-6339 FAX

Diane Rubin, Executive Director

Services

Arts and Crafts Instruction
Homework Help Programs
Recreational Activities
Sports, Individual
Sports, Team/Leagues

Ages: 5 to 11
Population Served: Attention Deficit Disorder (ADD/ADHD), Learning Disability
Area Served: Bronx
Program Hours: Monday - Thursday: 3-6 p.m.
Program Capacity: 20
Staff/Child Ratio: 1:10
Fees: Call for information.
Method of Payment: Cash, Check, Credit Card, Money Order
Medication Administered: No
Transportation Provided: Yes, within Riverdale District
Wheelchair Accessible: Yes
Contact: Leah Ferster, Contact

ROCKIN MAGICIAN

241 W. 134th St.
New York, NY 10030

(212) 862-7681 Administrative

William Brown, Executive Director
Languages Spoken: French, Spanish

Services

Homework Help Programs

Ages: 6 to 13
Area Served: All Boroughs
Service Description: Provides after school tutoring and homework help. Children with special needs are accepted on a case-by-case basis. Call for more information.

ROSE CENTER FOR EARTH SCIENCE AND SPACE - HAYDEN PLANETARIUM

81st St. at Central Park West
New York, NY 10024

(212) 873-1300 Administrative

Services

Arts and Crafts Instruction
Museums

Ages: All Ages
Area Served: All Boroughs
Program Hours: Vary depending on program.
Fees: Vary depending on program. Call museum for information.
Method of Payment: Cash, Checks, Credit Cards, Money Orders
Medication Administered: No
Transportation Provided: No
Wheelchair Accessible: Yes
Service Description: Provides a variety of weekend workshops for children of all ages. Accommodations can be made for children with disabilities.

S.T.A.G.E.S. - SPECIAL THEATRE ARTS GROUP FOR EXCEPTIONAL STUDENTS

56-15A Utopia Parkway
Fresh Meadows, NY 11365

(718) 357-4532 Administrative

www.theatrelearning.org/stages
TLstages@aol.com

Bob Calderon, Executive Director

Services

Art Therapy
Arts and Crafts Instruction
Drama Therapy

Ages: 9 to 14
Population Served: Asperger Syndrome, Attention Deficit Disorder (ADD/ADHD), Emotional Disability, Learning Disability, Pervasive Developmental Disorder (PDD/NOS), Speech/Language Disability
Program Hours: October - May, Monday: 4:30-6:30 p.m.
Program Capacity: 2 groups of 10
Staff/Child Ratio: 2:10
Fees: $895 for 28 two-hour sessions. $50 registration and evaluation fee
Method of Payment: 4 payments of $233.75 (October, November, January, and February)
Medication Administered: No
Transportation Provided: No. Programs meet at the Resurrection Lutheran Church, 44-10 192nd Street, North Flushing. Accessible by car, Northern Boulevard

bus or Long Island Railroad.
Wheelchair Accessible: No
Service Description: S.T.A.G.E.S. (Special Theatre Arts Group for Exceptional Students) uses drama and art to improve social skills of at-risk kids (learning disabled, oppositional/defiant, socially inhibited/withdrawn, hyperactive with attention deficit) and children with special needs (cognitive delays, autistic spectrum disorders, expressive language deficits, auditory processing difficulties).
Contact: Maxine Fields, Program Director

SACRED HEART ROMAN CATHOLIC CHURCH

41 Adelphi St.
Brooklyn, NY 11205

(718) 625-5115 Administrative
(718) 625-2918 FAX

Father Walter Murphy, Director
Languages Spoken: Spanish

Services

Homework Help Programs

Ages: 6 to 11
Program Hours: Monday-Thursday: 3:30-5:30 p.m.
Service Description: Mainstream after school program providing homework help. Children with special needs are considered on a case-by-case basis.

SAFE HAVEN WEST SIDE BASKETBALL LEAGUE'S CHAMPIONS TEAM

55 W. 92nd St.
New York, NY 10028

(212) 932-9377 Administrative

Eileen Palley, Director

Services

Sports, Team/Leagues

Ages: 6 to 21
Population Served: Attention Deficit Disorder (ADD/ADHD), Autism, Cerebral Palsy, Developmental Disability, Down Syndrome, Health Impairment, Mental Retardation (mild-moderate), Mental Retardation (severe-profound), Multiple Disability, Neurological Disability, Seizure Disorder, Speech/Language Disability
Area Served: All Boroughs
Service Description: A volunteer,

<continued...>

parent-organized program that provides children with special needs the opportunity to participate in sports. Games are held from January to March, in schools in Manhattan's Upper West Side. Call for more information.

SAMUEL FIELD YM-YWHA

58-20 Little Neck Parkway
Little Neck, NY 11362

(718) 225-6750 [259] Administrative
(718) 423-8276 FAX

samfield@aol.com

Robin Topol, C.S.W., Director of Special Services

Services

SPECIAL SERVICES FOR PEOPLE WITH DEVELOPMENTAL DISABILITIES
Homework Help Programs
Recreational Activities

Ages: 5 and up
Population Served: Autism, Cerebral Palsy, Deaf/Hard of Hearing, Developmental Delay, Developmental Disability, Down Syndrome, Learning Disability, Mental Retardation (mild-moderate), Mental Retardation (severe-profound), Neurological Disability
Program Hours: Monday - Thursday: 3-9 p.m.; Sundays: 10 a.m.-5 p.m.
Program Capacity: 100
Staff/Child Ratio: 1:6
Fees: Sliding Scale
Method of Payment: Medicaid
Transportation Provided: No
Service Description: After school program providing homework help and recreational activities for children with developmental disabilities.
Contact: Sue Jones, (728) 225-6750

CENTER FOR HELPING INDIVIDUALS WITH LEARNING DISABILITIES
Homework Help Programs
Recreational Activities

Ages: 5 to 12
Population Served: Attention Deficit Disorder (ADD/ADHD)
Program Hours: 3-6 p.m.
Program Capacity: 50
Staff/Child Ratio: 1:6
Fees: Sliding Scale
Method of Payment: Medicaid
Transportation Provided: Yes
Service Description: Programs are designed to provide socialization skills to children with attention deficit disorder.
Contact: John Smith, Program Coordinator (718) 225-6750

SEARCH BEYOND ADVENTURES

8 Common St., Suite 2
Waltham, MA 02451

(800) 800-9979 Administrative
(781) 647-5548 FAX

www.searchbeyond.com
travel@searchbeyond.com; search99@idt.net

Connie Magnuson, Director
Languages Spoken: French, Hindi, Sign Language, Tamil

Services

Travel

Ages: 18 and up
Population Served: Deaf/Hard of Hearing, Mental Retardation (mild-moderate), Mental Retardation (severe-profound), Seizure Disorder, Speech/Language Disability, Visual Disability/Blind
Staff/Child Ratio: 1:4 (average); 1:2 (for extra assistance trips)
Fees: Vary with tour
Method of Payment: Payment Plan
Medication Administered: Yes
Transportation Provided: Yes (varies with tour)
Wheelchair Accessible: Yes (some trips)
Service Description: Provides all-inclusive supervised tours for people with mental retardation or physical disabilities. Over 150 tours, by air, cruise, bus and train, ranging from 3 to 15 days, visit destinations in North America and overseas and depart from cities throughout the United States. Camping trips and urban tours are available. An extra assistance option is available.

SENECA NEIGHBORHOOD CENTER

1231 Lafayette Ave., 2nd Fl.
Bronx, NY 10474

(718) 378-1300 Administrative
(718) 893-2949 FAX

R. Edward Lee, Executive Director
Languages Spoken: Spanish

Services

Homework Help Programs
Recreational Activities

Ages: 6 to 18
Area Served: All Boroughs
Program Hours: Monday - Friday: 3:30-6 p.m. (6 to 12 years-olds); 7-10 p.m. (13 to 18 year-olds)
Wheelchair Accessible: Yes
Service Description: Provides after school programs for 6 to 12 year-olds and 13 to 18

< continued... >

year-olds which includes homework help, recreation and socialization with special activities on the weekends . Social workers and counselors are available for counseling, entitlement information and crisis intervention. All programs are mainstream, but children with special needs are accepted on a case-by-case basis.

SHADOW BOX THEATRE (THE)

325 West End Ave.
New York, NY 10023

(212) 724-0677 Administrative
(212) 724-0767 FAX

www.shadowboxtheatre.org
sbt@shadowboxtheatre.org

Sandra Robbins, Founder/Artistic Director

Services

Theater Performances

Ages: 4 to 11
Area Served: NYC Metro
Fees: $4.50-$4.75 per school group; $8 per individual
Method of Payment: Board of Education purchase order; school check; cash
Service Description: Theatre can provide your classroom with creative arts workshops in storytelling, puppetry, dramatics, dance and music for a multi-faceted learning experience integrated with the core curriculum.

SHIELD INSTITUTE (THE)

144-61 Roosevelt Ave.
Flushing, NY 11354

(718) 939-8700 Administrative
(718) 886-1534 Early Intervention
(718) 961-7669 FAX

www.shield.org

Susan Provenzano, Ed.D., Executive Director
Languages Spoken: French Creole, Greek, Italian, Portuguese, Romanian, Russian, Spanish, Turkish

Sites

1. SHIELD INSTITUTE (THE) - BRONX WEST EARLY LEARNING CENTER

200 W. Tremont Ave.
Bronx, NY 10453

(718) 294-3050 Administrative
(718) 716-6834 FAX

Ingrid Moodie, MS, Director

Services

Homework Help Programs
Recreational Activities

Ages: 5 to 8
Population Served: All Disabilities
Area Served: Districts 9 and 10 in the Bronx.
Program Hours: Monday - Friday: 3-5:45 p.m.
Program Capacity: 185
Staff/Child Ratio: 1:34
Medication Administered: No
Sites: 1

SID JACOBSON NORTH SHORE YM-YWHA

300 Forest Dr.
East Hills, NY 11548

(516) 484-1545 Administrative
(516) 484-7354 FAX

www.sjjcc.org

Lisa Hock, MSW, Supervisor of Special Services

Services

SPARK PROGRAM
Arts and Crafts Instruction
Homework Help Programs
Sports, Individual

Ages: 5 to 8
Population Served: Attention Deficit Disorder (ADD/ADHD), Learning Disability
Area Served: Queens, Nassau
Program Hours: Monday, Wednesday: 4-6 p.m.
Program Capacity: 10 participants
Staff/Child Ratio: 1:3
Fees: Call for fees
Wheelchair Accessible: Yes
Service Description: An after school program where high-functioning special needs children can get a head start on their homework and then participate in a creative activity class, such as sports skills and fundamentals of arts and crafts.

Field Trips/Excursions

Ages: 11-12, 13-18
Population Served: Attention Deficit Disorder (ADD/ADHD), Pervasive Developmental Disorder (PDD/NOS), Speech and Language Delay
Area Served: Queens, Nassau, Suffolk
Program Hours: Second Sunday of every month, 11 a.m.-5 p.m.
Program Capacity: 15 participants.
Staff/Child Ratio: 1:4
Fees: Call for fees.
Transportation Provided: Yes
Service Description: Supervised adventure with

< continued... >

new and old friends to a Mets game, museums, amusement parks, the Bronx Zoo, or an off Broadway play.

Recreational Activities
Social Skills Training
Sports, Team/Leagues

Ages: 4 to 9
Population Served: Attention Deficit Disorder (ADD/ADHD), Emotional Disability, Learning Disability, Speech and Language Delays
Area Served: Queens, Nassau
Program Hours: First and third Sunday of every month
Program Capacity: 15 per program.
Staff/Child Ratio: 1:3
Fees: Call for fees.
Service Description: Interpersonal relationships and social skills are developed through art, sports, cooking, discussions and special events led by social workers and special educators.

Social Skills Training

Ages: 11 to 18
Population Served: Attention Deficit Disorder (ADD/ADHD), Learning Disability
Area Served: Queens
Program Hours: Monday: 5-6:20 p.m.
Program Capacity: 10 participants
Staff/Child Ratio: 1:4
Fees: Call for fees.
Wheelchair Accessible: Yes
Service Description: Provide information and a positive, new way of looking at what it means to be a girl for the pre-teen/teen with ADHD or a social/learning disability.

SNUG HARBOR CULTURAL CENTER, INC.

1000 Richmond Terrace
Staten Island, NY 10301

(718) 448-2500 Administrative
(718) 442-8534 FAX

www.snug-harbor.org

Carrie Cooperider, Director of Education

Services

Arts and Crafts Instruction
Creative Writing
Storytelling
Theater Performances

Ages: All Ages
Population Served: All Disabilities
Area Served: Staten Island
Program Hours: Program takes place the 2nd Saturday of each month beginning in September, from 1-3 p.m.
Fees: Adults, $4; Children over 5, $3
Medication Administered: No

Transportation Provided: No
Service Description: Family Days at Snug Harbor Cultural Center provides a variety of activities and programs for all children and their parents or care givers. Children with special needs are considered on a case-by-case basis.

SOL GOLDMAN YM-YWHA

344 E. 14th St.
New York, NY 10003

(212) 780-0800 Administrative

Jeremy Lieberman

Services

Arts and Crafts Instruction
Homework Help Programs
Music Instruction
Recreational Activities

Ages: 4 to 12
Area Served: All Boroughs
Program Hours: Monday - Friday: 2:45-6 p.m.; Holidays: 8 a.m.-6 p.m.
Program Capacity: 100
Staff/Child Ratio: 1:4
Fees: Non-member, $300 per month; Member, $260 per month
Wheelchair Accessible: Yes
Service Description: Barrier-free facility that promotes the inclusion of children with special needs into socialization programs. Children with disabilities are accepted on a case-by-case basis. Activities include cooking, service projects, talent shows, trips, music and arts and crafts. Also has a roof top playground and gym. Snack provided.

SOUTH SHORE YMCA

3939 Richmond Ave.
Staten Island, NY 10312

(718) 227-3200 Administrative

Linda Allocco, Executive Director

Services

Arts and Crafts Instruction
Recreational Activities

Ages: 3 and up
Area Served: Staten Island
Wheelchair Accessible: Yes
Service Description: Full range of social, recreation and summer programs. Will include children with special needs on an individual basis. Call for more information.

SOUTH STREET SEAPORT MUSEUM (THE)

207 Front St.
New York, NY 10038

(212) 748-8600 Information
(212) 748-8610 FAX

www.southstseaport.org

Ken Struve, Director of School Programs

Services

Museums

Ages: 6 to 16
Service Description: Provides a variety of programs that enable students to explore a subject or concept by encouraging them to develop critical and creative thinking skills. Programs are designed to serve children with special needs.

SOUTHEAST BRONX NEIGHBORHOOD CENTER

955 Tinton Ave.
Bronx, NY 10456

(718) 589-5553 Administrative

Diane M. Herbert, Program Director
Languages Spoken: Spanish

Services

LEISURELY YOURS
Arts and Crafts Instruction
Computer Classes
Exercise Classes/Groups
Homework Help Programs
Recreational Activities

Ages: 12 to 21
Population Served: Developmental Disability, Mental Retardation (Mild/Moderate), Mental Retardation (Severe/Profound)
Area Served: Bronx
Program Hours: June - September, Monday - Friday: 3:30-6 p.m.
Program Capacity: 14
Staff/Child Ratio: 1:4
Transportation Provided: Yes. School transport vendor brings students to program site; program vendor drops student home.
Service Description: Leisurely Yours provides homework assistance and opportunities for structured and unstructured activities in music and dance, arts and crafts and table top games. Program focuses on social skills development and homework improvement.

SPECIAL OLYMPICS

1325 G St., NW, Suite 500
Washington, DC, 20005

(202) 628-3630 Administrative
(202) 824-0200 FAX

www.specialolympics.com

Languages Spoken: Spanish

Sites

1. SPECIAL OLYMPICS - NEW YORK
211 E. 43rd St., Suite 1205
New York, NY 10017

(212) 661-3963 Administrative
(212) 661-4658 FAX

www.nyso.org

Ruby Gary, Director of Field Service

Services

Sports, Individual
Sports, Team/Leagues
Swimming

Ages: 8 and up
Population Served: Developmental Disability, Mental Retardation (mild-moderate), Physical/Orthopedic Disability
Staff/Child Ratio: 1:3
Fees: None
Transportation Provided: Yes
Wheelchair Accessible: Yes
Service Description: Year-round sports program for people with mental retardation in a variety of Olympic-type sports, including soccer, swimming, track and field, basketball, cross-country skiing, bowling and bicycling. Transportation included for some programs. Call the New York City office for the contact in your borough.
Sites: 1

SPOKE THE HUB DANCING

748 Union St.
Brooklyn, NY 11215

(718) 857-5158 Administrative

www.spokethehub.org

Elise Long, Director

Services

<continued...>

Dancing Instruction

Ages: 2 to Adult
Area Served: All Boroughs
Program Capacity: 12 classes
Fees: Based on weeks of enrollment. Call for more information.
Service Description: Multi-faceted community arts organization which offers creative arts, i.e., dance, drama, and fitness classes. Willing to mainstream children with special needs on an individual basis.

SPROUT

893 Amsterdam Ave.
New York, NY 10025

(212) 222-9575 Administrative

www.gosprout.org
vacations@gosprout.org

Anthony DiSalvo, Executive Director

Services

BROOKLYN AND MANHATTAN SCHOOL VACATION PROGRAM
Field Trips/Excursions

Ages: 14 to 21
Population Served: Developmental Disabilities
Area Served: Brooklyn, Manhattan
Program Capacity: 10 participants per group.
Staff/Child Ratio: 3:10
Service Description: Offers extended trips during the school holiday periods for individuals with developmental disabilities (moderate to high functioning level). Participants must be able to function within the staff to participant ratio.

NEW YORK CITY PROGRAM
Field Trips/Excursions
Recreational Activities

Ages: 13 to Adult
Population Served: Developmental Disabilities
Area Served: Brookln, Manhattan, Queens
Program Capacity: 10 participants per group (moderate to high functioning level and ambulatory)
Staff/Child Ratio: 3:10
Service Description: Offers educational, recreational and cultural activities on weekday evenings and on Saturday and Sunday afternoons. Activities offered through this program includes: parties, theatre, museum visit, video club, bowling, sporting events, dinners, jazz brunches, picnics, and hikes.

ST. ALOYSIUS EDUCATION CLINIC

219 W. 132nd St.
New York, NY 10027

(212) 234-6495 Administrative
(212) 234-6495 FAX

Beth Pettit, Executive Director

Services

Arts and Crafts Instruction
Computer Classes
English as a Second Language
Remedial Education
Tutoring

Ages: 3.5 to 13
Population Served: Gifted, Learning Disability
Area Served: All Boroughs
Program Hours: Monday - Thursday: 8:15 a.m.-3:30 p.m., Friday: 8:15 a.m.-12 noon, July 1st - August 6th.
Program Capacity: 500
Staff/Child Ratio: 1:5
Fees: 8:30 a.m.-3:30 p.m. ($230); 8:30 a.m.-6 p.m. ($380)
Method of Payment: Money order, check, cash
Medication Administered: Yes, oral only
Service Description: Gifted academic summer program offering afternoon recreational activities. Tutoring done in a group setting.

ST. ANTHONY YOUTH CENTER

143 Thompson St.
New York, NY 10012

(212) 777-6177 Administrative

Languages Spoken: Sign Language

Services

Arts and Crafts Instruction
Recreational Activities
Remedial Education

Ages: 5 to 20
Population Served: Deaf/Hard of Hearing
Service Description: Provides recreational and educational activities for children and young adults. Call for more information.

ST. LUKE'S-ROOSEVELT HOSPITAL CENTER - ST. LUKE'S DIVISION

1111 Amsterdam Ave.
New York, NY 10025

(212) 523-4000 General Information
(212) 523-3062 Child Psychiatry
(212) 523-4728 Crime Victim Treatment Center
(212) 523-2876 HCBS Waiver
(212) 523-3847 Pediatrics

www.wehealnewyork.org

Services

CHILD PSYCHIATRY / ADOLESCENT ALTERNATIVE DAY PROGRAM
Recreational Activities

Ages: 6 to 13
Area Served: All Boroughs
Program Hours: Call for information
Fees: Call for information
Method of Payment: Medicaid
Transportation Provided: No
Wheelchair Accessible: Yes
Service Description: Provides a variety of recreational activities for children. Call center for further information.

ST. MARGARET'S CHURCH - LONGWOOD

940 E. 156th St.
Bronx, NY 10455

(718) 589-4430 Administrative
(718) 542-3013 FAX

Patricia Bryant, Director
Languages Spoken: Spanish

Services

Arts and Crafts Instruction
Field Trips/Excursions
Homework Help Programs
Music Instruction
Tutoring

Ages: 6 to 13
Population Served: Attention Deficit Disorder (ADD/ADHD), Learning Disability
Area Served: Bronx (Longwood section)
Program Hours: Monday - Friday: 3-6 p.m.
Program Capacity: 38
Fees: $50 per month plus $35 registration.
Method of Payment: Cash, check, money order
Transportation Provided: Yes, pick-ups for area schools.
Service Description: After school programs providing educational and recreational activities to children. Offers tutor in all subject areas and also offers ESL for spanish speaking students. Students participate in board games and trips to parks and recreation areas. Tutoring is

provided on a 1:1 basis.

ST. MATTHEWS AND ST. TIMOTHY'S NEIGHBORHOOD CENTER

26 W. 84th St.
New York, NY 10024

(212) 362-6750 Administrative
(212) 787-6196 FAX

Cindy Hatcher, Executive Director
Languages Spoken: Spanish

Services

STAR LEARNING CENTER
Tutoring

Ages: 6 to 18
Population Served: Learning Disability
Program Hours: Call for information
Program Capacity: 170/year
Staff/Child Ratio: 1:1
Transportation Provided: No
Service Description: Provides highly individualized tutoring in reading, math and writing to students who are behind grade level. Tutors are individually trained and supervised by reading/learning disabilities specialists.
Contact: Rita Spano, (212) 362-6750

STATEN ISLAND BROADWAY CENTER YMCA

651 Broadway
Staten Island, NY 10310

(718) 981-4933 Administrative

Services

Arts and Crafts Instruction
Dancing Instruction
Recreational Activities
Sports, Team/Leagues
Swimming

Ages: 5 to 12
Population Served: All Disabilities
Program Hours: Monday - Friday: 3-6 p.m.
Fees: Call for information
Medication Administered: No
Transportation Provided: No
Service Description: Provides after school recreational activities for children. In addition to typical recreation, offers dance classes and gymnastics. Children with disabilities are considered on a case-by-case basis. Call for more information.

STATEN ISLAND CHILDREN'S COUNCIL

420 Targee St.
Staten Island, NY 10304

(718) 447-8521 Administrative

Languages Spoken: Spanish

Sites

1. STATEN ISLAND CHILDREN'S COUNCIL
75 Victory Blvd.
Staten Island, NY 10301

(718) 447-3329 Administrative

Services

Arts and Crafts Instruction
Child Care Centers

Ages: 5 to 12
Population Served: Developmental Disability, Emotional Disability, Substance Abuse
Area Served: Staten Island
Program Hours: Call for information
Fees: Call for information
Transportation Provided: No
Wheelchair Accessible: Yes
Service Description: Provides day care and after school care. Willing to accept children with disabilities on an case-by-case basis.
Sites: 1

STATEN ISLAND CHILDREN'S MUSEUM

1000 Richmond Terrace
Staten Island, NY 10301

(718) 273-2060 Administrative
(718) 273-2836 FAX

Dina Rosenthal, Executive Director

Services

Museums

STATEN ISLAND HISTORICAL SOCIETY

441 Clarke Ave.
Staten Island, NY 10306

(718) 351-1611 Administrative

www.historicrichmondtown.org

Angela Russo, Director

Services

HISTORIC RICHMOND TOWN
Museums

Ages: 5 to Adult
Area Served: NYC Metro Area
Program Hours: Wednesday - Saturday: 10 a.m.-5 p.m. (July - August)
Wednesday - Sunday: 1-5 p.m. (September - June)
Program Capacity: Varies depending on event.
Staff/Child Ratio: 1:15
Fees: Children 6-18 $2.50, Adults $4.00.
Method of Payment: Check, cash, credit cards for advance payments.
Wheelchair Accessible: Partial accessibility, historical buildings were restored as is.
Service Description: An authentic village and museum complex interpreting three centuries of daily life and culture on the Island.

STATEN ISLAND MENTAL HEALTH SOCIETY, INC.

669 Castleton Ave.
Staten Island, NY 10301

(718) 442-2225 Administrative
(718) 442-2289 FAX

Dr. Kenneth Popler, Executive Director
Languages Spoken: Spanish

Sites

1. STATEN ISLAND MENTAL HEALTH SOCIETY, INC. - SLOSSON TERRACE
14 Slosson Terrace
Staten Island, NY 10301

(718) 720-6727 Administrative

Carol Briedel, Program Director, Family Support Services

Services

PROJECT FOR ACADEMIC STUDENT SUCCESS (PASS) / TEEN CENTER
Recreational Activities
Tutoring

Ages: 11 to 17
Program Hours: Monday - Thursday: 1-9 p.m., Friday: 9 a.m.-5 p.m.
Fees: None
Service Description: Offers a variety of services to families of at-risk children and/or adolescents receiving services in the community.
Sites: 1

STATEN ISLAND PARENT RESOURCE CENTER

2795 Richmond Ave.
Staten Island, NY 10314

(718) 698-5307 Administrative
(718) 370-1142 FAX

Eileen Duva, Coordinator

Services

Recreational Activities

Ages: 5 to 17
Population Served: Emotional Disability
Area Served: Staten Island
Program Hours: Monday - Friday: 9 a.m.-5 p.m.
Fees: None
Transportation Provided: No
Service Description: Provides a variety of services and programs for children with emotional disabilities and their parents.

STATEN ISLAND YMCA

651 Broadway
Staten Island, NY 10310

(718) 981-4933 Administrative

Services

Arts and Crafts Instruction
Recreational Activities

Ages: 6 to 12
Area Served: Staten Island
Program Hours: Monday - Friday and Saturday, hours vary depending on program.
Fees: $60 - $105 per 8 week class
Method of Payment: Cash, Check, Credit Card, Money Order
Medication Administered: No
Transportation Provided: No
Service Description: Offers after school recreational and educational activities. Provides job skill development and youth literacy program. Children with special needs are accepted on a case-by-case basis.

STATEN ISLAND ZOO

614 Broadway
Staten Island, NY 10310

(718) 442-3101 Administrative
(718) 442-3100 Administrative

Vincent Gatullo, Director

Services

Zoos/Wildlife Parks

Ages: 5 and up
Area Served: NYC Metro Area
Wheelchair Accessible: Yes
Service Description: Offers family workshops and educational programs. Call for more information.

STEINWAY CHILD AND FAMILY SERVICES - FAMILY SUPPORT PROGRAM

41-36 27th St.
Long Island City, NY 11101

(718) 389-5100 Administrative
(718) 391-9665 FAX

www.steinway.org

Michael Gerard, Director of Special Needs Program

Services

Social Skills Training

Ages: 5 and up
Population Served: Emotional Disability (severe)
Program Hours: Call for information
Fees: Sliding Scale
Medication Administered: No
Transportation Provided: Yes, for families residing in the Long Island City area.
Wheelchair Accessible: Yes
Service Description: Assists children with their social development in a mainstream program, providing support when needed.

SUNDAY SCHOOL FOR AUTISTIC SPECTRUM CHILDREN

c/o St. Philips Episcopal Church,
1072 80th St.
Brooklyn, NY 11228

(718) 745-2505 Church
(718) 236-9558 Administrative

bklyncandle@aol.com

Terrie Moseder, Sunday School Coordinator

Services

<continued...>

Religious Activities

Ages: 4 and up
Area Served: All Boroughs
Program Hours: October - May. Call for information
Wheelchair Accessible: No
Service Description: Sunday school classes for children with an autism spectrum disorder. Sign up the first week in October; classes run from October through May.

SUNDIAL SPECIAL VACATIONS

2609 Hwy 101 N, Suite #103
Seaside, OR 97138

(800) 547-9198 Toll Free
(503) 738-3324 Administrative
(503) 738-3369 FAX

www.sundial-travel.com

Bruce Conner, Administrator

Services

Travel

Ages: 16 and up
Population Served: Developmental Disability
Staff/Child Ratio: 1:6 (average)
Wheelchair Accessible: Yes
Service Description: Monthly trips to various destinations are offered. Extra assistance required for people using wheelchairs.

SUSAN E. WAGNER DAY CARE CENTER

1140 E. 229th St.
Bronx, NY 10466

(718) 547-1735 Administrative
(718) 547-0629 FAX

Joyce L. James, Director

Sites

1. SUSAN E. WAGNER DAY CARE CENTER

1140 E. 229th St.
Bronx, NY 10466

(718) 547-1735 Administrative
(718) 547-0629 FAX

Joyce L. James, Director

2. SUSAN E. WAGNER DAY CARE CENTER

4102 White Plains Rd.
Bronx, NY 10466

(718) 547-0501 Administrative
(718) 547-2013 FAX

3. SUSAN E. WAGNER DAY CARE CENTER

5401 Post Rd.
Bronx, NY 10471

(718) 601-5401 Administrative

Services

Arts and Crafts Instruction
Child Care Centers
Field Trips/Excursions
Homework Help Programs

Ages: Birth to 6
Population Served: Developmental Disability, Speech/Language Disability
Area Served: Bronx
Program Hours: Monday - Friday: 8 a.m.-2:30 p.m.
Program Capacity: 4 classes, 12 children per class
Staff/Child Ratio: 3:12
Medication Administered: Yes
Transportation Provided: Yes
Wheelchair Accessible: Yes
Service Description: Day care center offering child care services and homework help programs. Call for more information.
Sites: 1 2 3

SUTTON GYMNASTICS AND FITNESS CENTER

20 Cooper Square
New York, NY 10003

(212) 533-9390 Administrative
(212) 533-7342 FAX

Services

Recreational Activities
Sports, Individual

Ages: 1 and up
Area Served: All Boroughs
Program Hours: Call for information
Fees: Call for information
Medication Administered: No
Transportation Provided: No
Service Description: Gym that offers children's recreational programs. Children with special needs are considered on a case-by-case basis.

SYLVAN LEARNING CENTER

1556 3rd Ave.
New York, NY 10128

(888) 338-2283 Toll Free
(212) 828-1620 Administrative
(212) 828-1619 FAX

www.educate.com
info@sylvanhelp.com

Services

Remedial Education
Test Preparation

Ages: 5 to 18
Population Served: Learning Disability
Area Served: Manhattan
Fees: $59 per hour; $175 assessment fee; $50 registration fee
Method of Payment: Monthly payment plan, pre-payment program or loan
Service Description: Reading, math, study skills, SAT preparation, writing and state test preparation

TADA! THEATER

120 W. 28th St., 2nd Fl.
New York, NY 10001

(212) 627-1732 Administrative
(212) 243-6736 FAX

www.tadatheater.com
tada@tadatheater.com

Janine Nina Trevens, Artistic Director

Services

Acting Instruction
Creative Writing
Theater Performances

Ages: 3 to 18
Area Served: All Boroughs
Program Hours: Saturdays and Sundays. Times vary by program.
Fees: $185 - $260 (varies by program)
Transportation Provided: No
Wheelchair Accessible: Yes
Service Description: Programs in creative dramatics and musical theater are offered during the school year. There is also a year-long youth theater for children in grades 4 through 8, which produces original musicals performed by youth for family audiences and offers musical theater, acting and playwriting classes.

TAKE ME TO THE WATER

120 E. 89th St., Suite 1D
New York, NY 10128

(888) 794-6692 Information
(212) 828-8842 FAX

www.takemetothewater.com

Services

Swimming

Ages: All Ages
Population Served: All Disabilities (depending on severity of disability)
Program Hours: 7 days a week, after school hours.
Staff/Child Ratio: 1:1
Fees: $21/session
Method of Payment: Cash, Check, Credit Card, Money Order
Medication Administered: No
Transportation Provided: No
Wheelchair Accessible: No
Service Description: Swim program designed for all ages and abilities. Swim team, special needs instruction, and Baby & Me toddler classes.

TENDER CARE

5 W. 63rd St.
New York, NY 10023

(212) 875-4117 Administrative
(212) 580-0441 FAX

Peter Hoontis, Executive Director
Languages Spoken: Spanish

Services

Child Care Centers

Ages: 6 months to 5 years
Population Served: Asthma, Developmental Delay, Developmental Disability, Gifted, Speech/Language Disability
Area Served: All Boroughs
Service Description: Provides child care services on both a part-time and full time basis. Mainstreams children with special needs.

TENNIS FOR PEOPLE WITH PHYSICAL DISABILITIES

Flushing Meadows/Corona Park
Flushing Meadows, 11368

(718) 760-6200 Administrative

Tina Taps, Program Director

Services

Sports, Individual

Ages: All Ages
Population Served: Autism, Mental Retardation (mild-moderate), Physical/Orthopedic Disability
Area Served: Queens
Program Hours: Call for information
Fees: None
Medication Administered: No
Transportation Provided: No
Wheelchair Accessible: Yes
Service Description: Tennis lessons are provided for children and adults.

TENTH STREET TOTS CHILDCARE CENTER

297 E. 10th St.
New York, NY 10009

(212) 982-8701 Administrative

Angela Hughes, Director
Languages Spoken: Spanish

Services

Child Care Centers

Ages: 2 to 5
Area Served: Manhattan
Wheelchair Accessible: Yes
Service Description: Offers child care services. Will accepts children with special needs. Call for more information.

THIRD STREET MUSIC SCHOOL SETTLEMENT

235 E. 11th St.
New York, NY 10003

(212) 777-3240 Administrative
(212) 477-1808 FAX

Barbara E. Field, Executive Director

Services

Arts and Crafts Instruction
Dancing Instruction
Music Instruction

Ages: 2.5 and up
Service Description: Provides individual and group instruction in music, art, dance, voice and visual arts, regardless of ability or financial need. Call for more information.

TREASURE ISLAND

405 81st St.
Brooklyn, NY 11209

(718) 238-7676 Administrative
(718) 745-4365 FAX

Audrey Silberman, Executive Director
Languages Spoken: Italian, Russian, Spanish

Services

Child Care Centers

Ages: 2 to 6
Population Served: Developmental Delay, Learning Disability
Area Served: Brooklyn, Staten Island
Service Description: Provides child care services.

TRINITY PARISH PRESCHOOL

74 Trinity Place
New York, NY 10006

(212) 602-0829 Administrative
(212) 602-9601 FAX

Nadine Geyer, Executive Director
Languages Spoken: French, Italian, Spanish

Services

Child Care Centers

Ages: 6 months to 5 years
Wheelchair Accessible: Yes
Service Description: Provides child care services for infants, toddlers and preschool age children. Children with special needs accepted on a case-by-case basis.

TUESDAY NIGHT TEENS

300 Forest Drive
East Hills, NY 11548

(516) 484-1545 Administrative

Cara Greene, CSW, Executive Director

Services

Recreational Activities

Ages: 13 to 18
Population Served: Learning Disability
Area Served: Queens, Nassau, Suffolk
Fees: $195 for 15 2-hour sessions
Method of Payment: Payment Plan
Service Description: The program consists of unique groups, designed for high functioning teens. Focus is placed on the development of social skills. This program includes art, trips, sports, ongoing rap sessions and special projects.

TUTORING READING AND MATH CENTER

2525 Eastchester Road
Bronx, NY 10469

(718) 881-7964 Administrative

Services

Tutoring

Ages: 5 to 18
Population Served: Emotional Disability, Learning Disability
Service Description: Offers one-to-one tutorial services. Call for more information.

UNION SETTLEMENT ASSOCIATION

237 E. 104th St.
New York, NY 10029

(212) 828-6000 Administrative
(212) 828-6022 FAX

Ramon J. Rodríguez, Executive Director
Languages Spoken: Spanish

Services

Arts and Crafts Instruction
Computer Classes
English as a Second Language
Field Trips/Excursions
Homework Help Programs
Music Instruction

Ages: 6 to 12
Population Served: Attention Deficit Disorder (ADD/ADHD), Developmental Delay, Emotional Disability,
Learning Disability
Area Served: Manhattan
Program Hours: Monday - Friday: 3-6 p.m., 8-6 p.m. during summer
Program Capacity: 100
Staff/Child Ratio: 1:10
Fees: ACD determines fees.
Wheelchair Accessible: No
Service Description: Offers various after school and recreational activities including museum trips and games. Also has ESL for Spanish speaking participants.
Contact: Troy Calhoun, 212-828-6113

UNION THEOLOGICAL SEMINARY DAY CARE CENTER

90 LaSalle St.
New York, NY 10027

(212) 663-9318 Administrative
(212) 663-9326 FAX

Sarah Sexton, Executive Director

Services

Child Care Centers

Ages: 6 months to 5 years
Population Served: Learning Disability, Physical/Orthopedic Disability, Speech/Language Disability
Area Served: Manhattan
Program Capacity: 50
Staff/Child Ratio: 1:3 and 1:8
Fees: Call for information
Wheelchair Accessible: Yes
Service Description: Child care services offered to mainstream and special needs children.

UNITED CEREBRAL PALSY OF NEW YORK CITY

80 Maiden Lane, 8th Fl.
New York, NY 10038

(877) 827-2663 Information & Referral/Project Connect
(212) 683-6700 Administrative
(212) 679-0893 FAX

www.ucpnyc.org
infoucp@aol.com

Edward Matthews, Executive Director
Languages Spoken: Hebrew, French, Haitian Creole, Russian, Sign Language, Spanish

< continued...>

Sites

1. UNITED CEREBRAL PALSY OF NEW YORK CITY
80 Maiden Lane, 8th Fl.
New York, NY 10038

(212) 683-6700 Administrative
(212) 679-0893 FAX

www.ucpnyc.org

Edward Matthews, Executive Director

**2. UNITED CEREBRAL PALSY OF NEW YORK CITY -
BROOKLYN CENTER / HEALTH CARE SERVICES**
175 Lawrence Ave.
Brooklyn, NY 11230

(718) 436-7979 Administrative
(718) 436-9387 [100] Health Care Services
(718) 436-0071 FAX
(718) 436-8101 FAX - Health Care Services

**3. UNITED CEREBRAL PALSY OF NEW YORK CITY -
MANHATTAN CHILDREN'S CENTER / HEALTH CARE
SERVICES**
122 E. 23rd St.
New York, NY 10010

(212) 677-7400 Administrative
(212) 677-7400 [200] Health Care Services
(212) 529-2071 FAX

**4. UNITED CEREBRAL PALSY OF NEW YORK CITY -
STATEN ISLAND CHILDREN'S CENTER**
281 Port Richmond Ave.
Staten Island, NY 10302

(718) 442-6006 Administrative
(718) 273-5467 FAX

Clare Bonafede, Director

Services

S.P.I.R.I.T.
Arts and Crafts Instruction
Exercise Classes/Groups
Field Trips/Excursions
Recreational Activities
Sports, Individual
Sports, Team/Leagues
Swimming

Ages: 10 to 21
Population Served: Cerebral Palsy, Developmental
Disability, Down Syndrome, Mental Retardation
(mild/moderate), Mental Retardation (severe/profound),
Multiple Disability, Neurological Disability, Physical
Orthopedic Disability, Rare Disorders, Seizure Disorder,
Speech/Language Disability, Spina Bifida, Traumatic Brain
Injury, Visual Disability/Blind
Area Served: Manhattan, Brooklyn, Staten Island
Program Hours: 12 months, Saturday: 10 a.m.-3 p.m.
Program Capacity: Staten Island, 26; Brooklyn and
Manhattan, 34

Staff/Child Ratio: 1:3
Fees: None
Transportation Provided: Yes, must have
Medicaid number. Limited number of slots for
persons not Medicaid eligible.
Wheelchair Accessible: Yes
Service Description: S.P.I.R.I.T. offers the
opportunity to experience the diverse social and
recreational experiences available in the metro
area. Trips include-parks, zoos, movies, bowling,
Circle Line South Street Seaport and restaurants.
Once a month group members can swim in
UCP/NYC's accessible indoor pool. Activities in
our center include creative projects/arts and
crafts, sports/movement, cooking, discussion
groups, games, music, and parties.
Contact: Manhattan: Susan Rae, Assistant
Director of Recreation Services
Brooklyn & Staten Island: Michael Bolton,
Director of Recreation Services

Sites: 2 3 4

Arts and Crafts Instruction
Homework Help Programs
Music Instruction
Storytelling

Ages: 5 to 12
Population Served: Cerebral Palsy,
Develomental Disability, Down Sydrome, Mental
Retardation (mild/moder.), Mental
Retardation(severe/prof.), Multiple Disability,
Neurological Disability, Physical/Orthopedic
Disability, Rare Disorders, Seizure Disorder,
Speech/Language Disability, Spina Bifida,
Traumatic Brain Injury, Visual Disability/Blind.
Area Served: Brooklyn, Manhattan
Program Hours: October to early June, Monday
- Friday: 3-5:30 p.m.
Program Capacity: 22
Staff/Child Ratio: 1:2.75
Transportation Provided: Yes
Wheelchair Accessible: Yes
Service Description: The After School program
provides a stimulation array of recreational
activities for students 5 to 12. Students
participate in a variety of activities that enhance
peer interaction and social development. These
include: arts and crafts, cooking, gym,
playground time, movies and games. Snacks are
also provided. The program is a collaborative
effort between UCP/NYC and the New York City
Board of Education. Manhattan program serves
children who attend, P.S. 138 and P.79 only.
Brooklyn program serves children who attend
P.S. 396 only.

Brooklyn After School
110 Chester Street
Brooklyn, NY 11210

<continued...>

Manhattan After School
PS 136 @ 30
128th & Lexington Avenue
New York, NY 10035

Contact: Manhattan:Susan Rae, Assist. Director, Recreation Services.
Brooklyn: Michael Bolton, Director of Recreation Services.
Sites: 1

UNIVERSITY SETTLEMENT SOCIETY OF NEW YORK, INC.

184 Eldridge St.
New York, NY 10002

(212) 674-9120 Administrative
(212) 864-2350 FAX

Michael H. Zisser, Executive Director
Languages Spoken: Chinese, Spanish

Services

Arts and Crafts Instruction
Child Care Centers
Computer Classes
Homework Help Programs
Music Instruction
Tutoring

Ages: 6 to 12
Population Served: All Disabilities
Program Hours: Monday - Friday: 3-6 p.m.
Program Capacity: 100
Staff/Child Ratio: 3:25
Fees: $25 per month
Medication Administered: No
Transportation Provided: Yes, from P.S. 20 and St. Patrick's School
Wheelchair Accessible: Yes
Service Description: Provides an after school program where children with special needs are accepted on a case-by-case basis.

VALENTINE-VARIAN HOUSE

3266 Bainbridge Ave.
Bronx, NY 10467

(718) 881-8900 Administrative

Dr. Gary Hermelyn, Executive Director

Services

Museums

VALLEY, INC. (THE)

1047 Amsterdam Ave.
New York, NY 10025

(212) 222-2110 Administrative
(212) 222-4671 FAX

valleynyc@aol.com

John Bess, Founder/CEO

Services

Computer Classes
Dancing Instruction
Sports, Individual
Tutoring

Ages: 6 to 13
Program Hours: Call for information
Program Capacity: 20 - 30
Fees: None
Medication Administered: No
Transportation Provided: No
Service Description: Provides after school program offering martial arts, computer literacy classes, sports, dance, and tutoring. Children with special needs are considered on a case-by-case basis.

VAN CORTLANDT HOUSE MUSEUM

Van Cortlandt Park
Broadway at W. 246th St.
Bronx, NY 10471

(718) 543-3344 Administrative

Laura Correa-Carpenter, Director

Services

Museums

VANDERBILT YMCA

224 E. 47th St.
New York, NY 10017

(212) 756-9600 Administrative

Services

<continued...>

Arts and Crafts Instruction
Exercise Classes/Groups
Homework Help Programs
Swimming

Ages: 6 to 12
Population Served: All Disabilities
Area Served: All Boroughs
Program Hours: Monday - Friday: 2:30-6 p.m.
Fees: Call for information.
Medication Administered: No
Transportation Provided: No
Wheelchair Accessible: No
Service Description: Offers an after school program. Children with special needs are accepted on a case-by-case basis.
Contact: Kim Waldon, Youth-Teen Director

VANDER-ENDE ONDERDONCK HOUSE

c/o Greater Ridgewood Historical Society
1820 Flushing Ave.
Ridgewood, NY 11385

(718) 456-1776 Administrative

Joe Higgins
Languages Spoken: Spanish

Services

Museums

VANGUARD YOUTH CENTER

144 Macon St.
Brooklyn, NY 11216

(718) 783-1429 Administrative

Ms. Johnson, Director

Services

Recreational Activities

Ages: 6 to 13
Area Served: Brooklyn
Service Description: Offers after school recreation program. Children with special needs are accepted on a case-by-case basis.

VOLUNTEERS OF AMERICA

340 E. 85th St.
New York, NY 10024

(212) 873-2600 Administrative

www.voa-gny.org

Richard Salyer, Chief Executive Officer

Sites

1. VOLUNTEERS OF AMERICA - PARKCHESTER EARLY LEARNING CENTER
2433 E. Tremont Ave.
Bronx, NY 10461

(718) 931-0017 Administrative
(718) 824-6741 FAX

Rebecca Ramos, Program Director

2. VOLUNTEERS OF AMERICA - BRONX EARLY LEARNING CENTER
1166 River Ave.
Bronx, NY 10452

(718) 293-3665 Administrative
(718) 681-9710 FAX

Marianne Giordano, Director

Services

Respite, Children's Out-of-Home

Ages: 4 to 8
Population Served: Asperger Syndrome, Asthma, Autism, Blood Disorders, Developmental Delay, Developmental Disability, Emotional Disability, Learning Disability, Mental Retardation (mild-moderate), Pervasive Developmental Disorder (PDD/NOS), Physical/Orthopedic Disability, Seizure Disorder, Speech/Language Disability
Service Description: Provides educational and recreational programs for children.
Contact: Melissa Negron-Sims, (718) 892-7442
Sites: 1 2

WAVE HILL

675 W. 252nd St.
Bronx, NY 10471

(718) 549-3200 Administrative

Laura Koster, Garden Access Coordinator

Services

Arts and Crafts Instruction
Nature Centers/Walks
Parks/Recreation Areas

Ages: 6 and up
Population Served: Autism, Cerebral Palsy, Deaf-Blind, Deaf/Hard of Hearing, Developmental Delay, Developmental Disability, Down Syndrome, Emotional Disability, Learning Disability, Mental Retardation (Mild/Moderate), Multiple Disability, Neurological Disability, Physical/Orthopedic Disability.
Area Served: All Boroughs
Program Hours: Tuesday - Friday: 10 a.m.-4

<continued...>

p.m.
Staff/Child Ratio: 2:12
Fees: $100 per person (for special programs)
Method of Payment: Checks preferred
Wheelchair Accessible: Yes
Service Description: Nature/environmental program incorporating science, art and creative movement activities.
Contact: Laura Koster, Garden Access Coordinator

WE TRY HARDER BOWLING ASSOCIATION

6 Paerdegat 12th St.
Brooklyn, NY 11236

(718) 444-3795 Administrative

Mark Heiss, Coordinator

Services

Recreational Activities
Sports, Individual
Sports, Team/Leagues

Ages: 10 to 15
Population Served: Physical/Orthopedic Disability
Area Served: All Boroughs
Program Capacity: 40 to 50
Fees: Free, except for special event trips.
Service Description: A bowling and softball program that integrates children with physical disabilities. Call for more information.

WEST SIDE LITTLE LEAGUE CHALLENGER DIVISION

2472 Broadway, Box 333
New York, NY 10025-7449

(212) 678-2370 Administrative

Brenda Jordan, Challenger Division Head

Services

Sports, Team/Leagues

Ages: 5 to 18
Population Served: All Disabilities
Area Served: All Boroughs
Program Hours: Sundays: 9-11 a.m.
Fees: $10 - $75
Medication Administered: No
Transportation Provided: No
Wheelchair Accessible: Yes
Service Description: A volunteer, parent-organized program that provides children with special needs the opportunity to participate in sports.

WEST SIDE SOCCER LEAGUE'S VIP DIVISION

Various sites on the Upper West Side of Manhattan
(212) 577-3562 Administrative
(212) 479-7791
 Leave message for VIP Division

www.wssl.org
megger@legal-aid.org

Marcia Egger, Division Director

Services

VIP PLAYER DIVISION
Sports, Team/Leagues

Ages: 6 to 21
Population Served: Attention Deficit Disorder (ADD/ADHD), Autism, Cerebral Palsy, Developmental Disability, Down Syndrome, Health Impairment, Learning Disability, Mental Retardation (mild-moderate), Mental Retardation (severe-profound), Multiple Disability, Neurological Disability, Physical/Orthopedic Disability, Seizure Disorder, Speech/Language Disability, Spina Bifida, Technology Supported
Area Served: All Boroughs
Service Description: Volunteer parent-organized groups providing children with special needs a chance to play sports. Soccer is played September to November in parks around Manhattan's Upper West Side.

WEST SIDE YMCA

5 W. 63rd St.
New York, NY 10023

(212) 875-4100 Administrative
(212) 875-4291 FAX

Shannon Cussen, Executive Director

Services

Arts and Crafts Instruction
Child Care Centers
Sports, Individual
Swimming

Ages: 6 months to 18 years
Population Served: Developmental Disability, Physical/Orthopedic Disability
Area Served: All Boroughs
Program Hours: Hours vary depending on program. Call for information
Fees: Fees vary depending on program. Call for information
Method of Payment: Cash, Check, Credit Card, Money Order
Medication Administered: No

< continued... >

Transportation Provided: No
Service Description: Children from pre-kindergarten to high school can expand their minds with inspirational classes in the arts, music and theater. Children also strengthen their bodies and spirits with swimming, gymnastics and martial arts.

WHITNEY MUSEUM OF AMERICAN ART

945 Madison Ave. at 75th St.
New York, NY 10021

(212) 570-3676 Administrative
(877) 944-8639 Ticketing

www.whitney.org

Services

Museums

Ages: 7 to 11
Area Served: All Boroughs
Program Hours: Year round, Saturdays: 11:30 a.m.-12:30 p.m.
Program Capacity: 15
Fees: Admission fee. Please call for information.
Transportation Provided: No
Wheelchair Accessible: Yes
Service Description: Offers "Look Out," a drawing class for children where they learn directly by discussing and sketching works in the exhibition. Parents are encouraged to participate. Accommodations can be made for children with special needs.
Contact: Sophie Sanders, Family Weekend Program Director

WILDLIFE CONSERVATION SOCIETY - BRONX ZOO

2300 Southern Blvd.
Bronx, NY 10460

(718) 220-5141 Administrative
(718) 733-4460 FAX

www.wcs.org

Languages Spoken: Spanish

Services

Zoos/Wildlife Parks

Ages: All Ages
Area Served: All Boroughs
Program Hours: Vary depending on program
Program Capacity: Varies depending on program
Fees: Vary depending on program.
Method of Payment: Cash, Check, Credit Card, Money Order
Medication Administered: No

Transportation Provided: No
Wheelchair Accessible: Yes
Service Description: Provides a variety of programs for all children. Please call for a complete listing of programs and activities. Children with special needs can be accommodated.

WOMEN IN NEED, INC.

115 W. 31st St., 4th Fl.
New York, NY 10001

(212) 695-4758 Administrative

www.women-in-need.org

Rita Zimmer, Founder
Languages Spoken: Spanish

Services

CHILDREN'S DAY CARE
Arts and Crafts Instruction
Homework Help Programs
Tutoring

Ages: 5 to 12
Area Served: Manhattan
Program Hours: Monday - Friday: 3-6 p.m.
Fees: Call for information
Transportation Provided: No
Service Description: Mainstream, after school program for school-age children of working parents who reside in Manhattan.

WONGARATTA, INC.

132 State Route 365
Remsen, NY 13438

(315) 831-3621 Administrative

www.nwood.com
campinfo@nwood.com

Gordon Felt, Executive Director

Services

Field Trips/Excursions
Recreational Activities
Social Skills Training
Travel

Ages: 11 to 18
Population Served: Attention Deficit Disorder (ADD/ADHD), Developmental Disability, Learning Disability, Neurological Disability
Area Served: NYC Metro Area
Program Hours: Call for information
Fees: Call for information
Medication Administered: No
Transportation Provided: No

<continued...>

Service Description: Socialization programs for children with learning challenges, including day trips on Saturdays and school holidays and a summer teen travel program.

WOODSIDE ON THE MOVE

3942 69th St.
Woodside, NY 11377

(718) 476-8449 Administrative
(718) 476-6946 FAX

Don Ryan
Languages Spoken: Spanish

Services

Arts and Crafts Instruction
Computer Classes
Exercise Classes/Groups
Homework Help Programs
Recreational Activities
Sports, Team/Leagues

Ages: 5 to 12
Area Served: All Boroughs
Program Hours: Monday - Thursday: 3-5 p.m.
Program Capacity: 200
Fees: None
Medication Administered: No
Transportation Provided: No
Wheelchair Accessible: Yes
Service Description: This after school program is offered at P.S. 11, Monday - Thursday for grades 4, 5 and 6; and P.S. 12, Tuesday, Wednesday and Thursday for grades 2 - 5. This program accepts children with special needs on a case-by-case basis.
Contact: Heather Strafer

WORKING ORGANIZATION FOR RETARDED CHILDREN AND ADULTS (WORC)

1979 Marcus Ave., Suite E140
Lake Success, NY 11042

(516) 327-9560 Administrative
(516) 327-9582 FAX

www.worca.org

Matthew Zebatto, Assistant Executive Director

Services

QUEENS SPECIAL NEEDS RESPITE / RECREATION
Arts and Crafts Instruction
Computer Classes
Field Trips/Excursions
Recreational Activities

Ages: 6 to 12
Population Served: Autism
Area Served: Queens

Program Hours: Saturday: 9 a.m.-3 p.m.
Service Description: Individuals in this program enjoy activities such as Broadway shows, museums, movies, circus and other events. Center-based activities include arts and crafts, computers and educational games.

WYCKOFF GARDENS YOUTH PROGRAM

272 Wyckoff St.
Brooklyn, NY 11217

(718) 522-2431 Administrative

Languages Spoken: Spanish

Services

Arts and Crafts Instruction
Dancing Instruction
Film Presentations
Homework Help Programs
Recreational Activities
Tutoring

Ages: 6 to 12
Area Served: Brooklyn
Program Hours: Monday - Friday: 3-6 p.m. July - August, Monday - Friday: 9 a.m.-4 p.m.
Program Capacity: 22
Fees: None
Medication Administered: No
Transportation Provided: No
Wheelchair Accessible: Yes
Service Description: Wyckoff Gardens offers a variety of educational and recreational activities for children. Children with special needs are accepted on a case-by-case basis.

YAI/NATIONAL INSTITUTE FOR PEOPLE WITH DISABILITIES

460 W. 34th St., 11th Fl.
New York, NY 10001

(212) 273-6182 YAI LINK
(212) 563-7474 Administrative
(212) 268-1083 FAX
(212) 290-2787 TDD

www.yai.org
link@yai.org

Joel Levy, CEO
Languages Spoken: Chinese, Russian, Spanish

<continued...>

Services

BROOKLYN EXTEND-A-FAMILY / MANHATTAN WEEKEND RESPITE
Respite, Children's Out-of-Home

Ages: 16 and up
Population Served: All Disabilities
Staff/Child Ratio: 1:3
Fees: $1.00 per hour plus activity cost
Transportation Provided: Yes
Service Description: Recreation activities on Saturday evenings for people 16 years of age and older. Activities include arts and crafts, drama groups, trips, ball games, and other community events.

YESHIVA UNIVERSITY MUSEUM

15 W. 16th St.
New York, NY 10011

(212) 294-8330 Administrative
(212) 294-8335 FAX

www.yu.edu/museum

Judy Dick, Assistance Education Curator
Languages Spoken: French, German, Hebrew, Spanish, Yiddish

Services

Museums

Ages: All ages
Area Served: All boroughs
Wheelchair Accessible: Yes
Service Description: An art and history museum with a special focus on Jewish art and history. The education department runs programs for students in grades 1 through 12. The museum will provide accommodations for special needs students. Teachers should call in advance for group tours and workshop information and reservations. There is a once-a-month family workshop that can accommodate children with special needs. Call for information on programs and times.

YM-YWCA - LA PUERTA ABIERTA DAY CARE CENTER

2864 W. 21st St.
Brooklyn, NY 11224

(718) 373-1100 Administrative
(718) 449-0538 FAX

Jane Doyle, Director
Languages Spoken: Spanish

Services

Child Care Centers

Ages: 2.6 to 5
Area Served: Brooklyn
Program Hours: Monday - Friday: 8 a.m.-6 p.m.
Fees: Call for information
Medication Administered: No
Transportation Provided: No
Service Description: Child care services provided for mainstream children. Children with special needs are considered on a case-by-case basis.

YM-YWHA OF WASHINGTON HEIGHTS AND INWOOD

54 Nagle Ave.
New York, NY 10040

(212) 569-6200 Administrative
(212) 567-5915 FAX

Robert Liebeskind, Associate Executive Director
Languages Spoken: Hebrew, Russian, Spanish

Services

Arts and Crafts Instruction
Computer Classes
Cooking Classes
Homework Help Programs
Recreational Activities
Sports, Team/Leagues
Swimming

Ages: 5 to 12
Population Served: Emotional Disability, Physical/Orthopedic Disability
Area Served: All Boroughs
Program Hours: Monday - Thursday: 3-5:30 p.m., Friday: 3-5 p.m.
Fees: Call for information
Transportation Provided: Yes, from PS 18, 48, 98, 131, and 187, plus Good Shepherd, Muscota, St. Judes, and Manhattan Christian Academy. Additional schools can be added. Call for information
Wheelchair Accessible: Yes
Service Description: Offers small age appropriate group activities, designed to increase awareness, encourage social interaction and help develop physical skills. Provides children with the opportunity to participate in a well-balanced afternoon of recreational, socialization, cultural, and educational activities. Accepts children with emotional and physical disabilities on an individual basis. Call for more information.

YOUNG AUDIENCES INC.

115 E. 92nd St.
New York, NY 10128

(212) 831-8110 Administrative
(212) 289-1202 FAX

www.youngaudiences.org
ya4kids@ya.org

Richard Bell, Executive Director
Languages Spoken: American Sign Language, Spanish

Sites

1. YOUNG AUDIENCES INC. - NEW YORK

1 E. 53rd St.
New York, NY 10022

(212) 319-9269 Administrative

Joanne Bernstein-Cohen, Director

Services

SPECIAL EDUCATION PROGRAM
Theater Performances

Ages: 5 to 21
Population Served: Autism, Deaf/Hard of Hearing, Developmental Disability, Emotional Disability, Physical/Orthopedic Disability, Visual Disability/Blind
Area Served: All Boroughs
Program Hours: Call for information
Fees: Call for information
Wheelchair Accessible: Yes
Service Description: The special education program brings together specifically trained YA/NY artists and student populatons: seeing or hearing impaired, physically challenged or emotionally, educationally or developmentally disabled. YA/NY offers residencies in all art forms that are designed to meet the needs of special education students at different SIE levels, developmental stages and inclusion classrooms.
Sites: 1

YWCA OF NEW YORK CITY

610 Lexington Ave.
New York, NY 10022

(212) 735-9702 Administrative
(212) 223-5187 FAX

www.ywcanyc.org

Rae Linefsky, Executive Director

Services

SUMMER SAILS - SEAPORT SAILS & OVERNIGHT RESPITE
Respite, Children's Out-of-Home Swimming

Ages: 10 to 20
Population Served: Physical Disabilities
Program Hours: 5 overnight stays. Call for information
Program Capacity: 20
Fees: Call for information
Service Description: Offers five overnight stays and seven 3-hour sails into the New York Harbor aboard the tall ships of the South Street Seaport.
Contact: Angela Perez (212) 735-9766

NETWORKING PROJECT FOR YOUNG ADULTS WITH DISABILITIES
Mentoring Programs

Ages: 13 to 21
Service Description: Links young participants with adult mentors who have developmental, physical and sensory problems. Participants and mentors meet twice monthly to share experience and expertise in areas ranging from self-advocacy to self-defense to self-expression through the arts.
Contact: Barbara Perez (212) 735-9767

Appendix
Legal Services

ADVOCATES FOR CHILDREN OF NEW YORK, INC.
151 W. 30th St., 5th Fl. New York, NY 10001
(212)947-9779 Administrative
(212)947-9790 FAX

AMERICAN CIVIL LIBERTIES UNION
125 Broad St. New York, NY 10036
(212)549-2500 Administrative

ASIAN AMERICAN LEGAL DEFENSE AND EDUCATION FUND
99 Hudson St., 12th Fl. New York, NY 10013-2869
(212)966-5932 Administrative
(212)966-4303 FAX

LEGAL ADVICE CLINIC
50-16 Parsons Blvd. Flushing, NY 11355
(718)460-5600 Administrative
(718)445-0032 FAX

ASSOCIATION OF THE BAR OF THE CITY OF NEW YORK
42 W. 44th St. New York, NY 10036-6689
(212)626-7373 Administrative
(212)575-5676 FAX

BRONX COUNTY BAR ASSOCIATION
851 Grand Concourse, Rm. 124 Bronx, NY 10451
(718)293-5600 Administrative
(718)681-0098 FAX

BROOKLYN BAR ASSOCIATION LAWYER REFERRAL SERVICE
123 Remsen St. Brooklyn, NY 11201-4212
(718)624-0843 Administrative
(718)797-1713 FAX

CARDOZA BET TZEDEK LEGAL SERVICES
55 Fifth Ave. New York, NY 10003
(212)790-0240 Administrative
(212)790-0256 FAX

CENTER FOR DISABILITY ADVOCACY RIGHTS (CEDAR)
841 Broadway, Suite 605 New York, NY 10003
(212)979-0505 Administrative
(212)979-8778 FAX
(212)979-7880 TDD

FAMILY LAW CENTER
53 Stanton St. New York, NY 10002
(212)254-8228   Administrative
(212)254-8346   FAX

LAWYERS ALLIANCE FOR NEW YORK
330 Seventh Ave., 19th Fl. New York, NY 10001
(212)219-1800   Administrative
(212)941-7458   FAX

LAWYERS FOR CHILDREN (LFC)
110 Lafayette St., 8th Fl. New York, NY 10013
(212)966-6420   Administrative
(212)966-0531   FAX

LEGAL AID SOCIETY CIVIL DIVISION
111 Livingston St., Brooklyn, NY 11201
(212)577-3300   Administrative
(212)577-7999   FAX

LEGAL AID SOCIETY - BRONX JUVENILE RIGHTS DIVISION
900 Sheridan Ave., 6C12 Bronx, NY 10451
(718)579-7900   Administrative
(718)293-8744   FAX

LEGAL AID SOCIETY - BRONX NEIGHBORHOOD OFFICE CIVIL DIVISION
953 Southern Blvd. Bronx, NY 10451
(718)991-4758   Administrative
(718)842-2867   FAX

LEGAL AID SOCIETY - BROOKLYN NEIGHBORHOOD OFFICE CIVIL DIVISION
166 Montague St. Brooklyn, NY 11201
(718)722-3100   Administrative
(212)722-3093   FAX

LEGAL AID SOCIETY - COMMUNITY LAW OFFICE
230 E. 106th St., 1st Fl. New York, NY 10029
(212)426-3000   Administrative
(212)876-5365   FAX

LEGAL AID SOCIETY - FAR ROCKAWAY NEIGHBORHOOD OFFICE CIVIL DIVISION
1600 Central Ave., 1st Fl. Far Rockaway, NY 11691
(718)337-4900   Administrative
(718)327-3415   FAX

LEGAL AID SOCIETY - HARLEM NEIGHBORHOOD OFFICE CIVIL DIVISION
2090 Seventh Ave., 8th Fl. New York, NY 10027
(212)663-3293   Administrative
(212)749-7038   FAX

LEGAL AID SOCIETY - MANHATTAN JUVENILE RIGHTS DIVISION
60 Lafayette St., 9A New York, NY 10013
(212)312-2260   Administrative
(212)349-0874   FAX

LEGAL AID SOCIETY - QUEENS JUVENILE RIGHTS DIVISION
90-04 161 St., 4th Fl. Jamaica, NY 11432
(718)298-8900   Administrative
(718)657-0537   FAX

LEGAL AID SOCIETY - QUEENS NEIGHBORHOOD OFFICE CIVIL DIVISION
120-46 Queens Blvd. Kew Gardens, NY 11415
(718)286-2450   Administrative
(718)263-4234   FAX

LEGAL AID SOCIETY - STATEN ISLAND NEIGHBORHOOD OFFICE CIVIL DIVISION
60 Bay St. Staten Island, NY 10301
(718)273-6677   Administrative
(718)442-2679   FAX

LEGAL SERVICES FOR CHILDREN, INC.
271 Madison Ave., Rm. 1007 New York, NY 10016
(212)683-7999   Administrative
(212)683-5544   FAX

LEGAL SERVICES FOR NEW YORK CITY
350 Broadway, 6th Fl. New York, NY 10013-9998
(212)431-7200   Administrative
(212)966-9571   FAX
     (212)431-7232   FAX

LEGAL SERVICES FOR NEW YORK CITY - BEDFORD STUYVESANT COMMUNITY LEGAL SERVICES
1368-90 Fulton St., 2nd Fl. Brooklyn, NY 11216
(718)636-1155   Administrative
(718)398-6414   FAX

LEGAL SERVICES FOR NEW YORK CITY - BRIGHTON OFFICE
30-49 Brighton 6th St. Brooklyn, NY 11235
(718)934-2989   Administrative
(718)858-1786   FAX

**LEGAL SERVICES FOR NEW YORK CITY - BRONX LEGAL SERVICES
NORTH OFFICE**
2605 Grand Concourse Bronx, NY 10468
(718)220-0030 Administrative
(718)993-5427 FAX

**LEGAL SERVICES FOR NEW YORK CITY - BRONX LEGAL SERVICES
SOUTH OFFICE**
579 Courtlandt Ave. Bronx, NY 10451
(718)993-6250 Administrative
(718)993-3672 FAX

**LEGAL SERVICES FOR NEW YORK CITY - BROOKLYN LEGAL SERVICES
CORP. A EAST**
BROOKLYN OFFICE
80 Jamaica Ave. Brooklyn, NY 11207
(718)487-1300 Administrative
(718)342-1780 FAX

**LEGAL SERVICES FOR NEW YORK CITY - BROOKLYN LEGAL SERVICES
CORP. A**
WILLIAMSBURG OFFICE
260 Broadway Brooklyn, NY 11211
(718)782-6195 Administrative
(718)782-6790 FAX

**LEGAL SERVICES FOR NEW YORK CITY - BROOKLYN LEGAL SERVICES
CORP. B**
105 Court St., 3rd Fl. Brooklyn, NY 11201
(718)237-5500 Administrative
(718)855-0733 FAX
(718)237-5546 HIV Project

LEGAL SERVICES FOR NEW YORK CITY - BROOKLYN BRANCH
180 Livingston St., Rm. 302 Brooklyn, NY 11201
(718)852-8888 Administrative
(718)858-1786 FAX

**LEGAL SERVICES FOR NEW YORK CITY - HARLEM LEGAL SERVICES,
INC.**
55 W. 125th St., 10th Fl. New York, NY 10027
(212)348-7449 Administrative
(212)348-4093 FAX

LEGAL SERVICES FOR NEW YORK CITY - MFY LEGAL SERVICES
299 Broadway, 4th Fl. New York, NY 10007
(212)417-3700 Administrative
(212)417-3890 FAX
(212)417-3891 FAX

LEGAL SERVICES FOR NEW YORK CITY - QUEENS LEGAL SERVICES LONG ISLAND CITY OFFICE

42-15 Crescent St., 9th Fl. Long Island City, NY 11101
(718)392-5646 Administrative
(718)937-5350 FAX

LEGAL SERVICES FOR NEW YORK CITY - QUEENS LEGAL SERVICES SOUTH JAMAICA OFFICE

89-00 Sutphin Blvd., Rm. 206 Jamaica, NY 11435
(718)657-8611 Administrative
(718)526-5051 FAX

MENTAL HYGIENE LEGAL SERVICES

c/o Bronx Psychiatric Center 1500 Waters Pl., Thompson Bldg. 7th Fl. Bronx, NY 10461
(718)931-0600 Main Number
(718)792-0444 Administrative
(718)792-5639 Administrative

NEW YORK CITY COMMISSION ON HUMAN RIGHTS

40 Rector St., 10th Fl. New York, NY 10006
(212)662-2427 Bias Hotline
(212)306-7450 Discrimination Complaints
(212)306-7500 Administrative

NEW YORK LAWYERS FOR THE PUBLIC INTEREST, INC. (NYLPI)

151 W. 30th St., 11th Fl. New York, NY 10001-4007
(212)244-4664 Administrative
(212)244-4570 FAX
(212)244-3692 TDD

NEW YORK LEGAL ASSISTANCE GROUP

130 E. 59th St., 14th Fl. New York, NY 10022
(212)750-0800 Administrative
(212)750-0820 FAX

NEW YORK STATE COMMISSION ON QUALITY OF CARE (CQC)

401 State St. Schenectady, NY 12305-2397
(800)624-4143 Toll Free
(518)381-7098 Administrative
(518)381-7095 FAX (Advocacy)

NEW YORK STATE COMMISSION ON QUALITY OF CARE (CQC) - NEW YORK CITY

55 Hanson Pl., Rm. 1069 Brooklyn, NY 11217
(718)923-4305 Administrative
(800)624-4143 Hotline
(718)923-4306 FAX

NEW YORK STATE DIVISION OF HUMAN RIGHTS

One Fordham Plaza, 4th. Fl. Bronx, NY 10458
(718)741-8400 Administrative
(718)741-3214 FAX

NEW YORK STATE DIVISION OF HUMAN RIGHTS - BROOKLYN

55 Hanson Pl., Rm. 304 Brooklyn, NY 11217
(718)722-2856 Administrative
(718)722-2869 FAX

NEW YORK STATE DIVISION OF HUMAN RIGHTS - OFFICE OF AIDS DISCRIMINATION

20 Exchange Place, 2nd Fl. New York, NY 10005
(212)480-2522 Administrative
(212)480-0143 FAX

NEW YORK STATE DIVISION OF HUMAN RIGHTS - UPPPER MANHATTAN

State Office Building 163 W. 125th St., Rm. 415 New York, NY 10027
(212)961-8650 Administrative
(212)961-4425 FAX

NEW YORK STATE TRIAL LAWYERS ASSOCIATION

132 Nassau St., 2nd Fl. New York, NY 10038-2486
(212)349-5890 Administrative
(212)608-2310 FAX

NORTHERN MANHATTAN COALITION FOR IMMIGRANT RIGHTS

2 Bennett Ave., 2nd Fl. New York, NY 10033
(212)781 0355 Administrative
(212)781-0943 FAX

NORTHERN MANHATTAN IMPROVEMENT CORPORATION (NMIC)

76 Wadsworth Ave. New York, NY 10033
(212)822-8300 Administrative
(212)740-9646 FAX

PUERTO RICAN LEGAL DEFENSE AND EDUCATION FUND

99 Hudson St., 14th Fl. New York, NY 10013
(212)219-3360 Administrative
(212)431-4276 FAX

QUEENS COUNTY BAR ASSOCIATION

90-35 148th St. Jamaica, NY 11435
(718)291-4500 Administrative
(718)657-1789 FAX

RICHMOND COUNTY BAR ASSOCIATION

152 Stuyvesant Pl., PO Box 140593 Staten Island, NY 10301
(718)442-4500 Administrative
(718)442-2019 FAX

SOUTH BRONX ACTION GROUP
384 E. 149th St., #220 Bronx, NY 10455
(718)993-5869 Administrative
(718)993-7904 FAX

WASHINGTON SQUARE LEGAL SERVICES
161 Ave. of the Americas, 4th Fl. New York, NY 10013
(212)998-6430 Administrative
(212)995-4031 FAX

Service Index

Child Care Centers

Child Care Resource and Referral

Computer Classes

Cooking Classes

Creative Writing

Dance Therapy

Dancing Instruction

Drama Therapy

English as a Second Language

Equestrian Therapy

Exercise Classes/Groups

Field Trips/Excursions

Film Making Instruction

Film Presentations

Homework Help Programs

Mentoring Programs

Museums

Music Instruction

Music Performances

Music Therapy

Nature Centers/Walks

Religious Activities

Remedial Education

Respite, Children's Out-of-Home

Social Skills Training

Sports, Individual

Sports, Team/Leagues

Storytelling

Wilderness Training

Youth Development

Zoos/Wildlife Parks

Population Served Index

AIDS/HIV +

Association to Benefit Children
Bedford Haitian Community Center
Bedford Stuyvesant Community Mental Health Center
Chai Lifeline
Crown Heights Service Center, Inc.
Door (The) - A Center of Alternatives
Greenwich Village Youth Council, Inc. (GUYC)
Hamilton-Madison House
Heartshare Human Services of New York
Henry Street Settlement

Herbert G. Birch Services
Hero, Inc.
Highbridge Advisory Council
Joseph P. Addabbo Family Health Center
New Alternatives for Children
Pratt Institute
Queens County Farm Museum
R.E.A.C.H. (Recreation, Education, Athletics and
Creative Arts for the Handicapped) – Staten Island

All Disabilities

Actors Theatre Workshop, Inc. (The)
After-School Corporation, The (TASC)
American Craft Museum
Aspira of New York
Bedford Stuyvesant YMCA
Brooklyn Bureau of Community Service
Brooklyn Central YMCA
Brooklyn Children's Museum
Brooklyn Public Library - The Child's Place for Children With
Special Needs
Caribbean and American Family Services, Inc.
Children's Aid Society
Creative Music Therapy Studio
Def Dance Jam Workshop
Department of Parks and Recreation of New York City
Door (The) - A Center of Alternatives
El Faro Beacon Community Center
Evelyn Douglin Center for Serving People in Need, Inc.
Flying Wheels Travel
Friends of Crown Heights #3
Funworks for Kids
Harlem YMCA
Heartshare Human Services of New York
Hero, Inc.
Hudson Guild, Inc.
Hudson River Museum
Inspirica
Lincoln Center for the Performing Arts, Inc.
Lincoln Road Playground
Maimonides Medical Center
New Alternatives for Children
New York Aquarium

New York Botanical Garden
New York City Administration for Children's Services
New York City Department of Health
New York Hall of Science
Nordoff-Robbins Center for Music Therapy
Padres Para Padres
Pedro Albizu Campos Community Center
Playground for All Children (The) - Manhattan
Playground for All Children (The) - Queens
Playground for All Children (The) – Staten Island
Polish and Slavic Center, Inc.
Presbyterian Infant and Child Care Center
Queens Botanical Garden
R.E.A.C.H. (Recreation, Education, Athletics and
Creative Arts for the Handicapped) – Staten Island
Resources for Children with Special Needs, Inc.
Riverdale Neighborhood House
Rose Center for Earth Science and Space - Hayden
Planetarium
Shadow Box Theatre (The)
Snug Harbor Cultural Center, Inc.
Staten Island Broadway Center YMCA
Staten Island YMCA
Sutton Gymnastics and Fitness Center
Take Me to the Water
University Settlement Society of New York, Inc.
Valley, Inc. (The)
Vanderbilt YMCA
West Side Little League Challenger Division
YAI/National Institute for People with Disabilities
YM-YWCA - La Puerta Abierta Day Care Center

Allergies

Brookwood Child Care

Arthritis

Empire State Games for the Physically Challenged

Asperger Syndrome

Association for Neurologically Impaired Brain Injured Children,
Inc. (ANIBIC)
Association to Benefit Children
Autism Foundation of New York
City Lights Program, Inc.
Dream Catchers - Therapeutic Riding
Eden II Programs
Heartshare Human Services of New York
Kings Bay YM-YWHA

Lindamood-Bell Learning Center
Professional Service Centers for the Handicapped
(PSCH)
Riverdale Equestrian Center
S.T.A.G.E.S. - Special Theatre Arts Group for
Exceptional Students
Sunday School for Autistic Spectrum Children
Volunteers of America

Asthma

Association to Benefit Children
Brookwood Child Care
Chai Lifeline
Church Avenue Merchants Block Association (CAMBA)
Citizens Care Day Care Center
Columbia University - Teacher's College - Educational and
Psychological Services
Community Opportunities and Development Agency (CODA)
Dr. White Community Center
East Harlem Tutorial Program, Inc.
Hamilton-Madison House
Herbert G. Birch Services
Highbridge Advisory Council
Interfaith Neighbors, Inc.

Kings Bay YM-YWHA
Lenox Hill Neighborhood House
National Theater Workshop of the Handicapped
New Alternatives for Children
North Bronx Family Service Center
Playing 2 Win (P2W)
Pratt Institute
Public School 274 After School Program
Public School 81 After School Program
Puerto Rican Council Day Care
Queens County Farm Museum
Tender Care
Volunteers of America

At Risk

Actors Theatre Workshop, Inc. (The)
Bank Street College of Education - Family Center
Bronx Organization for the Learning Disabled (BOLD)
Colony-South Brooklyn Houses, Inc.
ENACT (Educational Network of Artists in Creative Theatre)

Institute for Theatre-Learning, Inc.
Interfaith Neighbors, Inc.
Neighborhood Care Team
New York City Mission Society

Attention Deficit Disorder (ADD/ADHD)

A - 1 Universal Care, Inc.
A Plus Center for Learning
A.D.D. Resource Center, Inc. (The)
After School Workshop, Inc.
Alianza Dominicana, Inc.
Association for Neurologically Impaired Brain Injured Children,
Inc. (ANIBIC)
Autism Foundation of New York
Bais Aharon - The Creative Academics and Remedial
Education Center
Bedford Stuyvesant Community Mental Health Center
Beekman School
Beth Handler Associates
Brookwood Child Care
Carol's Educare Child Care Center, Inc.
Carver Community Center
Castle Hill Community Center
Center for Computerized Cognitive Enhancement
Children and Adults with Attention Deficit Disorders (CHADD)
Children's Museum of the Arts
Church Avenue Merchants Block Association (CAMBA)
Churchill School and Center, Inc. (The)
Citizens Care Day Care Center
City Lights Program, Inc.
Columbia University - Teacher's College - Educational and
Psychological Services
Community Opportunities and Development Agency (CODA)
Community Service Council of Greater Harlem, Inc.
Dr. White Community Center
Dream Catchers - Therapeutic Riding
East Harlem Tutorial Program, Inc.
ENACT (Educational Network of Artists in Creative Theatre)
Fun Time Vacation Tours, Inc.
Hamilton-Madison House
Heartshare Human Services of New York
Hebrew Educational Society
Herbert G. Birch Services

Highbridge Advisory Council
Huntington Learning Center
Institute for Theatre-learning, Inc.
Interfaith Neighbors, Inc.
James Weldon Johnson Community Center
Jespy Tours, Inc.
Jewish Community House of Bensonhurst
Joseph Demarco Child Care Center
Joseph P. Addabbo Family Health Center
Kings Bay YM-YWHA
Learning for Life
Learning Tree
Lenox Hill Neighborhood House
Lindamood-Bell Learning Center
Neighborhood Care Team
New Alternatives for Children
North Bronx Family Service Center
Northside Center for Child Development
Organized Student (The)
Padres Para Padres
Pal-O-Mine Equestrian, Inc.
Public School 274 After School Program
Public School 81 After School Program
Queens County Farm Museum
R.E.A.C.H. (Recreation, Education, Athletics and
Creative Arts for the Handicapped) – Staten Island
Riverdale YM-YWHA
S.T.A.G.E.S. - Special Theatre Arts Group for
Exceptional Students
Safe Haven West Side Basketball League's Champions
Team
Samuel Field YM-YWHA
Sid Jacobson North Shore YM-YWHA
St. Margaret's Church - Longwood
Union Settlement Association
West Side Soccer League's VIP Division
Wongaratta, Inc.

Autism

92nd Street YM-YWHA
A - 1 Universal Care, Inc.
A Plus Center for Learning

Association for Children with Down Syndrome
Association for Neurologically Impaired Brain Injured
Children, Inc. (ANIBIC)

Association in Manhattan for Autistic Children, Inc. (AMAC)
Association to Benefit Children
Autism Foundation of New York
Bedford Haitian Community Center
Boy Scouts of America - Greater New York Council
Bronx Developmental Center
Bronx Organization for Autistic Citizens
Brooklyn Children's Museum
Brooklyn School for Special Children
Brooklyn Services for Autistic Citizens, Inc.
Central Family Life Center
Chama Child Development Center
Community Opportunities and Development Agency (CODA)
Douglaston After School Center
Dream Catchers - Therapeutic Riding
Eden II Programs
Eihab Human Services, Inc.
El Faro Beacon Community Center
ENACT (Educational Network of Artists in Creative Theatre)
General Human Outreach in the Community, Inc. (GHO)
Heartshare Human Services of New York
Herbert G. Birch Services
Hero, Inc.
James Weldon Johnson Community Center
Jespy Tours, Inc.
Kingsbridge Heights Community Center, Inc.
Lindamood-Bell Learning Center

Music for Living Center for Music Therapy
National Jewish Council for the Disabled
New Directions
New York Families for Autistic Children, Inc.
North Bronx Family Service Center
Northside Center for Child Development
On Your Mark
Padres Para Padres
Pal-O-Mine Equestrian, Inc.
Playing 2 Win (P2W)
Professional Service Centers for the Handicapped (PSCH)
Quality Services for the Autism Community (QSAC)
Queens County Farm Museum
R.E.A.C.H. (Recreation, Education, Athletics and Creative Arts for the Handicapped) – Staten Island
Respite Foundation, Inc.
Riverdale Equestrian Center
Safe Haven West Side Basketball League's Champions Team
Samuel Field YM-YWHA
Sunday School for Autistic Spectrum Children
Tennis for People with Physical Disabilities
Volunteers of America
Wave Hill
West Side Soccer League's VIP Division
Working Organization for Retarded Children and Adults (WORC)
Young Audiences Inc.

Blood Disorders

Volunteers of America

Cancer

Chai Lifeline
Hamilton-Madison House
James Weldon Johnson Community Center
New Alternatives for Children

Playing 2 Win (P2W)
Pratt Institute
Queens County Farm Museum

Cardiac Disorder

Chai Lifeline
James Weldon Johnson Community Center
National Theater Workshop of the Handicapped

New Alternatives for Children
Queens County Farm Museum

Cerebral Palsy

A - 1 Universal Care, Inc.
Association for Neurologically Impaired Brain Injured Children, Inc. (ANIBIC)
Association to Benefit Children
Bedford Haitian Community Center
Boy Scouts of America - Greater New York Council
Brooklyn Children's Museum
Brooklyn School for Special Children
Chai Lifeline
Douglaston After School Center
Dream Catchers - Therapeutic Riding
El Faro Beacon Community Center
Empire State Games for the Physically Challenged
General Human Outreach in the Community, Inc. (GHO)
Heartshare Human Services of New York
Hebrew Institute of Riverdale
Hero, Inc.
Institutes of Applied Human Dynamics - Centers for the Multiply Handicapped
James Weldon Johnson Community Center
Joseph Demarco Child Care Center
My Friend's House of Douglaston, New York Inc.

National Theater Workshop of the Handicapped
Networking Project for Young Adults With Disabilities
New Alternatives for Children
New Directions
New York Services for the Handicapped
New York State Parks Games for the Physically Challenged
North Bronx Family Service Center
On Your Mark
Padres Para Padres
Pal-O-Mine Equestrian, Inc.
Professional Service Centers for the Handicapped (PSCH)
Queens County Farm Museum
Respite Foundation, Inc.
Riverdale Equestrian Center
Safe Haven West Side Basketball League's Champions Team
Samuel Field YM-YWHA
United Cerebral Palsy of New York City
Wave Hill
West Side Soccer League's VIP Division

Cystic Fibrosis

Association to Benefit Children
Chai Lifeline
James Weldon Johnson Community Center

New Alternatives for Children
Queens County Farm Museum

Deaf/Hard of Hearing

Achilles Track Club, Inc.
Association for Neurologically Impaired Brain Injured Children, Inc. (ANIBIC)
Association to Benefit Children
Big Apple Circus
Brooklyn Children's Museum
Brooklyn School for Special Children
Chai Lifeline
Children's Aid Society
Children's Heimeshe Workshop
Church of St. Mark - School District 17
Community Opportunities and Development Agency (CODA)
Def Dance Jam Workshop
Dream Catchers - Therapeutic Riding
Empire State Games for the Physically Challenged
Families First, Inc.
Heartshare Human Services of New York
Hero, Inc.

Martial Arts for the Deaf
Midwood Development Corporation
National Jewish Council for the Disabled
National Theater Workshop of the Handicapped
Networking Project for Young Adults With Disabilities
New Alternatives for Children
New York State Parks Games for the Physically Challenged
North Brooklyn YMCA
Queens County Farm Museum
Queens Museum
R.E.A.C.H. (Recreation, Education, Athletics and Creative Arts for the Handicapped) – Staten Island
Samuel Field YM-YWHA
Search Beyond Adventures
St. Anthony Youth Center
Wave Hill
Young Audiences Inc.

Deaf-Blind

Brooklyn Children's Museum
Chai Lifeline
Lenox Hill Neighborhood House
National Theater Workshop of the Handicapped

New Alternatives for Children
Queens County Farm Museum
Wave Hill

Developmental Delay

Association for Neurologically Impaired Brain Injured Children, Inc. (ANIBIC)
Association to Benefit Children
Bedford Haitian Community Center
Bedford Stuyvesant Community Mental Health Center
Bellport Area Community Action Committee
Brooklyn Children's Museum
Brooklyn School for Special Children
Carol's Educare Child Care Center, Inc.
Chama Child Development Center
Church Avenue Merchants Block Association (CAMBA)
Citizens Care Day Care Center
City Lights Program, Inc.
Columbia University - Teacher's College - Educational and Psychological Services
Community Opportunities and Development Agency (CODA)
Dream Catchers - Therapeutic Riding
Dyckman Farm House Museum
El Faro Beacon Community Center
ENACT (Educational Network of Artists in Creative Theatre)
Family Learning Center, Inc.
General Human Outreach in the Community, Inc. (GHO)
Hamilton-Madison House
Heartshare Human Services of New York
Hebrew Educational Society

Herbert G. Birch Services
Hero, Inc.
Highbridge Advisory Council
Institutes of Applied Human Dynamics - Centers for the Multiply Handicapped
Interfaith Neighbors, Inc.
Lindamood-Bell Learning Center
Lucille Murray Child Development Center
Music for Living Center for Music Therapy
My Friend's House of Douglaston, New York Inc.
North Bronx Family Service Center
On Your Mark
Otsar Family Services, Inc.
Padres Para Padres
Pal-O-Mine Equestrian, Inc.
Professional Service Centers for the Handicapped (PSCH)
Queens County Farm Museum
Queensbridge Day Care Center
Samuel Field YM-YWHA
Tender Care
Union Settlement Association
Volunteers of America
Wave Hill

Developmental Disability

92nd Street YM-YWHA
A - 1 Universal Care, Inc.
A Plus Center for Learning
Achilles Track Club, Inc.
African American Parent Council
After School Workshop, Inc.

Agudath Israel of America
All Children's House Family Center
Association for Children with Down Syndrome
Association for Neurologically Impaired Brain Injured Children, Inc. (ANIBIC)
Association for the Advancement of Blind and Retarded, Inc.

Association for the Help of Retarded Children (AHRC)
Association in Manhattan for Autistic Children, Inc. (AMAC)
Association to Benefit Children
Autism Foundation of New York
Bais Ezra
Bedford Haitian Community Center
Bedford Stuyvesant Community Mental Health Center
Bellport Area Community Action Committee
Boy Scouts of America - Greater New York Council
Bronx Organization for Autistic Citizens
Bronx YMCA
Brooklyn Children's Museum
Brooklyn School for Special Children
Brooklyn Services for Autistic Citizens, Inc.
Carol's Educare Child Care Center, Inc.
Catholic Guardian Society
Central Family Life Center
Chama Child Development Center
Children's Museum of the Arts
Church Avenue Merchants Block Association (CAMBA)
Churchill School and Center, Inc. (The)
City Lights Program, Inc.
Community Opportunities and Development Agency (CODA)
Def Dance Jam Workshop
Douglaston After School Center
Dream Catchers - Therapeutic Riding
Dyckman Farm House Museum
East Harlem Council for Community Improvement
East Side House Settlement
El Faro Beacon Community Center
ENACT (Educational Network of Artists in Creative Theatre)
Evelyn Douglin Center for Serving People in Need, Inc.
Fun Time Vacation Tours, Inc.
General Human Outreach in the Community, Inc. (GHO)
Guild for Exceptional Children (GEC)
Harlem Dowling Westside Center for Children and Family Services
Heartshare Human Services of New York
Hebrew Institute of Riverdale
Herbert G. Birch Services
Hero, Inc.
Huntington Learning Center
Institutes of Applied Human Dynamics - Centers for the Multiply Handicapped
Interfaith Neighbors, Inc.
James Weldon Johnson Community Center
Jespy Tours, Inc.

Jewish Board of Family and Children's Services (JBFCS)
Joseph Demarco Child Care Center
Kings Bay YM-YWHA
Lenox Hill Neighborhood House
Lifespire/ACRMD
Lindamood-Bell Learning Center
Lucille Murray Child Development Center
Midwood Development Corporation
Music for Living Center for Music Therapy
My Friend's House of Douglaston, New York Inc.
Networking Project for Young Adults with Disabilities
New York Families for Autistic Children, Inc.
New York Services for the Handicapped
North Bronx Family Service Center
On Your Mark
Organized Student (The)
Otsar Family Services, Inc.
Padres Para Padres
Pal-O-Mine Equestrian, Inc.
Playing 2 Win (P2W)
Professional Service Centers for the Handicapped (PSCH)
Project Independence of Queens
Queens County Farm Museum
Queens Parent Resource Center
Queensbridge Day Care Center
R.E.A.C.H. (Recreation, Education, Athletics and Creative Arts for the Handicapped) - Brooklyn
R.E.A.C.H. (Recreation, Education, Athletics and Creative Arts for the Handicapped) – Staten Island
Reading Reform Foundation
Riverdale Equestrian Center
Safe Haven West Side Basketball League's Champions Team
Samuel Field YM-YWHA
Southeast Bronx Neighborhood Center
Special Olympics
Sprout
Staten Island Children's Council
Sundial Special Vacations
Susan E. Wagner Day Care Center
Tender Care
Tennis for People With Physical Disabilities
Treasure Island
United Cerebral Palsy of New York City
Volunteers of America
Wave Hill
West Side Soccer League's VIP Division
West Side YMCA
Wongaratta, Inc.
Young Audiences Inc.

Diabetes

Brooklyn Children's Museum
Cambria Center for the Gifted Child
Chai Lifeline
Columbia University - Teacher's College - Educational and Psychological Services
Community Opportunities and Development Agency (CODA)
Heartshare Human Services of New York

James Weldon Johnson Community Center
Jespy Tours, Inc.
Kingsbridge Heights Community Center, Inc.
National Theater Workshop of the Handicapped
New Alternatives for Children
North Bronx Family Service Center
Playing 2 Win (P2W)

Down Syndrome

Association for Children with Down Syndrome
Association for Neurologically Impaired Brain Injured Children, Inc. (ANIBIC)
Association to Benefit Children
Bedford Haitian Community Center
Brooklyn Children's Museum
Brooklyn School for Special Children
Carol's Educare Child Care Center, Inc.

Chama Child Development Center
Children's Museum of the Arts
Douglaston After School Center
Dream Catchers - Therapeutic Riding
Dyckman Farm House Museum
El Faro Beacon Community Center
ENACT (Educational Network of Artists in Creative Theatre)

General Human Outreach in the Community, Inc. (GHO)
Heartshare Human Services of New York
Hebrew Institute of Riverdale
Herbert G. Birch Services
Hero, Inc.
James Weldon Johnson Community Center
Lucille Murray Child Development Center
Midwood Development Corporation
My Friend's House of Douglaston, New York Inc.
New Alternatives for Children
New Directions
On Your Mark
Padres Para Padres

Pal-O-Mine Equestrian, Inc.
Professional Service Centers for the Handicapped (PSCH)
Queens County Farm Museum
R.E.A.C.H. (Recreation, Education, Athletics and Creative Arts for the Handicapped) – Staten Island
Riverdale Equestrian Center
Safe Haven West Side Basketball League's Champions Team
Samuel Field YM-YWHA
United Cerebral Palsy of New York City
Wave Hill
West Side Soccer League's VIP Division

Emotional Disability

Aguadilla Day Care Center
All Children's House Family Center
Association to Benefit Children
Astor Home for Children
Bedford Stuyvesant Community Mental Health Center
Big Brothers/Big Sisters of New York City, Inc.
Boy Scouts of America - Greater New York Council
Brooklyn Children's Museum
Brooklyn School for Special Children
Carver Community Center
Certified Tutoring Service
Children's Museum of the Arts
Church Avenue Merchants Block Association (CAMBA)
Citizens Care Day Care Center
City Lights Program, Inc.
Columbia University - Teacher's College - Educational and Psychological Services
Community Service Council of Greater Harlem, Inc.
Concord Family Services
Crown Heights Service Center, Inc.
Dr. White Community Center
Dream Catchers - Therapeutic Riding
Dyckman Farm House Museum
El Faro Beacon Community Center
ENACT (Educational Network of Artists in Creative Theatre)
Forest Hills Community House
Greenwich Village Youth Council, Inc. (GUYC)
Hamilton-Madison House
Harlem Children's Zone
Harlem Dowling Westside Center for Children and Family Services
Hebrew Educational Society
Henry Street Settlement
Herbert G. Birch Services

Hero, Inc.
Institute for Theatre-Learning, Inc.
Interfaith Neighbors, Inc.
James Weldon Johnson Community Center
Jewish Child Care Association (jcca)
Joseph Demarco Child Care Center
Joseph P. Addabbo Family Health Center
Kings Bay YM-YWHA
Langston Hughes Community Library and Cultural Center
Lenox Hill Neighborhood House
Neighborhood Care Team
New Directions
Pal-O-Mine Equestrian, Inc.
Playing 2 Win (P2W)
Puerto Rican Council Day Care
Queens Child Guidance Center
Queens County Farm Museum
Queens Museum
Queens Parent Resource Center
R.E.A.C.H. (Recreation, Education, Athletics and Creative Arts for the Handicapped) – Staten Island
S.T.A.G.E.S. - Special Theatre Arts Group for Exceptional Students
Staten Island Children's Council
Staten Island Parent Resource Center
Steinway Child and Family Services - Family Support Program
Tutoring Reading and Math Center
Union Settlement Association
Volunteers of America
Wave Hill
YM-YWHA of Washington Heights and Inwood
Young Audiences Inc.

Epilepsy

Epilepsy Institute (The)

Fragile X Syndrome

Heartshare Human Services of New York

Gifted

Brooklyn Children's Museum
Cambria Center for the Gifted Child
Church Avenue Merchants Block Association (CAMBA)
Citizens Care Day Care Center
City Lights Program, Inc.
Columbia University - Teacher's College - Educational and Psychological Services
Dr. White Community Center
Dyckman Farm House Museum
Hamilton-Madison House
Hebrew Educational Society
Highbridge Advisory Council
Huntington Learning Center
Interfaith Neighbors, Inc.

Lenox Hill Neighborhood House
Lindamood-Bell Learning Center
North Brooklyn YMCA
Northside Community Development Council, Inc.
Playing 2 Win (P2W)
Pratt Institute
Project Bridge
Prospect Park
Prospect Park YMCA
Public School 274 After School Program
Public School 81 After School Program
Puerto Rican Council Day Care
Queens County Farm Museum
Reading Reform Foundation

St. Aloysius Education Clinic   Tender Care

Health Impairment

Association for Neurologically Impaired Brain Injured Children, Inc. (ANIBIC)
Association for the Help of Retarded Children (AHRC)
Association to Benefit Children
Brooklyn School for Special Children
Chai Lifeline
Children's Museum of the Arts
Citizens Care Day Care Center
Community Opportunities and Development Agency (CODA)
Douglaston After School Center
Heartshare Human Services of New York
Henry Street Settlement
James Weldon Johnson Community Center
Kingsbridge Heights Community Center, Inc.

Laurelton Theatre of Performing & Visual Arts
Lenox Hill Neighborhood House
My Friend's House of Douglaston, New York Inc.
Padres Para Padres
Pal-O-Mine Equestrian, Inc.
Playing 2 Win (P2W)
Puerto Rican Council Day Care
Queens County Farm Museum
R.E.A.C.H. (Recreation, Education, Athletics and Creative Arts for the Handicapped) – Staten Island
Safe Haven West Side Basketball League's Champions Team
West Side Soccer League's VIP Division

Juvenile Offender

Bedford Stuyvesant Community Mental Health Center
Crown Heights Service Center, Inc.
Dr. White Community Center
Goodwill Industries of Greater New York, Inc.

Lenox Hill Neighborhood House
Queens County Farm Museum
Ridgewood Bushwick Senior Citizens Council, Inc.

Learning Disability

A Plus Center for Learning
After School Workshop, Inc.
Alianza Dominicana, Inc.
Association for Neurologically Impaired Brain Injured Children, Inc. (ANIBIC)
Association for the Help of Retarded Children (AHRC)
Association to Benefit Children
Astor Home for Children
Bais Aharon - The Creative Academics and Remedial Education Center
Balin Mann Associates
Bedford Stuyvesant Community Mental Health Center
Bellport Area Community Action Committee
Beth Elohim
Beth Handler Associates
Booker T. Washington Learning Center
Bronx Organization for the Learning Disabled (BOLD)
Brooklyn Children's Museum
Brooklyn School for Special Children
Brookwood Child Care
Brownstone School and Day Care Center
Carver Community Center
Center for Computerized Cognitive Enhancement
Certified Tutoring Service
Chama Child Development Center
Children's Museum of the Arts
Church Avenue Merchants Block Association (CAMBA)
Church of St. Mark - School District 17
Churchill School and Center, Inc. (The)
Citizens Care Day Care Center
City Lights Program, Inc.
Claremont Neighborhood Center
Columbia University
Columbia University - Teacher's College - Educational and Psychological Services
Community Opportunities and Development Agency (CODA)
Community Service Council of Greater Harlem, Inc.
Concord Family Services
Dream Catchers - Therapeutic Riding
East Harlem Tutorial Program, Inc.
East Side House Settlement
El Faro Beacon Community Center
Empire Learning Services of Manhattan

ENACT (Educational Network of Artists in Creative Theatre)
Families First, Inc.
Forest Hills Community House
Fulton Day Care Center
Fun Time Vacation Tours, Inc.
Grace Church School
Grosvenor Neighborhood House, Inc.
Guided Tour, Inc.
Hamilton-Madison House
Harlem Children's Zone
Heartshare Human Services of New York
Hebrew Educational Society
Herbert G. Birch Services
Hero, Inc.
Highbridge Advisory Council
Huntington Learning Center
Institute for Theatre-Learning, Inc.
Interfaith Neighbors, Inc.
James Weldon Johnson Community Center
Jewish Board of Family and Children's Services (JBFCS)
Jewish Child Care Association (JCCA)
Jewish Community House of Bensonhurst
Joseph Demarco Child Care Center
Kings Bay YM-YWHA
Learning for Life
Lehman College
Lenox Hill Neighborhood House
Lindamood-Bell Learning Center
Lucille Murray Child Development Center
Manhattan Center for Learning
Mary McDowell Center for Learning
Mcburney YMCA
Midwood Development Corporation
Music for Living Center for Music Therapy
My Friend's House of Douglaston, New York Inc.
Neighborhood Care Team
Networking Project for Young Adults With Disabilities
North Bronx Family Service Center
North Brooklyn YMCA
Northside Center for Child Development
Northside Community Development Council, Inc.

On Your Mark
Organized Student (The)
Padres Para Padres
Park Slope Tutorial Services
Pratt Institute
Public School 274 After School Program
Public School 81 After School Program
Puerto Rican Council Day Care
Queens County Farm Museum
Queens Museum
R.E.A.C.H. (Recreation, Education, Athletics and Creative Arts for the Handicapped) – Staten Island
Reading Reform Foundation
Riverdale YM-YWHA
S.T.A.G.E.S. - Special Theatre Arts Group for Exceptional Students

Samuel Field YM-YWHA
Sid Jacobson North Shore YM-YWHA
St. Aloysius Education Clinic
St. Margaret's Church - Longwood
St. Matthews and St. Timothy's Neighborhood Center
Sylvan Learning Center
Treasure Island
Tuesday Night Teens
Tutoring Reading and Math Center
Union Settlement Association
Union Theological Seminary Day Care Center
Volunteers of America
Wave Hill
West Side Soccer League's VIP Division
Wongaratta, Inc.

Mental Retardation (mild-moderate)

92nd Street YM-YWHA
A - 1 Universal Care, Inc.
A Plus Center for Learning
After School Workshop, Inc.
Association for Neurologically Impaired Brain Injured Children, Inc. (ANIBIC)
Association for the Help of Retarded Children (AHRC)
Association to Benefit Children
Bedford Haitian Community Center
Bedford Stuyvesant Community Mental Health Center
Bellport Area Community Action Committee
Boy Scouts of America - Greater New York Council
Brooklyn Children's Museum
Brooklyn School for Special Children
Carol's Educare Child Care Center, Inc.
Chama Child Development Center
Children's Museum of the Arts
Citizens Care Day Care Center
City Lights Program, Inc.
Columbia University - Teacher's College - Educational and Psychological Services
Community Opportunities and Development Agency (CODA)
Douglaston After School Center
Dream Catchers - Therapeutic Riding
Dyckman Farm House Museum
Eihab Human Services, Inc.
El Faro Beacon Community Center
ENACT (Educational Network of Artists in Creative Theatre)
Evelyn Douglin Center for Serving People in Need, Inc.
Fun Time Vacation Tours, Inc.
General Human Outreach in the Community, Inc. (GHO)
Guided Tour, Inc.
Haitian Americans United for Progress, Inc. (HAUP)
Heartshare Human Services of New York
Hebrew Institute of Riverdale

Herbert G. Birch Services
Hero, Inc.
Institutes of Applied Human Dynamics - Centers for the Multiply Handicapped
James Weldon Johnson Community Center
Jespy Tours, Inc.
Jewish Board of Family and Children's Services (JBFCS)
Kingsbridge Heights Community Center, Inc.
Leisure Trax
Midwood Development Corporation
Music for Living Center for Music Therapy
My Friend's House of Douglaston, New York Inc.
National Jewish Council for the Disabled
New Directions
On Your Mark
Padres Para Padres
Pratt Institute
Professional Service Centers for the Handicapped (PSCH)
Project Happy
Queens County Farm Museum
Queens Museum
Queens Parent Resource Center
R.E.A.C.H. (Recreation, Education, Athletics and Creative Arts for the Handicapped) – Staten Island
Respite Foundation, Inc.
Safe Haven West Side Basketball League's Champions Team
Samuel Field YM-YWHA
Search Beyond Adventures
Southeast Bronx Neighborhood Center
Special Olympics
Tennis for People With Physical Disabilities
United Cerebral Palsy of New York City
Volunteers of America
Wave Hill
West Side Soccer League's VIP Division

Mental Retardation (severe-profound)

A - 1 Universal Care, Inc.
A Plus Center for Learning
Bedford Haitian Community Center
Bellport Area Community Action Committee
Boy Scouts of America - Greater New York Council
Brooklyn School for Special Children
Chama Child Development Center
Community Opportunities and Development Agency (CODA)
Dyckman Farm House Museum
El Faro Beacon Community Center

ENACT (Educational Network of Artists in Creative Theatre)
General Human Outreach in the Community, Inc. (GHO)
Haitian Americans United for Progress, Inc. (HAUP)
Heartshare Human Services of New York
Hebrew Institute of Riverdale
Herbert G. Birch Services
Hero, Inc.
Institutes of Applied Human Dynamics - Centers for the Multiply Handicapped

James Weldon Johnson Community Center
Kingsbridge Heights Community Center, Inc.
Music for Living Center for Music Therapy
My Friend's House of Douglaston, New York Inc.
National Jewish Council for the Disabled
New Directions
Padres Para Padres
Professional Service Centers for the Handicapped (PSCH)
Queens County Farm Museum

R.E.A.C.H. (Recreation, Education, Athletics and Creative Arts for the Handicapped) – Staten Island
Respite Foundation, Inc.
Safe Haven West Side Basketball League's Champions Team
Samuel Field YM-YWHA
Search Beyond Adventures
Southeast Bronx Neighborhood Center
United Cerebral Palsy of New York City
West Side Soccer League's VIP Division

Multiple Disability

Association for the Advancement of Blind and Retarded, Inc.
Association to Benefit Children
Bellport Area Community Action Committee
Brooklyn Children's Museum
Brooklyn School for Special Children
Chai Lifeline
Citizens Care Day Care Center
Douglaston After School Center
Dream Catchers - Therapeutic Riding
Eden II Programs
El Faro Beacon Community Center
General Human Outreach in the Community, Inc. (GHO)
Hebrew Institute of Riverdale
Herbert G. Birch Services
Hero, Inc.

James Weldon Johnson Community Center
Joseph Demarco Child Care Center
Kings Bay YM-YWHA
My Friend's House of Douglaston, New York Inc.
New Alternatives for Children
North Bronx Family Service Center
Padres Para Padres
Professional Service Centers for the Handicapped (PSCH)
Queens County Farm Museum
Safe Haven West Side Basketball League's Champions Team
United Cerebral Palsy of New York City
Wave Hill
West Side Soccer League's VIP Division

Neurological Disability

A Plus Center for Learning
Achilles Track Club, Inc.
After School Workshop, Inc.
Association for Neurologically Impaired Brain Injured Children, Inc. (ANIBIC)
Autism Foundation of New York
Bellport Area Community Action Committee
Brooklyn Children's Museum
Brooklyn School for Special Children
Carol's Educare Child Care Center, Inc.
Chai Lifeline
Children's Museum of the Arts
City Lights Program, Inc.
Douglaston After School Center
Dream Catchers - Therapeutic Riding
General Human Outreach in the Community, Inc. (GHO)
Heartshare Human Services of New York
Hebrew Institute of Riverdale
Hero, Inc.
Huntington Learning Center
James Weldon Johnson Community Center
Jespy Tours, Inc.
Kingsbridge Heights Community Center, Inc.

Lindamood-Bell Learning Center
My Friend's House of Douglaston, New York Inc.
National Jewish Council for the Disabled
Networking Project for Young Adults With Disabilities
New Alternatives for Children
New York Services for the Handicapped
On Your Mark
Organized Student (The)
Padres Para Padres
Pal-O-Mine Equestrian, Inc.
Professional Service Centers for the Handicapped (PSCH)
Queens County Farm Museum
R.E.A.C.H. (Recreation, Education, Athletics and Creative Arts for the Handicapped) – Staten Island
Respite Foundation, Inc.
Safe Haven West Side Basketball League's Champions Team
Samuel Field YM-YWHA
United Cerebral Palsy of New York City
Wave Hill
West Side Soccer League's VIP Division
Wongaratta, Inc.

Oral Disorders

Institute for Theatre-Learning, Inc.

Pervasive Developmental Disorder (PDD/NOS)

A - 1 Universal Care, Inc.
Association in Manhattan for Autistic Children, Inc. (AMAC)
Autism Foundation of New York
Bedford Haitian Community Center
Boy Scouts of America - Greater New York Council
Center for Computerized Cognitive Enhancement
Dream Catchers - Therapeutic Riding
Eden II Programs

Heartshare Human Services of New York
Herbert G. Birch Services
Institute for Theatre-learning, Inc.
James Weldon Johnson Community Center
Lindamood-Bell Learning Center
Neighborhood Care Team
New Alternatives for Children
New York Families for Autistic Children, Inc.

Professional Service Centers for the Handicapped (PSCH)
S.T.A.G.E.S. - Special Theatre Arts Group for Exceptional Students

Sid Jacobson North Shore YM-YWHA
Sunday School for Autistic Spectrum Children
Volunteers of America

Physical/Orthopedic Disability

Accessible Journeys
Achilles Track Club, Inc.
After School Workshop, Inc.
Association for the Advancement of Blind and Retarded, Inc.
Association to Benefit Children
Bronx YMCA
Brooklyn Children's Museum
Brooklyn School for Special Children
Chai Lifeline
Children's Museum of the Arts
Citizens Care Day Care Center
Community Service Council of Greater Harlem, Inc.
Douglaston After School Center
Dream Catchers - Therapeutic Riding
Empire State Games for the Physically Challenged
General Human Outreach in the Community, Inc. (GHO)
Hamilton-Madison House
Heartshare Human Services of New York
Hebrew Institute of Riverdale
James Weldon Johnson Community Center
Jespy Tours, Inc.
Laurelton Theatre of Performing & Visual Arts
My Friend's House of Douglaston, New York Inc.
National Theater Workshop of the Handicapped
New Alternatives for Children

New York Services for the Handicapped
New York State Parks Games for the Physically Challenged
Northside Center for Child Development
Padres Para Padres
Pal-O-Mine Equestrian, Inc.
Project Happy
Prospect Park
Queens County Farm Museum
Queens Museum
R.E.A.C.H. (Recreation, Education, Athletics and Creative Arts for the Handicapped) – Staten Island
Special Olympics
Tennis for People with Physical Disabilities
Union Theological Seminary Day Care Center
United Cerebral Palsy of New York City
Volunteers of America
Wave Hill
We Try Harder Bowling Association
West Side Soccer League's VIP Division
West Side YMCA
YM-YWHA of Washington Heights and Inwood
Young Audiences Inc.
YWCA of New York City

Rare Disorder

Association to Benefit Children
Chai Lifeline
New Alternatives for Children

Pal-O-Mine Equestrian, Inc.
United Cerebral Palsy of New York City

Seizure Disorder

Association for Neurologically Impaired Brain Injured Children, Inc. (ANIBIC)
Association to Benefit Children
Brooklyn School for Special Children
Chai Lifeline
Douglaston After School Center
Dream Catchers - Therapeutic Riding
Epilepsy Institute (The)
General Human Outreach in the Community, Inc. (GHO)
Hamilton-Madison House
Heartshare Human Services of New York
Herbert G. Birch Services
James Weldon Johnson Community Center
Jespy Tours, Inc.
Kingsbridge Heights Community Center, Inc.
My Friend's House of Douglaston, New York Inc.
National Jewish Council for the Disabled

National Theater Workshop of the Handicapped
New Alternatives for Children
On Your Mark
Padres Para Padres
Pal-O-Mine Equestrian, Inc.
Professional Service Centers for the Handicapped (PSCH)
R.E.A.C.H. (Recreation, Education, Athletics and Creative Arts for the Handicapped) – Staten Island
Respite Foundation, Inc.
Safe Haven West Side Basketball League's Champions Team
Search Beyond Adventures
United Cerebral Palsy of New York City
Volunteers of America
West Side Soccer League's VIP Division

Sickle Cell Anemia

Brooklyn Children's Museum
Cambria Center for the Gifted Child
Chai Lifeline
Children's Museum of the Arts
Crown Heights Service Center, Inc.
Hamilton-Madison House
Heartshare Human Services of New York

Herbert G. Birch Services
James Weldon Johnson Community Center
New Alternatives for Children
North Bronx Family Service Center
Pal-O-Mine Equestrian, Inc.
Playing 2 Win (P2W)
Queens County Farm Museum

Speech/Language Disability

92nd Street YM-YWHA
After School Workshop, Inc.
Aguadilla Day Care Center
Alianza Dominicana, Inc.
Association for Children With Down Syndrome
Association for Neurologically Impaired Brain Injured Children,
Inc. (ANIBIC)
Association to Benefit Children
Bais Aharon - The Creative Academics and Remedial
Education Center
Balin Mann Associates
Bellport Area Community Action Committee
Beth Elohim
Brooklyn Children's Museum
Brooklyn School for Special Children
Brookwood Child Care
Carver Community Center
Children's Heimeshe Workshop
Children's Museum of the Arts
Church Avenue Merchants Block Association (CAMBA)
Churchill School and Center, Inc. (The)
Citizens Care Day Care Center
Columbia University - Teacher's College - Educational and
Psychological Services
Community Opportunities and Development Agency (CODA)
Douglaston After School Center
Dream Catchers - Therapeutic Riding
ENACT (Educational Network of Artists in Creative Theatre)
Family Learning Center, Inc.
General Human Outreach in the Community, Inc. (GHO)
Grand Street Settlement
Grosvenor Neighborhood House, Inc.
Hamilton-Madison House
Hartley House
Heartshare Human Services of New York
Herbert G. Birch Services

Hero, Inc.
Highbridge Advisory Council
Institute for Theatre-Learning, Inc.
Interfaith Neighbors, Inc.
James Weldon Johnson Community Center
Jespy Tours, Inc.
Joseph Demarco Child Care Center
Kingsbridge Heights Community Center, Inc.
Lenox Hill Neighborhood House
Lindamood-Bell Learning Center
Lucille Murray Child Development Center
Music for Living Center for Music Therapy
My Friend's House of Douglaston, New York Inc.
National Theater Workshop of the Handicapped
Neighborhood Care Team
Nicholas Cardell Day Care Center
Northside Center for Child Development
Padres Para Padres
Pal-O-Mine Equestrian, Inc.
Puerto Rican Council Day Care
Queens County Farm Museum
Queensbridge Day Care Center
R.E.A.C.H. (Recreation, Education, Athletics and
Creative Arts for the Handicapped) – Staten Island
S.T.A.G.E.S. - Special Theatre Arts Group for
Exceptional Students
Safe Haven West Side Basketball League's Champions
Team
Search Beyond Adventures
Sid Jacobson North Shore YM-YWHA
Susan E. Wagner Day Care Center
Tender Care
Union Theological Seminary Day Care Center
United Cerebral Palsy of New York City
Volunteers of America
West Side Soccer League's VIP Division

Spina Bifida

Association to Benefit Children
Brooklyn Children's Museum
Brooklyn School for Special Children
Chai Lifeline
Heartshare Human Services of New York
Herbert G. Birch Services
My Friend's House of Douglaston, New York Inc.
National Theater Workshop of the Handicapped

New Alternatives for Children
New York Services for the Handicapped
North Bronx Family Service Center
Padres Para Padres
Pal-O-Mine Equestrian, Inc.
United Cerebral Palsy of New York City
West Side Soccer League's VIP Division

Substance Abuse

Crown Heights Service Center, Inc.
Harlem Children's Zone
Heartshare Human Services of New York
Hero, Inc.
Interfaith Neighbors, Inc.

James Weldon Johnson Community Center
Pal-O-Mine Equestrian, Inc.
Playing 2 Win (P2W)
Queens County Farm Museum
Ridgewood Bushwick Senior Citizens Council, Inc.

Technology Supported

Chai Lifeline
My Friend's House of Douglaston, New York Inc.
New Alternatives for Children
Padres Para Padres
Pal-O-Mine Equestrian, Inc.

Queens County Farm Museum
R.E.A.C.H. (Recreation, Education, Athletics and
Creative Arts for the Handicapped) – Staten Island
West Side Soccer League's VIP Division

Tourette Syndrome

Association for Neurologically Impaired Brain Injured Children, Inc. (ANIBIC)
Brooklyn Children's Museum
Chai Lifeline

City Lights Program, Inc.
James Weldon Johnson Community Center
Queens County Farm Museum

Traumatic Brain Injury (TBI)

Association for Neurologically Impaired Brain Injured Children, Inc. (ANIBIC)
Association to Benefit Children
Chai Lifeline
City Lights Program, Inc.
Dream Catchers - Therapeutic Riding

Hero, Inc.
National Theater Workshop of the Handicapped
New Alternatives for Children
Professional Service Centers for the Handicapped (PSCH)
United Cerebral Palsy of New York City

Underachiever

A Plus Center for Learning
After School Workshop, Inc.
Asian Professional Extension, Inc.
Association to Benefit Children
Bank Street College of Education - Family Center
Big Sister Educational Action and Service Center
Brooklyn Children's Museum
Brownstone School and Day Care Center
Carver Community Center
Children's Museum of the Arts
Church Avenue Merchants Block Association (CAMBA)
Church of St. Mark - School District 17
Churchill School and Center, Inc. (The)
Citizens Care Day Care Center
City Lights Program, Inc.
Claremont Neighborhood Center
Columbia University - Teacher's College - Educational and Psychological Services
Community Service Council of Greater Harlem, Inc.
Concord Family Services
Dr. White Community Center
East Harlem Tutorial Program, Inc.

Fulton Day Care Center
Hamilton-Madison House
Harlem Center for Education, Inc.
Hartley House
Herbert G. Birch Services
Highbridge Advisory Council
Huntington Learning Center
Interfaith Neighbors, Inc.
James Weldon Johnson Community Center
Lenox Hill Neighborhood House
Lindamood-Bell Learning Center
Northside Community Development Council, Inc.
Pal-O-Mine Equestrian, Inc.
Pratt Institute
Project Bridge
Prospect Park YMCA
Public School 274 After School Program
Public School 81 After School Program
Puerto Rican Council Day Care
Queens County Farm Museum
Reading Reform Foundation
Staten Island Historical Society

Visual Disability/Blind

Achilles Track Club, Inc.
Association for the Advancement of Blind and Retarded, Inc.
Big Apple Circus
Boy Scouts of America - Greater New York Council
Brooklyn Children's Museum
Brooklyn School for Special Children
Chai Lifeline
Children's Museum of the Arts
Dyckman Farm House Museum
Empire State Games for the Physically Challenged
Families First, Inc.
Heartshare Human Services of New York
James Weldon Johnson Community Center
Lenox Hill Neighborhood House

National Theater Workshop of the Handicapped
New Alternatives for Children
New Directions
New York State Parks Games for the Physically Challenged
Pal-O-Mine Equestrian, Inc.
Queens County Farm Museum
Queens Museum
R.E.A.C.H. (Recreation, Education, Athletics and Creative Arts for the Handicapped) – Staten Island
Search Beyond Adventures
United Cerebral Palsy of New York City
Young Audiences Inc.

Mainstream Index

Laguardia Community College
Langston Hughes Community Library and Cultural Center
Laurelton Theatre of Performing & Visual Arts
Liberty Science Center
Lincoln Road Playground
Long Island City YMCA
Long Island Museum of American Art, History and Carriages
Lucy Moses School for Music and Dance
Manhattan Valley Youth Program
Mcburney YMCA
Mentoring USA
Metropolitan Museum of Art (The)
Morningside Children's Center
Morris-Jumel Mansion
Mount Vernon Hotel Museum and Garden
Museum of American Financial History
Museum of American Folk Art
Museum of Jewish Heritage (The)
Museum of Modern Art
Museum of Television & Radio
Museum of the City of New York
Museum of the Moving Image
National Museum of the American Indian
Neighborhood Service and Development Agency
Nevins Day Care Center, Inc.
New Museum of Contemporary Arts
New Victory Theatre
New York Aquarium
New York Botanical Garden
New York City Fire Department Museum
New York City Mission Society
New York Hall of Science
New York State Office of Parks, Recreation and Historic Preservation
Nicholas Cardell Day Care Center
North Bronx Family Service Center
North Brooklyn YMCA
Northside Center for Child Development
Northside Community Development Council, Inc.
Pedro Albizu Campos Community Center
Pesach Tikvah
Pierpont Morgan Library
Playground for All Children (The) - Manhattan
Playground for All Children (The) - Queens
Playing 2 Win (P2W)
Police Athletic League, Inc. (PAL)
Polish and Slavic Center, Inc.
Pratt Institute
Presbyterian Infant and Child Care Center
Project Teen Aid
Prospect Park
Prospect Park YMCA
Protectors of Pine Oak Woods
Puerto Rican Council Day Care
Purple Circle Day Care Center
Queens Botanical Garden
Queens Child Guidance Center
Queens County Farm Museum
Queens Museum
Queens Wildlife Center
Reading Reform Foundation
Riverdale Community Center
Riverdale Neighborhood House
Riverdale YM-YWHA
Rockin Magician
Rose Center for Earth Science and Space
Sacred Heart Roman Catholic Church
Seneca Neighborhood Center
Shadow Box Theatre (The)
Snug Harbor Cultural Center, Inc.

South Shore YMCA
South Street Seaport Museum (The)
Spoke the Hub Dancing
St. Aloysius Education Clinic
Staten Island Broadway Center YMCA
Staten Island Children's Council
Staten Island Children's Museum
Staten Island Historical Society
Staten Island YMCA
Staten Island Zoo
Susan E. Wagner Day Care Center
Sutton Gymnastics and Fitness Center
Sylvan Learning Center
Take Me to the Water
Tender Care
Tenth Street Tots Child Care Center
Third Street Music School Settlement
Trinity Parish Preschool
Union Settlement Association
University Settlement Society of New York, Inc.
Valentine-Varian House
Valley, Inc. (The)
Van Cortlandt House Museum
Vanderbilt YMCA
Vander-Ende Onderdonck House
Vanguard Youth Center
Wave Hill
West Side YMCA
Wildlife Conservation Society- Bronx Zoo
Whitney Museum of American Art
Women in Need, Inc.
Woodside on the Move
Wyckoff Gardens Youth Program
Yeshiva University Museum
YM-YWCA - La Puerta Abierta Day Care Center
YM-YWHA of Washington Heights and Inwood

Program Time Index

After School

81st Precinct Community Affairs
92nd Street YM-YWHA
A Plus Center for Learning
Actors Theatre Workshop, Inc. (The)
Add Joy to Learning
African American Parent Council
After School Workshop, Inc.
After-School Corporation, The (TASC)
Aguadilla Day Care Center
Alianza Dominicana, Inc.
All Children's House Family Center
Alley Pond Environmental Center
American Craft Museum
Archdiocese of New York
Aspira of New York
Association for Children with Down Syndrome
Association for Neurologically Impaired Brain Injured Children, Inc. (ANIBIC)
Association for the Help of Retarded Children (AHRC)
Association in Manhattan for Autistic Children, Inc. (AMAC)
Association to Benefit Children
Autism Foundation of New York
Bais Ezra
Balin Mann Associates
Bank Street College of Education - Family Center
Bayside YMCA
Bedford Haitian Community Center
Bedford Stuyvesant Community Mental Health Center
Bedford Stuyvesant YMCA
Beekman School
Beth Elohim
Big Sister Educational Action and Service Center
Booker T. Washington Learning Center
Boston Secor Community Center
Boys and Girls Clubs of America
Boys and Girls Harbor
Bridgewood Tutoring Service
Bronx House Jewish Community Center
Bronx Organization for Autistic Citizens
Bronx Organization for the Learning Disabled (BOLD)
Bronx River Art Center and Gallery
Bronx YMCA
Brooklyn Bureau of Community Service
Brooklyn Center for the Urban Environment (BCUE)
Brooklyn Central YMCA
Brooklyn Children's Museum
Brooklyn Historical Society (The)
Brooklyn Public Library -The Child's Place for Children with Special Needs
Brooklyn School for Special Children
Brownstone School and Day Care Center
Cambria Center for the Gifted Child
Caribbean and American Family Services, Inc.
Carol's Educare Child Care Center, Inc.
Carver Community Center
Casita Maria
Castle Hill Community Center
Catalpa YMCA
Center for Family Support, Inc. (The)
Central Queens YM-YWHA
Chama Child Development Center
Chelsea Piers - Pier 62
Child Development Support Corporation
Children's Aid Society

Children's Museum of Manhattan (CMOM)
Children's Museum of the Arts
Chinatown YMCA
Church Avenue Merchants Block Association (CAMBA)
Church of St. Mark - School District 17
Churchill School and Center, Inc. (The)
Citizens Advice Bureau (CAB)
Claremont Neighborhood Center
Cluster, Inc.
Community Association for Progressive Dominicans
Community Opportunities and Development Agency (CODA)
Community Service Council of Greater Harlem, Inc.
Community United Methodist Church
Concord Family Services
Concourse House
Cross Island YMCA
Crown Heights Service Center, Inc.
Def Dance Jam Workshop
Department of Parks and Recreation of New York City
Digital Clubhouse
Discovery Programs, Inc.
Douglaston After School Center
Dr. White Community Center
East Harlem Block Schools, Inc.
East Harlem Tutorial Program, Inc.
East Side House Settlement
Eastern District YMCA
Eden II Programs
Eihab Human Services, Inc.
El Faro Beacon Community Center
El Museo Del Barrio
Elmcor After School Program
Empire Learning Services of Manhattan
Evelyn Douglin Center for Serving People in Need, Inc.
Families First, Inc.
Family Dynamics, Inc.
Featherbed Lane Youth Center, Inc.
Flatbush YMCA
Flushing Club House
Flushing YMCA
Forest Hills Community House
Friends of Crown Heights #3
Friends of Crown Heights Daycare
Good Shepherd Services
Grace Church School
Grand Street Settlement
Greenpoint YMCA
Grosvenor Neighborhood House, Inc.
Guild for Exceptional Children (GEC)
Haitian Americans United for Progress, Inc. (HAUP)
Harlem Center for Education, Inc.
Harlem Children's Zone
Harlem Dowling Westside Center for Children and Family Services
Harlem School of the Arts
Harlem YMCA
Hartley House

Heartshare Human Services of New York
Hebrew Educational Society
Henry Street Settlement
Herbert G. Birch Services
Hetrick-Martin Institute
Highbridge Advisory Council
Highbridge Community Life Center
Hudson Guild, Inc.
Immigrant Social Service, Inc.
Interfaith Neighbors, Inc.
Jacob Riis Neighborhood Settlement House
Jamaica Center for Arts and Learning
James Weldon Johnson Community Center
Kids with a Promise
Kings Bay YM-YWHA
Langston Hughes Community Library and Cultural Center
Lenox Hill Neighborhood House
Long Island City YMCA
Maimonides Medical Center
Manhattan Valley Youth Program
Mcburney YMCA
Midwood Development Corporation
Morningside Children's Center
Museum of Modern Art
My Friend's House of Douglaston
National Theater Workshop of the Handicapped
Neighborhood Care Team
Neighborhood Service and Development Agency
Nevins Day Care Center, Inc.
New York Botanical Garden
New York City Department of Youth and Community
Development
New York City Mission Society
North Bronx Family Service Center
North Brooklyn YMCA
Northside Community Development Council, Inc.
On Your Mark
Pedro Albizu Campos Community Center
Pesach Tikvah
Playing 2 Win (P2W)
Polish and Slavic Center, Inc.
Pratt Institute

Professional Service Centers for the
Handicapped (PSCH)
Project Bridge
Project Teen Aid
Public School 274 After School Program
Public School 81 After School Program
Puerto Rican Council Day Care
Purple Circle Day Care Center
Queens Child Guidance Center
Queens Parent Resource Center
Reading Reform Foundation
Ridgewood Bushwick Senior Citizens Council,
Inc.
Riverdale Community Center
Riverdale Equestrian Center
Riverdale Neighborhood House
Riverdale YM-YWHA
(S.T.A.G.E.S). - Special Theatre Arts Group for
Exceptional Students
Sacred Heart Roman Catholic Church
Samuel Field YM-YWHA
Seneca Neighborhood Center
Sid Jacobson North Shore YM-YWHA
Sol Goldman YM-YWHA
Southeast Bronx Neighborhood Center
Sprout
St. Margaret's Church - Longwood
Staten Island Broadway Center YMCA
Staten Island Children's Council
Staten Island YMCA
Take Me to the Water
Union Settlement Association
United Cerebral Palsy of New York City
University Settlement Society of New York, Inc.
Valley, Inc. (The)
Vanderbilt YMCA
Vanguard Youth Center
Women in Need, Inc.
Woodside on the Move
Wyckoff Gardens Youth Program
YM-YWHA of Washington Heights and Inwood

All Year

A Plus Center for Learning
A.D.D. Resource Center, Inc. (The)
Accessible Journeys
Achilles Track Club, Inc.
Alianza Dominicana, Inc.
Alley Pond Environmental Center
American Museum of Natural History
Asia Society
Asian Professional Extension, Inc.
Asphalt Green
Association for Neurologically Impaired Brain Injured Children,
Inc. (ANIBIC)
Association for the Advancement of Blind and Retarded, Inc.
Association for the Help of Retarded Children (AHRC)
Astor Home for Children
Bais Aharon -The Creative Academics and Remedial
Education Center
Bais Ezra
Ballet Hispanico
Bartow-Pell Mansion Museum Carriage House and Garden
Basketball City
Belvedere Castle in Central Park
Big Apple Circus
Big Apple Games
Big Brothers/Big Sisters of New York City
Bloomingdale School of Music

Boy Scouts of America - Greater
New York
Boys and Girls Harbor
Bridgewood Tutoring Service
Bronx Museum of the Arts
Bronx River Art Center and
Gallery
Bronx YMCA
Brooklyn Arts Exchange
Brooklyn Botanic Garden
Brooklyn Children's Museum
Brooklyn College
Brooklyn Gymnastics Center
Brooklyn Learning Center
Brooklyn Museum of Art (The)
Brookwood Child Care
Cardinal Mccloskey Services
Carol's Educare Child Care Center, Inc.
Castle Clinton National Monument
Catholic Big Brothers of New York
Catholic Big Sisters
Central Family Life Center
Central Park - Charles A. Dana Discovery
Central Park Wildlife Center
Certified Tutoring Service
Chelsea Piers - Pier 62

Child Care Council of Nassau County, Inc.
Child Care Council of Suffolk
Child Care Council of Westchester
Children and Adults With Attention Deficit Disorders (CHADD)
Children's Heimeshe Workshop
Children's Museum of Manhattan (CMOM)
Children's Museum of the Arts
Children's Zoo at Flushing Meadow Corona Park
Church Avenue Merchants Block Association (CAMBA)
Citizens Care Day Care Center
Cloisters (The)
Columbia University
Columbia University - Teacher's College
Committee for Hispanic Children and Families, Inc.
Concourse House
Cooper-Hewitt National Design Museum
Creative Music Therapy Studio
Dairy in Central Park (The)
Day Care Council of New York, Inc.
Dial-A-Teacher
Dome Project, Inc. (The)
Door (The) - A Center of Alternatives
Dream Catchers - Therapeutic Riding
Dyckman Farm House Museum
East Harlem Council for Community Improvement
East Harlem Council for Human Services, Inc.
East Harlem Tutorial Program, Inc.
East Side Creative Arts Studio
Eden II Programs
Empowerment Institute for Mentally Retarded of Greater New York, Inc.
ENACT (Educational Network of Artists in Creative Theatre)
Family Learning Center, Inc.
Flying Wheels Travel
Funworks for Kids
Gateway National Recreation Area
Goodwill Industries of Greater New York, Inc.
Greenwich House, Inc.
Guggenheim Museum
Guided Tour, Inc.
Hamilton-Madison House
Harlem Children's Zone
Heartshare Human Services of New York
Herbert G. Birch Services
Hero, Inc.
Hudson River Museum
Hudson Valley Children's Museum
Huntington Learning Center
Inspirica
Institute for Theatre-Learning, Inc.
Interfaith Neighbors, Inc.
Jamaica Center for Arts and Learning
Jespy Tours, Inc.
Jewish Board of Family and Children's Services (JBFCS)
Jewish Child Care Association (JCCA)
Jewish Museum (The)
Joseph P. Addabbo Family Health Center
Kaplan, Inc.
Kingsland Homestead - Queens Historical Society
Laguardia Community College
Learning for Life
Learning Tree
Lehman College
Leisure Trax
Lenox Hill Neighborhood House
Liberty Science Center
Lincoln Road Playground
Lindamood-Bell Learning Center
Literacy Assistance Center, Inc.

Long Island Museum of American Art, History and Carriages
Lucille Murray Child Development Center
Manhattan Center for Learning
Manhattan Valley Youth Program
Mary Mcdowell Center for Learning
Mentoring USA
Metropolitan Museum of Art (The)
Morris-Jumel Mansion
Mount Vernon Hotel Museum and Garden
Museum of American Financial History
Museum of American Folk Art
Museum of Jewish Heritage (The)
Museum of Television & Radio
Museum of the City of New York
Museum of the Moving Image
Music for Living Center for Music Therapy
National Museum of the American Indian
National Theatre of the Deaf
New Directions
New Museum of Contemporary Arts
New Victory Theatre
New York Aquarium
New York Botanical Garden
New York City Fire Department Museum
New York City Mission Society
New York Services for the Handicapped
New York State Parks Games for the Physically Challenged
Nicholas Cardell Day Care Center
Nordoff-Robbins Center for Music Therapy
Organized Student (The)
Outward Bound USA
Pal-O-Mine Equestrian, Inc.
Park Slope Tutorial Services
Pierpont Morgan Library
Playground for All Children (The)
Police Athletic League, Inc. (PAL)
Presbyterian Infant and Child Care Center
Princeton Review (The)
Prospect Park YMCA
Protectors of Pine Oak Woods
Queens Botanical Garden
Queens County Farm Museum
Queens Museum
Queens Parent Resource Center
Queens Wildlife Center
Queensbridge Day Care Center
R.E.A.C.H.- Brooklyn
R.E.A.C.H.- Staten Island
Reading Reform Foundation
Resources for Children with Special Needs
Ridgewood Bushwick Senior Citizens Council
Rockin Magician
Rose Center for Earth Science and Space - Hayden Planetarium
Safe Haven West Side Basketball League's Champions Team
Search Beyond Adventures
Shadow Box Theatre (The)
Sid Jacobson North Shore YM-YWHA
South Shore YMCA
South Street Seaport Museum (The)
Spoke the Hub Dancing
St. Anthony Youth Center
St. Matthews and St. Timothy's Neighborhood Center
Staten Island Children's Museum
Staten Island Historical Society
Staten Island Mental Health Society, Inc.

Staten Island Parent Resource Center
Staten Island YMCA
Staten Island Zoo
Steinway Child and Family Services - Family Support Program
Steven Sales Day Care Center
Sundial Special Vacations
Susan E. Wagner Day Care Center
Sutton Gymnastics and Fitness Center
Sylvan Learning Center
Take Me to the Water
Tennis for People with Physical Disabilities
Third Street Music School Settlement
Treasure Island
Trinity Parish Preschool
Tuesday Night Teens
Tutoring Reading and Math Center
Union Settlement Association
Union Theological Seminary Day Care Center
Valentine-Varian House
Van Cortlandt House Museum

Vander-Ende Onderdonck House
Volunteers of America
Wave Hill
We Try Harder Bowling Assoc.
West Side Soccer League's VIP
West Side YMCA
Whitney Museum of American Art
Wildlife Conservation Society - Bronx Zoo
Working Organization for Retarded Children and Adults (WORC)
YAI/National Institute for People with Disabilities
Yeshiva University Museum
YM-YWCA - La Puerta Abierta Day Care Center
Young Audiences Inc.
YWCA of New York City

Evening

Association for the Help of Retarded Children (AHRC)
Flushing Club House
Harlem Center for Education, Inc.
Harlem School of the Arts
Harlem YMCA

Herbert G. Birch Services
Interfaith Neighbors, Inc.
Kings Bay Little League Challenger
Lenox Hill Neighborhood House
Midwood Development Corporation

Holidays

Aguadilla Day Care Center
Alianza Dominicana, Inc.
Bank Street College of Education - Family Center
Big Apple Games
Bronx YMCA
Chai Lifeline
Children's Zoo at Flushing Meadow Corona Park
Dyckman Farm House Museum
El Museo Del Barrio
Empire State Games for the Physically Challenged
Flushing YMCA
Friends of Crown Heights #3
Friends of Crown Heights Daycare
Girl Scouts of the USA
Grosvenor Neighborhood House, Inc.

Guggenheim Museum
Guided Tour, Inc.
Heartshare Human Services of New York
Hebrew Educational Society
Kingsbridge Heights Community Center, Inc.
Leisure Trax
Nevins Day Care Center, Inc.
New Directions
Otsar Family Services, Inc.
Search Beyond Adventures
Sol Goldman YM-YWHA
Sprout
St. Aloysius Education Clinic
Wongaratta, Inc.
YAI/National Institute for People With Disabilities

Weekends

A - 1 Universal Care, Inc.
A Plus Center for Learning
Agudath Israel of America
Asian Professional Extension, Inc.
Association for Neurologically Impaired Brain Injured Children, Inc. (ANIBIC)
Association for the Help of Retarded Children (AHRC)
Association in Manhattan for Autistic Children, Inc. (AMAC)
Autism Foundation of New York
Bank Street College of Education - Family Center
Basketball City
Bedford Stuyvesant Community Mental Health Center
Big Sister Educational Action and Service Center
Bridgewood Tutoring Service
Bronx Community College
Bronx Developmental Center
Bronx Organization for the Learning Disabled
Bronx YMCA
Brooklyn College
Brooklyn Gymnastics Center
Brooklyn Learning Center
Brooklyn Services for Autistic Citizens, Inc.

Catholic Guardian Society
Central Park Wildlife Center
Children's Aid Society
Children's Zoo at Flushing Meadow-Corona Park
Church Avenue Merchants Block Association (CAMBA)
City Lights Program, Inc.
Colony-South Brooklyn Houses, Inc.
Craft Students League of the YWCA
Digital Clubhouse
Dream Catchers -Therapeutic Riding
Dyckman Farm House Museum
East Harlem Council for Community Improvement
El Faro Beacon Community Center
El Museo Del Barrio
Elmcor After School Program
Empire Learning Services of Manhattan
Empire State Games for the Physically Challenged
Epilepsy Institute (The)

Evelyn Douglin Center for Serving People in Need, Inc.
General Human Outreach in the Community, Inc. (GHO)
Harlem Center for Education, Inc.
Heartshare Human Services of New York
Herbert Berghof Studio
Herbert G. Birch Services
Highbridge Advisory Council
Hudson River Museum
Hunter College
Institutes of Applied Human Dynamics - Centers for the Multiply Handicapped
Interfaith Neighbors, Inc.
Jewish Museum (The)
Kings Bay Little League Challenger
Leisure Trax
Lifespire/ACRMD
Maimonides Medical Center
Midwood Development Corporation
My Friend's House of Douglaston
National Jewish Council for the Disabled
National Theater Workshop of the Handicapped
Networking Project for Young Adults with Disabilities
New York Botanical Garden
New York City Mission Society
New York Families for Autistic Children, Inc.
New York Hall of Science

Northside Center for Child Development
On Your Mark
Otsar Family Services, Inc.
Padres Para Padres
Pesach Tikvah
Professional Service Centers for the Handicapped (PSCH)
Project Happy
Quality Services for the Autism Community (QSAC)
Reading Reform Foundation
Respite Foundation, Inc.
Riverdale Equestrian Center
Sid Jacobson North Shore YM-YWHA
Snug Harbor Cultural Center, Inc.
Sprout
Staten Island YMCA
Sunday School for Autistic Spectrum Children
United Cerebral Palsy of New York City
West Side Little League Challenger Division
Whitney Museum of American Art
Wongaratta, Inc.
YAI/National Institute for People With Disabilities

City/Town Index

ZIP Code Index

Resources
for Children with
Special Needs, Inc.

116 East 16th Street, 5th Floor, New York, NY 10003
Phone (212) 677-4650 • FAX (212) 254-4070
E-mail: info@resourcesnyc.org • Website: resourcesnyc.org

FACT SHEET

Resources for Children with Special Needs is a comprehensive, independent, not-for-profit information, referral, advocacy, training and support center for New York City parents and professionals looking for all kinds of programs and services for children from birth to 21 with learning, developmental, emotional or physical disabilities. In 1992, Resources was designated by the U.S. Department of Education as one of a national network of 90 Parent Training and Information Centers.

Information & Referral • Direct Help • Support • Advocacy • Workshops • An Annual Training Series • A Comprehensive Database • A Library • Publications • Outreach

---

Help For Parents and Professionals
We help locate and obtain appropriate programs and services for children and youth with disabilities and special needs. We
• help identify the child's and family's needs.
• provide accurate, up-to-date information.
• provide guidance in selecting programs and services.
• provide ongoing parent support.
• act as advocate and case manager.
• follow through and follow up on all assistance given.

Just Call Us
We provide information and assistance in person, by phone, and by mail, in English and Spanish. Call (212) 677-4650. We are open Monday through Friday from 9:00 a.m. to 5:30 p.m. An answering machine will take messages after hours. All telephone help is free. Our *sliding scale waivable* fee for an office consultation for parents is $0 to $50 and covers all help given around a particular issue. We work with people of all income levels, all ethnic and racial groups, in all of New York City's boroughs.

Finding Programs and Services of All Kinds
We maintain New York City's largest comprehensive computerized database of programs and services for children with disabilities or special needs and their families. We help find schools and educational programs, public and private, day and residential, general and special • infant and preschool programs • day care and child care services • vocational and job training programs • independent living programs • camps and summer programs • recreational, afterschool and other social programs • cultural resources • family support and respite services • social services • evaluation and diagnostic services • therapies and remedial services • medical

and health services • individual professionals • legal and advocacy services • toys, equipment and educational materials • and more.

Advocacy and Support
We provide individual advocacy, including representation at Committee on Special Education meetings and procedural hearings when necessary. We support parents through the process of obtaining help, however long the process might take.

Training and Workshops for Parents and Professionals
We conduct workshops on laws, regulations, rights, entitlements and procedures for obtaining educational and other services; on the systems serving children with disabilities; and on the many kinds of resources available in communities. Every year we present a free training series in English and Spanish, and respond to hundreds of requests for specialized training from parent groups, community organizations, and public agencies. With the New York City Training Collaborative for Early Intervention, we conduct New York State's training about the Early Intervention program at workshops in all boroughs.

Library
Our library and information services are supervised by our Director of Information Services, a professional librarian. Parents, professionals and students are welcome.

Publications
•*Camps 2002 , A Directory of Camps and Summer Programs for Children and Youth with Disabilities and Special Needs in the Metro New York Area*, published February 3, 2002.
•*Schools for Children with Autism Spectrum Disorders, A Directory of Educational Programs in New York City and the Lower Hudson Valley*, 2001.
•*The Comprehensive Directory, A Directory of Programs and Services for Children with Disabilities and Their Families in the Metro New York Area,* December 2001.
These will be followed by additional directories and guides covering schools, afterschool programs early intervention, and more. To order our publications call Resources at 212-677-4650.

Outreach and Special Events
•*Special Camp Fair.* At our annual Special Camp Fair each February, over 3000 parents and professionals talk with camp directors, learn about camps and summer programs for children with disabilities, and receive a free copy of our *Camp Directory*.

•*Center Without Walls.* With Resources' database on laptop computers, a bilingual mobile Access Team from Resources for Children and Advocates for Children of New York takes the information, training and advocacy services of both organizations to communities of immigrant, minority and at risk families throughout the city.

•*The New York City Information and Advocacy Clearinghouse for Children and Youth with Special Needs.* A continually updated computerized city and region wide database of agencies, organizations and individuals providing information and advocacy services promotes information exchange and access for parents of children with disabilities.

Funding
We are funded by foundations, corporations, the local, state and federal government, earned income, and many generous individuals.

Let Us Know What You Think

Resources for Children with Special Needs wants to know what you need.

If you have ideas for directories or for guidebooks covering issues, strategies, systems or services for children and youth with special needs and their families, let us know. Tell us if you like our directories, or if you don't, so we can improve them.

Send us your ideas by mail, fax, or email.

And, please send your suggestions for updates to *After School and More*. We would like to know about additional programs to include, additional information you'd like to see in the descriptions, or any features that would make the directory more helpful in finding the right program for your child.

Comments and Suggestions:

_____

_____

_____

_____

_____

_____

_____

Optional:

Name _____

Address _____

City _____ State _____ Zip Code _____

Phone _____ E-mail _____

Mail or fax your suggestions to:
Dianne Littwin
Director of Publications

Resources for Children with
Special Needs, Inc.
116 East 16 Street, 5th Floor
New York, NY 10003
212 677-4650 ▪ 212 254-4070 Fax

Or email to:
dlittwin@resourcesnyc.org

Publications Order Form

The Comprehensive Directory: *Programs and Services for Children and Youth with Disabilities and Special Needs and Their Families in the Metro New York Area*

This all-inclusive directory has more than 2,500 listings of services, programs and agencies that serve children from birth to 21 with disabilities. Education, recreation, medical and social services are all be included.
ISBN 0-9678365-1-4. Publication Jan. 2002. $55.00 plus $7.00 P&H

                                                  _____ copies $ _____ total

Schools for Children with Autism Spectrum Disorders: *A Directory of Educational Programs in New York City and the Lower Hudson Valley*

Detailed descriptions of more than 350 schools and educational services for children and youth with autism spectrum disorders. Glossary and resource sections included.
ISBN 0-9678365-3-0. Publication March 2001. $20.00 plus $7.00 P&H

   _____ copies $ _____ total

After School and More: *After School, Weekend and Holiday Programs for Children and Youth with Disabilities and Special Needs in the Metro New York Area*

Serving the out-of-school time for children with recreation, sports, and educational programs. Zip code index.
ISBN 0-9678365-5-7. Publication Sept. 2002. $25.00 plus $7.00 P&H

   _____ copies $ _____ total

Camps 2003: *A Directory of Camps and Summer Programs for Children and Youth with Disabilities and Special Needs in the Metro New York Area*

The standard reference for camps in the New York Metro area for children with special needs. Special and mainstream programs are included. Indexed by disability and program type.
ISBN 0-9678365-7-3. Publication Feb. 2003. $22.00 plus $7.00 P&H

   _____ copies $ _____ total

Transition Matters: Moving toward Independence: *Programs and Services for Youth with Disabilities and Special Needs in the Metro New York Area*

A guide and directory providing information on the rights, entitlements, and services available for children (and their families) transitioning from school to adult life.
ISBN 0-9678365-6-5. Publication March 2003. Tentative price $35.00 plus $7.00 P&H

Total Publications $_____
Total Postage and Handling $_____
Total Enclosed/Charged $_____

All orders must be prepaid by check, money order, or credit card to:

Resources for Children with Special Needs, Inc.,
Dept AFS1 116 East 16th Street, 5th Floor
New York, NY 10003   **212 254-4070 Fax**

Name

Organization

Address

City   State   Zip code

Daytime phone number

Credit Card Type   Visa   MasterCard   Am Ex   Diners Club   JCC

Account Number   Exp date   Signature

Billing name and address if different from above